MECHANICS-
MERCANTILE
LIBRARY.

Arthur F. Mathews '06

SPEND 'Til THE END

THE REVOLUTIONARY GUIDE TO RAISING YOUR LIVING STANDARD— TODAY AND WHEN YOU RETIRE

Laurence J. Kotlikoff and Scott Burns

SIMON & SCHUSTER

New York • London • Toronto • Sydney

Simon & Schuster
1230 Avenue of the Americas
New York, NY 10020

Copyright © 2008 by Scott Burns and Laurence J. Kotlikoff.

All rights reserved, including the right to reproduce this book or
portions thereof in any form whatsoever. For information address
Simon & Schuster Subsidiary Rights Department,
1230 Avenue of the Americas, New York, NY 10020.

First Simon & Schuster hardcover edition June 2008

SIMON & SCHUSTER and colophon are registered trademarks of
Simon & Schuster Inc.

For information about special discounts for bulk purchases,
please contact Simon & Schuster Special Sales at
1-800-456-6798 or business@simonandschuster.com.

Designed by Dana Sloan

Manufactured in the United States of America

10 9 8 7 6 5 4 3 2 1

Library of Congress Cataloging-in-Publication Data

Kotlikoff, Laurence J.
    Spend 'til the end: the revolutionary guide to raising your living
standard—today and when you retire / by Laurence J. Kotlikoff and
Scott Burns.
        p. cm.
    Includes bibliographical references and index.
    1. Finance, Personal—Handbooks, manuals, etc. I. Burns, Scott
II. Title.
HG179.B849 2008
332.024—dc22   2007051823

ISBN-13: 978-1-4165-4890-4
ISBN-10:   1-4165-4890-4

To Dayle and Carolyn,
with our deep love and affection

Acknowledgments

We thank our oustanding editor, Bob Bender, and our terrific agent, Alice Martell, for helping us make this book a reality. We also thank our many friends and colleagues in the academic, journalism, and financial planning communities for their encouragement and suggestions.

Larry Kotlikoff wishes to express his deep appreciation to Boston University for a quarter century's support of his research in economics.

Contents

Introduction:
The Three Commandments of Economics   1

Part 1   SMOOTH FINANCIAL PATHS   15

1. "I Am Financially Sick"   17
2. Consumption Smoothing   21
3. Conventional Consumption Disruption   27
4. Pimping Risk   39
5. Financial Mind-benders   44

Part 2   FINANCIAL PATHOLOGY   53

6. What, Me Worry?   55
7. Understanding Financial Disease   76
8. Financial Snake Oil   94

Part 3   RAISING YOUR LIVING STANDARD   107

9. My Son the Plumber   109
10. Does College Really Pay?   115
11. Fire Your Job   118
12. Location, Location   122
13. Whether 'Tis Wiser   127
14. Pay It Down, Way Down   133

15. Does It Pay to Play?   141
16. Converting   156
17. Cashing Out   160
18. Double Dip on Social Security   169
19. Russian Roulette for Keeps   175
20. Learning Your Bs and Ds   183
21. Holding Your Nuts   186
22. Fire Your Broker   191
23. Downsize   196
24. Equitable Alimony   199

Part 4 PRICING YOUR PASSIONS   203

25. Ciao, Baby   205
26. Shacking Up   208
27. Take the Leisure and Run   214
28. Pricing Procreation   219
29. Can We Help the Kids?   224
30. Charity Stays at Home   228

Part 5 PRESERVING YOUR LIVING STANDARD   233

31. Are Stocks Safer Than Bonds in the
    Long Run?   237
32. Diversify Your Resources, Not Your
    Portfolio   243
33. Spending Down   250
34. Beware of Averages   256
35. Portfolio Choice   263
36. Public Policy Risk   267
37. Sell Your Boss Short (or Long)   272
38. The Troll Under the Bridge   277
39. Should I Care About Long-Term Care?   283
40. A Safety-First Strategy   287

Epilogue: Is There an Economist in the House?   295
Index   301

SPEND 'Til THE END

Introduction:

The Three Commandments of Economics

THIS BOOK MAY change your life. If you follow its simple prescriptions—the surprising rules of true financial planning—you'll live a more relaxed and happier life. You'll do so by achieving a higher and more stable living standard and a better lifestyle.

These are big claims for a small book. But we aren't offering the revolutionary solution of the moment. This isn't the miracle diet of the week or the sex trick of the month. It isn't even the six mutual funds guaranteed to fix your future. Instead we're providing something with a great pedigree: an economics-based, three-part prescription for personal financial health:

- Maximize your spending power.
- Smooth your living standard.
- Price your love.

Economists have been developing and refining their approach to financial planning for over a century. But few people know about it, and for good reason: it's been impossible to implement this refined approach from a computational perspective. But times change, and today PCs can calculate in seconds what used to take mainframes weeks. With these new power tools, economists can finally move from describing financial problems to prescribing solutions. In particular, they can now help people improve both their financial and personal lives by finding them a higher, smoother, and more rewarding spending path.

"Higher, smoother, more rewarding spending" sounds good. So what's the catch?

There is no catch.

Maximizing your spending power doesn't require working yourself to the bone or even working an extra hour. It means making a host of decisions regarding education, career, job, location, housing, mortgage, retirement account, insurance, portfolio, tax, and Social Security, among others, that provide you more money—potentially *a lot* more money—to spend for the same effort.

Take the decision of whether to collect a smaller Social Security retirement benefit starting at age sixty-two or a larger one starting at a later age. Making the right choice doesn't take any more time or effort than making the wrong one, but the consequences for your living standard can be spectacular. The same holds for choosing between jobs, mortgages, retirement accounts, and so on.

Smoothing your living standard means spreading your spending power evenly over time, so you never need worry about running out. It doesn't mean starving now to gorge later or vice versa. Economists call this spreading of your spending power over time *consumption smoothing.* It is based on the law of diminishing returns—the well-known proposition that you *can* have too much of a good thing. Six-year-olds have this down. Put them in front of a plate of cupcakes. They'll inhale the first, gulp down the second, struggle through the third, and then save the rest for tomorrow. In making this spending/saving decision, six-year-olds are smoothing their consumption. They are trying to even out their pleasure from consuming today, when times are good (Dad's been shopping), with their pleasure from consuming tomorrow, when times are bad (Mom's going shopping).

Smoothing your consumption also means protecting your living standard—making sure it stays relatively steady in good and bad times. For six-year-olds, living-standard protection means hiding the remaining cupcakes from Mom. For us grown-ups, it means inoculating our living standard against adverse changes in income, healthcare costs, taxes, government benefits, and inflation, and making sure that risky investments are truly worth the gamble.

Pricing love doesn't mean selling your firstborn for ready cash. It means knowing what it costs, measured in terms of your living standard, to do things that you'd really love to do. These include taking a wonderful but low-paying job, retiring early, having kids, buying a vacation home, getting divorced, signing up for an Alaska cruise, moving to Arizona, and contributing to charity, among many other things.

Pricing your passions is critical to getting the most out of your spending power. Imagine having to buy the week's groceries at a market that doesn't post prices. You'd surely end up spending too much on things you thought were cheap but were actually expensive, and perhaps too little on things you thought were expensive but were actually cheap. You'd be spending blind and buying too little love for your money.

Maximize your spending power; smooth your living standard; price your love—these are the Three Commandments of economics. Although the economics lingo may be foreign, the concepts are familiar. We all try to follow these rules most of the time. Just consider the kinds of financial questions we ask:

- Does contributing to my 401(k) pay?
- Is this mortgage the cheapest?
- Should I go back to school?
- Should I convert my IRA (Individual Retirement Account) to a Roth IRA?
- Am I saving enough to sustain my living standard?
- Will my kids suffer financially if I die?
- Does holding stock make sense at my age?

- Can I afford a cabin cruiser?
- Is working until sixty-five worth it?
- Can I swing living downtown?
- What's a safe rate of retirement spending?

Each of these questions tests compliance with the Three Commandments. Each involves economics' bottom line: your living standard. And each is a version of: Can I raise my living standard? Can I preserve my living standard? Can I sacrifice my living standard?

Posing living-standard questions is easy. Answering them is tough. Take contributing to a regular 401(k) versus a Roth 401(k). The former option means paying less tax now but more later. The latter means the opposite. Which option generates a higher living standard? And how do these choices compare if taxes are increased later on?

Getting the right answer to these seemingly straightforward questions is immensely complicated. But thanks to new economics technology—technology that calculates your highest sustainable living standard—such questions can now be answered in seconds.

This book is going to use this new technology to teach you the Three Commandments. It's going to do so in general and specific terms. And it's going to do so in plain English. So even though one of us—Larry—is an economist, there won't be any geek talk or equations, just the repeated application of economic common sense.

Economic common sense, you'll come to see, is at complete odds with conventional financial planning, which, frankly, has as much connection to proper saving, insurance, and investment decisions as French fries with melted cheese have to a healthy diet. Indeed, this book will argue that virtually every bit of conventional financial wisdom you've heard over the years is simply wrong.

So get ready. This book is going to turn your financial thinking upside down. Here's a sample of some of the financial mind-benders you'll shortly encounter—and understand:

- Setting retirement spending targets is asking for big trouble.
- The poor and middle class should hold relatively more stock than the rich.
- Diversifying your portfolio is generally a bad idea.
- Stock holdings should rise, fall, rise, and fall again with age.
- Having children may lower your need for life insurance.
- Spouses/partners with the highest earnings may need the least life insurance.
- The rich have bigger saving and insurance problems than average people.
- Maximizing retirement account contributions is generally undesirable.
- Waiting to take Social Security can dramatically raise your living standard.
- Oversaving and overinsuring are risky.
- Mortgages offer no tax advantages for most households.

How Come?

This book is full of practical steps to improve your financial life. Most of these steps, ironically, have nothing to do with investing in stocks or bonds. Indeed, we don't get to portfolios until part 5. But this book is far more than just a "how-to" financial formulary. It also implants a wee bit of economic theory in your cranium to help you understand economics-based financial planning. Also, expect to get a sense of the computational challenges inherent in proper planning. Once you do, you will realize the primitive nature of conventional planning tools and why it's taken economists so long to develop useful software.

Finally, get ready for a sobering survey, spiced with gallows humor, of financial pathology American style—a survey that will leave no doubt: *Homo Americanus* is not *Homo economicus*. Americans have personalities, feelings, desires, cravings, appetites, crazes, addictions—you name it—none of which enters standard economic theory. To the contrary, standard economic theory presumes that we are super-rational automatons who never crack a smile, never grab a kiss, never get angry, never suffer a lapse in financial judgment, and never get an urgent need to shop till we drop. But, as we'll discuss, *neuroeconomics*—the new economics subfield that uses brain waves to study economic choices—shows that our emotions are fully engaged when we make financial decisions.

This is not to denigrate the ability of standard economic theory to predict general financial behavior. A great deal of such behavior lines up well with theoretical predictions. For example, the theory predicts that people will save for retirement—and most people do. But when it comes down to comparing what any given household should do with what that household is actually doing, the gulf is huge. For example, household A should be saving 5 percent of its income, not 20 percent. Household B needs life insurance and is holding $500K, but really needs $1.5 million. Household A should diversify its financial assets and is holding 30 percent stock and 70 percent bonds, but the portfolio shares should be reversed. In other words, most of us try to do the right thing, but we often miss the target—badly.

The huge gulf between actual and prescribed behavior tells us we need help in determining and implementing precise economics-based, household-specific recommendations.

Our survey of Americans' financial ills will reassure you that whatever financial problems you face, they could be worse. It should also convince you that whatever else one might say about conventional financial planning, it has failed miserably in securing the financial health of tens of millions of Americans. In short, it's time for a financial-planning approach that actually works and that is guided by an overall framework—economic theory—that makes sense.

The Game Plan

Our book has five parts. Part 1, "Smooth Financial Paths," takes you on a trip—actually, a drug trip—to illustrate in the simplest possible setting what we mean by living standard, consumption, and consumption smoothing. We're going to start you out as a drug dealer (to avoid tax and Social Security complications) and then gradually transform you into a more familiar Middle American. During each of your metamorphoses, you will not only be smoothing your consumption, but also maximizing your spending power, pricing your love, or both. By the end of your trip, you'll have a clear sense of financial health and be poised to learn why conventional financial planning promotes the opposite: financial pathology.

Conventional planning, as you may already know, asks people to set their own retirement spending target. Then it asks you to predict what your survivors should spend. What you probably don't know is that setting one's targets correctly is virtually impossible. Worse, even small targeting mistakes can generate major upheavals in your standard of living as you proceed through life.

The planning/investment/insurance industry knows that making you set your own targets is asking you to do all the hard work. So the industry provides quick targeting advice. This "advice" invariably involves wildly high saving and insurance recommendations. No surprise—the industry is trying to sell you a product. It is not trying to help you smooth your consumption.

Once the industry cons you into accepting impossibly high saving and insurance goals, it "helps" you achieve them by terribly misusing what's called *Monte Carlo analysis* to con you into buying high-cost and high-risk investments. Follow this advice, and you'll face far too much variability in your living standard.

The financial industry's practice of soliciting risk is no minor matter. It can gravely damage your financial health and constitutes serious financial malpractice. The industry, by the way, ranges from your neighborhood financial planner to major financial companies, including "good guy" companies, such as TIAA-CREF, Fidelity Investments, and Vanguard—three of the nation's largest vendors of mutual funds and insurance. All are systematically violating the Hippocratic oath: "First, do no harm." Indeed, conventional financial planning is virtually guaranteed to make us financially sick. Some firms do far more harm than others, but all of them call what they do financial planning.

Whether conventional planning or our own decision making is the cause, we are all financially sick. This "we" includes you.

We don't care if you're Suze Ormond (the best-selling financial author), Jane Bryant Quinn (*Newsweek*'s acclaimed financial columnist), or any other self-proclaimed financial healer with millions of acolytes. We don't care if you're Peter Lynch (Fidelity's all-time top money manager), David Swensen (Yale's brilliant endowment investor), or any other renowned investment guru: you are financially sick.

How do we know this?

Because nobody—not Suze, not Jane, not Peter, not David, not us, and not you—can maximize her spending, smooth her consumption, or price her love on her own. It's too damn tough, just as it's too damn tough to think thirty moves ahead in chess. Deep Blue—IBM's supercomputer—can think that far ahead. But no human on earth, not even Garry Kasparov, can come close.

Skeptics should consider this brief list of interrelated factors in determining one's financial future: household demographics; labor earnings; retirement dates; federal, state, and local taxes; Social Security retirement, survivor, and dependent benefits; private pension benefits; annuities; regular and retirement account assets; retirement account contributions and withdrawals; home ownership and mortgage payments; borrowing constraints; economies in shared living; dates for taking Social Security; Medicare Part B premiums; the relative costs of children; planned changes in housing; the choice of a state in which to live; the financing of college and weddings; the role of inflation in lowering the real cost of mortgage payments; the real value of one's pension (if it's not fully inflation-indexed); paying for one's dream boat; and so on.

Now multiply all that by another factor: each of these variables demands consideration in each and every survival state—situations in which the household head or spouse/partner has died. And up until now, at least, only a small number of people have used the right software to get anywhere near consumption smoothing.

Our financial pathology doesn't begin and end, however, with the wrong financial objectives and the wrong planning tools, although these deficiencies can easily put us in the economic ER. As psychologists have been telling us for years, most of us are, to put it politely, just plain nuts. We're compulsive, irrational, depressed, stressed, manic, addicted, bipolar, panicked, and anxious. Any one of these maladies can lead us to create a first-rate financial mess.

This point—that the world is populated by economic neurotics and psychotics rather than fabled rational economic man—has only recently dawned on economists. (The profession is only 330 years old.) Indeed, in recent years economists have created a whole new field *behavioral finance*—to study the financial decisions of crazy people—namely, us and you.

Part 2, "Financial Pathology," provides the aforementioned quick tour of financial illness and its causes. It then pushes on to discuss financial malpractice and its practitioners, and quantifies just how bad conventional advice can be.

We hope this book advances the standard of care that financial planners and the companies we mentioned above provide their clients. But the fact is that you don't need these companies or financial planners to give you advice. If you own a personal computer, you can raise your living standard, smooth your consumption, and price your passions far better than *any* financial planner or company you might hire.* And if you don't own a PC, you can get much closer to true financial health by basing your financial decisions on the examples presented here and at www.esplanner.com, and www.assetbuilder.com.

---

* The professional standard of care will change when financial-planning clients insist on plans that make economic sense and when major financial institutions perceive that their Web "tools" and other financial elixirs are an embarrassment, if not a legal liability.

Part 3, "Raising Your Living Standard," tells you, among other things, how to decide, from a financial perspective:

- whether education pays
- which career to pursue
- which job delivers the highest spending power
- where to live
- how to finance your home
- how much to contribute to retirement accounts
- whether to save in regular or Roth retirement accounts
- the best age to begin collecting Social Security
- whether to annuitize your retirement assests
- whether to take out a reverse mortgage
- whether to pay down your mortgage
- whether to hold stocks or bonds in your retirement account
- whether to use a broker

Part 4, "Pricing Your Passions," helps you make a variety of life-style decisions that can make you much happier even if they reduce your living standard. These decisions include:

- getting married
- getting divorced
- retiring early
- having kids
- assisting your kids financially
- contributing to charity

Part 5, "Preserving Your Living Standard," is about risk taking and risk avoidance. Consumption smoothing is biased toward risk avoidance. This goes back to the law of diminishing returns. If you're famished and sitting in front of three cupcakes, you'd surely turn down a 50-50 chance of either losing one or winning an extra.

Why? Well, if you lose the gamble, you'll get to eat only two cupcakes and really wish you had a third. If you win, you'll already have eaten three when you reach for the fourth. With three in your gut, you'll probably say, "Gee, I'm getting a bit stuffed." So the fourth cupcake—the upside—has much less value than the third cupcake—the downside.

This is why taking fair gambles is an economics no-no. But if the gamble is sufficiently favorable—if you have, say, a 50 percent chance of losing one cupcake and a 50 percent chance of winning ten cupcakes, flipping the coin may be worth it. So economics doesn't counsel absolute prudence. Gambling is OK, but only when the odds are favorable enough to overcome your risk aversion—your desire to avoid loss.

Investing in stocks is an example of a favorable bet. Historically, stocks have provided a much higher return than bonds. But investing in stocks can entail lots of living-standard risk. Part 5 lets you see this risk with your own eyes via a living standard risk-reward diagram. For those used to thinking about portfolio choice based on the risk-return (mean-variance) efficiency frontier diagram, now five decades old, this new diagram will be an eye-opener. It shows how the level and variability of our living standards change as we age, based on how we invest our assets and how we spend them.

We'll use the living-standard-risk diagram to consider whether stocks are safer the longer you hold them (they aren't), whether life-cycle funds properly adjust your portfolio holdings as you age (they don't), and whether you should follow a popularly recommended 4 percent asset-spend-down rule in retirement (you shouldn't).

Part 5 also examines the other major risks to your economic life: the risks of losing your earnings, dying too soon, living too long, experiencing inflation, tax hikes and Social Security benefit cuts, and long-term care. Although it might seem impossible to limit many of these risks, there are, as we'll explain, novel ways to inoculate yourself against (hedge) each of them.

Deciding which risks to take and which to avoid is particularly tough for two reasons. First, we face a goodly number of different risks. Second, how we evaluate any given risk depends on how we're handling the others. Thus, holding lots of stock in our portfolio is one thing if we're in a highly secure job. It's another thing if we're in a job that could disappear overnight.

Part 5's parting advice is to take a safety-first approach to risk taking. The idea is to start from a position of maximum risk insulation and consider from this vantage point if any risky opportunities make sense, be they investing in the stock market, canceling expensive insurance policies, switching to riskier employment, or taking off the inflation and policy hedges we'll tell you about. If none does—if a maximally safe and secure financial future floats your boat—stick with it. There's no shame in playing it safe.

Full Disclosure

Much of the book contains examples based on ESPlanner™, the only publicly available personal financial-planning software program developed by economists. ESPlanner, which stands for Economic Security Planner™, is marketed to individuals, financial planners, educators, and employers at www.esplanner.com by Economic Security Planning Inc.*

Larry is president of the company and has a financial stake in the software we'll be using to illustrate the Three Commandments. Scott does not. He likens ESPlanner to VisiCalc, the first spreadsheet program created in the late 1970s. VisiCalc launched the personal computer industry and played a major role in driving sales of the Apple II. But over time it was supplanted by Lotus 1-2-3, which was supplanted by Excel. ESPlanner, while the first commercial consumption smoother, will surely not be the last and may not even retain top market share in the long run. As with VisiCalc, the importance of ESPlanner is what it portends.

So please don't view this book as a sales pitch for ESPlanner. You can read and benefit from this book even if you never buy ESPlanning. Regard this book instead as a sales pitch for an economics-

---

* Larry and Stanford economist Douglas Bernheim started the company in the mid-nineties. Larry and Cato economist Jagadeesh Gokhale designed and developed the program's basic code.

based approach to financial health. You should also know that economic science has only one prescription when it comes to financial planning—namely, consumption smoothing—and all consumption-smoothing computer programs (there are hundreds, if not thousands being used in research) that carefully calculate taxes and Social Security benefits will generate the same recommendation as ESPlanner for the same inputs.

This book's examples and those posted (under Case Studies) at www.esplanner.com and www.assetbuilder.com will give you a pretty clear sense of how much to save, how much to insure, and how much to invest in risky securities. You'll also learn about a wide range of moves that can raise your living standard. Finally, you'll start to see the true living-standard price of a host of lifestyle decisions.

That said, since ESPlanner will be used to produce our examples, it's important to point out that the program has been well vetted. It's been on the market for several years and has been sold to thousands of households. The program has been featured in leading newspapers, magazines, and Web sites, including the *New York Times,* the *Wall Street Journal,* the *Washington Post,* the *Boston Globe, USA Today, Consumer Reports,* the *Dallas Morning News,* the *Baltimore Sun, Time, BusinessWeek, Forbes, Fortune, Money,* MSN Money, *SmartMoney, Kiplinger's Personal Finance, Investor's Business Daily,* Fox News, NBC News, MarketWatch, *CFO Magazine,* CNNMoney, Bloomberg.com, Motley Fool, Yahoo–Finance, *InvestmentNews, Financial Advisor,* and *The Journal of Financial Planning.* ESPlanner has also been strongly endorsed by top economists, including the late Franco Modigliani, who won the 1985 Nobel Prize in Economic Sciences for work on the life-cycle model of saving.

ESPlanner's patented algorithm actually features two dynamic programs—one to smooth the household's living standard and one to determine the life insurance holdings needed to protect that living standard—that iterate with (talk to) each other. In less than five seconds the program generates either a perfectly smooth living standard path or the smoothest living standard path consistent with not going into debt (apart from borrowing for a home). In these five seconds, the program not only does iterative dynamic programming but also calculates taxes and Social Security benefits in thousands of survivor states.*

How do we know that the answers ESPlanner yields are accurate? We can verify from the financial plan's balance sheets and other reports that (a) the recommended living standard path is either perfectly smooth or as smooth as it can be absent borrowing; (b) the financial plan considers all household assets, earnings, special expenditures, housing expenses, college, estate plans, taxes, and Social Security retirement benefits; and (c) survivors receive precisely enough life insurance to maintain their former living standard.

Now it's our turn to ask a question: How does the conventional method of financial planning stack up against the economics approach? Read on and find out.

---

* Dynamic programming is a mathematical technique developed in 1953 by mathematician Richard Bellman. An example of a survivor state is the husband dies at forty-seven and his widow is alive at seventy-one.

PART 1

Smooth
Financial Paths

Whether we're young or old, rich or poor, smart or cranially challenged, we all must decide how to lead a secure financial life without hoarding or squandering. Getting it right can be pretty tough.

Just ask George Foreman, two-time heavyweight boxing champion of the world and the oldest man ever to win the championship (at age forty-five!). In 1973, at the age of twenty-four, Foreman beat Joe Frazier for his first heavyweight title and had millions. By the mid-1980s he was broke.

As the fighter told the *New York Times* in 2006: "It was frightening, the most horrible thing that can happen to a man, as far as I am concerned. . . . I had a family, people to take care of—my wife, my children, my mother. I haven't gotten over that yet. . . . It was that scary because you hear about people being homeless, and I was only fractions, fractions from being homeless."

Foreman's far from the only rich luminary to squander his/her riches. The list of famous spendthrifts includes Thomas Jefferson, Buffalo Bill Cody, Mark Twain, Ulysses S. Grant, Michael Jackson, Dorothy Hamill, Robert Maxwell, and Mike Tyson.

There are also extreme misers. Take Hetty Green. At the turn of the last century, Hetty was the wealthiest woman in America. Dubbed "the witch of Wall Street," Hetty was notorious for her stinginess, never turning on the heat, never using hot water, and never changing her clothes. Her diet consisted of 15-cent pies. When her son, Ned, broke a leg and had to be hospitalized, she took him home because of the expense. As a result, poor Ned lost his leg to gangrene.

Obviously, Hetty was nuts. George Foreman was too, at least when he was blowing his wad. (He's since rebuilt his wealth in part by selling the Lean Mean Grilling Machine.) You, we're sure, are neither a spendthrift nor a miser. But given that you're reading this book, you are probably worried whether you are saving the right amount, holding the right amount of insurance, and investing wisely.

You should be.

1. "I Am Financially Sick"

EVER OFFER AN AA member a drink? The first words out of his mouth are "I'm an alcoholic." And a good thing too. Fessing up to having a drinking problem is tough stuff. But doing so has great curative powers. It eliminates the internal BS. It identifies the condition as medical. And it keeps the booze from flowing.

Owning up to financial disease is as curative. It makes us examine our financial decisions and seek financial advice.

So, please, repeat after us: "I am financially sick."

You're not alone. We're all financially sick. We spend too much, save too little, underinsure, invest foolishly on hot tips, fail to diversify, try to beat the market, gamble, buy lottery tickets, shop compulsively, hold on to losers, max out our credit cards, get hooked on Starbucks, and spend as little time as humanly possible thinking about the future. Plenty of us end up living off Social Security.

Or we do the opposite. We pinch every penny, worry endlessly about our finances, oversave, buy too much insurance, take no risks, and avoid debt like the plague—only to wind up in a retirement home with far more money than we can possibly spend. We squander our youth instead of our money.

Either way, we screw things up. There is a good reason why. We each have two personalities at war within our brains: a current self and a future self. The future self is constantly yelling at the current self to behave, to be careful, and to worry about tomorrow. The current self is constantly telling the future self that life's too short, that it's party time, and that the future will take care of itself. Sometimes one wins, sometimes the other.

The struggle is continuous. Should we buy that Krispy Kreme donut? Should we eat out tonight? (MasterCard is always ready to give us a "priceless" experience.) Should we upgrade our cell phone? Can we afford a new car? Are we saving enough for the kids' college? Wouldn't a trip to Europe be fun? Should we contribute more to our 401(k)? Even the personal finance magazines are divided. The covers of *Kiplinger's, Money,* and *SmartMoney* yell at us to save, but inside they run articles telling us to spend.

To make matters worse, all manner of commercial enterprises are pitching their wares to our current and future selves. The sales effort is unrelenting. Buy this. Buy that. Save here. Insure with us. Invest now. Get in on the ground floor.

Conflicting advertising lures us simultaneously toward instant and deferred gratification. But the real trouble begins when our inner spender or inner saver always prevails—that's when we start playing extreme games with our financial health.

Even those of us able to keep our spend now/spend later schizophrenia at bay can be financially sick. Financial health isn't God-given, like good genes. It requires making the right spending, saving, and investment decisions, not once, not twice, but on an ongoing basis. Doing so is incredibly difficult. Sometimes we think we're making the right financial moves, but we're doing just the opposite. Or we can wait too long to move and miss golden opportunities.

Sounds hopeless, doesn't it? It isn't. Stick with us, and we'll show you, in simple terms, what you need to do to improve both your present and your future. And we'll explain how to use consumption smoothing to make lifestyle decisions that will raise your living standard.

Consumption smoothing means being able to spend 'til the end. Specifically, it means being able to sustain your family's living standard over time, as you age, and across times, as you experience good ones and bad ones. Obviously you can spend only what you can afford. And what you can afford depends on your earnings, assets, pensions, Social Security benefits, taxes, and other economic resources, both positive and negative.

Trying to spend more than your economic resources permit spells trouble: bill collectors, a bad credit rating, and, ultimately, bankruptcy. But spending less is also a problem. Why work hard your whole life and die without spending what you've earned?

No one wants to splurge today and starve tomorrow—or starve today and splurge tomorrow. Instead most of us seek a *smooth* consumption ride—a stable living standard—throughout our lives. We want to live at the highest and safest level given our resources and tolerance for risk. Figuring out how is the true path to financial health. But doing so with just your brain isn't easy—even for economists.

Clueless in Ann Arbor

Recently Larry attended a conference at the University of Michigan's Retirement Research Center. The participants included fifteen of the world's top economic experts on retirement saving. Their papers covered saving adequacy, health expenditures, retirement, and 401(k) contributions.

During one of the breaks, Larry gave the economists a quiz. He described a middle-aged, middle-class Ohio couple with an extremely simple set of demographic and economic characteristics, living in a world of perfect certainty—a world with no earnings, health expenditure, rate of return, inflation, tax, or Social Security surprises on the horizon.

Larry instructed each economist to write down on a piece of paper ("with no talking to your neighbor") how much the household should spend in the current year as part of a plan to achieve a smooth (stable) living standard per person through time.

The correct answer was $87,549. The answers that came back

ranged from \$42,712 to \$135,943, with an average value of \$73,211. The closest response was off the mark by \$12,872. Given the time allotted, the economists weren't able to use calculators, computers, or equations. They were forced to make their spending decision with the same tool most people use for these matters: their brains.

The fact that every one of these expert brains preformed so miserably in such a simple setting speaks volumes for our ability to make highly complex financial decisions on our own. Evolution didn't wire our brains to make sophisticated financial calculations. Our actual saving and insurance choices fall very wide of the computer-generated, economically optimal mark. Indeed, the statistical correlation between actual and economically appropriate financial decisions is close to zero. To put it bluntly, when it comes to dealing with our finances using just our brains, no one, including economists, has a clue!

2. Consumption Smoothing

A PICTURE TELLS a thousand words. So do examples. To understand consumption smoothing, please forget who you are, where you are, what you have, and what you want. Come with us on a trip—a drug trip.

Close your eyes. Now open them. *Voilà!* You're a forty-year-old drug dealer. You're single. You live in Chicago. You've got two kids living with an ex, whom you've totally abandoned. You have zero assets. But you're not poor. You earn $100K a year—an excellent living—and the best part is, *it's tax free!*

Your business is a bit unusual, but, hey, everyone's gotta make a buck. You're good at what you do. You consider yourself a professional. You follow the latest just-in-time inventory practices. You maintain quality control by sampling your wares. You wear a suit to work, which makes you feel good and reassures your upscale clients. And to bond with your customers, you read the financial press—the *Wall Street Journal, Forbes, Business Week, Fortune, Barron's*, and all the rest—each of which hits you with endless ads about retirement planning.

These ads have done their job. You've decided to take retirement planning seriously. Indeed, after considerable reflection, you've arrived at a simple and serious strategy. Your plan is to retire on your sixtieth birthday and celebrate by mainlining a lethal dose of heroin. Yes, this is grim. But this is your plan, and we're not going to argue with it.

How should you smooth your consumption between now and your termination date? Easy. Save nothing, and just spend $100K per year. Your living standard will be a perfectly stable $100K per year, year after year, right up to your going-away party.

Living Life to the Longest

Now suppose that you have a mind-altering (read chemical) experience. Suddenly you realize that life's a bowl of cherries. Suddenly you want to live as long as possible. In your case that's age ninety.

Your consumption-smoothing problem has gotten tougher. It's now going to require some middle school math.

Let's start by recalling that because you still want to retire at sixty, you have twenty years to work but up to fifty years to live. And though the chances are small, given your habits, that you'll live to ninety, you have to plan for that possibility. The alternative is living that long and starving.

What to do? Well, your earnings over the next twenty years come to $2 million ($100K × 20). Dividing this amount by the fifty years you have left equals $40,000 per year—the amount you can spend each year without running out. (We're assuming zero inflation and that you save money under your pillow to keep the government in the dark about your assets.)

Given your annual $100K earnings, this means you'll have to save $60K per year before you retire. By age sixty, you'll have saved $1.2 million, which will cover your annual $40K spending tab for your thirty years of retirement.

Note that your new passion—making it to age ninety—comes at a price: namely, a 60 percent reduction in your living standard for the next twenty years.

Finding Religion

Now suppose you have another "experience." This time you find religion. Religion tells you that it's time to grow up, get clean, and accept responsibility for your ten- and fifteen-year-old children. You agree, and within a week you find yourself feeding, clothing, and housing your two children, who are thrilled to be sharing your income.

How much should you spend, given that there are now two more mouths to feed? Good question. Here's what you have to consider: The kids will live with you until they turn nineteen. The kids don't eat as much. (Wrong!) Their clothes aren't as expensive. (Wrong!) They don't have your special pharmacological needs. (You hope!) And two can live more cheaply than one; in other words, the kids can share your apartment, television, heating, and so on. (Right!) So you need to factor in the relative costs of your kids as well as the economies of shared living.

But what's your goal? Is it spending exactly the same total amount each year? Or is it having the same living standard *per person* now and in the future?

It's the latter.

Consumption smoothing means achieving the same living standard per person when there are three of you at home, when there are two of you at home, and when you're by yourself. But that means more *total* spending when the kids are at home.

When the two kids are at home, you should spend $59,759 each year. When your older child leaves home (at nineteen), you should spend $47,299 per year. And once the younger kid leaves, you should spend $33,006 annually. This amount—$33,006—is, by the way, your household's living standard per person. It's your own annual living standard through all your remaining years of life as well as that of your kids when they are at home.

So taking in the kids costs you. Your annual living standard was $40,000. It's now $33,006. Your living standard dropped by 17.5 percent. But the kids are happier, you're happier on balance, and money's not everything.

Becoming a Republican

Having the kids at home is great, except for one thing. They keep asking what you do for a living. Explaining that you're a drug dealer doesn't cut it. After several days of agonizing about getting an honest job (the idea of paying taxes drives you nuts), you arrange to work for one of your former clients, who owns—guess what—a drug company!

You still earn $100K per year up to age sixty, but joy for joy, you now get to pay federal income taxes, federal payroll taxes, and state income taxes. After seething about the high cost of government, you suddenly realize two good things. First, you'll be eligible to collect Social Security retirement benefits. Second, you'll be able to invest your savings because you won't have to hide them from the feds. Let's assume you can earn 3 percent for sure above inflation on your savings and that you elect to start collecting Social Security at sixty-five.

How big an economic mistake did you make in taking an honest job and opting to pay taxes? In fact, you made no mistake. Going legit was the right move in terms of maximizing your spending power. Your living standard actually *rises* by 7 percent, from $33,006 to $35,362! True, you end up paying over $26K in taxes this year alone. But you also end up collecting over $21K per year in Social Security benefits from age sixty-five right through age ninety, if you make it that far. And earning a 3 percent real (above inflation) return provides you with what economists call the miracle of compound interest.

You're stunned and thrilled to learn that honesty is actually the best policy. You decide the straight and narrow life is the only way to go. You immediately join the Elks Club, the Lions Club, the Rotary Club, the Masons, the Kiwanis Club, and the Templars (yes, they are still around, albeit in hiding), and start delivering free lectures titled "Take It from Me—Crime *Really* Doesn't Pay." The audiences love you. They give you standing Os night after night. And then you do something you swore you'd never do: You become a Republican. (We'll get you Democrats later.)

Maximizing Your Living Standard

Just when you're sure life can't get any better, it does. You meet Irvina Fisher at the Youngish Republicans Club and fall head over heels in love. Irvina is your exact double. She has two kids the same ages as yours, earns $100K a year, wants to retire at sixty, and has a storied past that we won't mention. Better still, she's an economist who knows how to work every angle when it comes to raising one's living standard.

On your second date Irvina proposes marriage. She drops down on one knee, looks up at you with tears in her eyes, hands you a small jewelry box, and asks, "Will you marry me?" Shocked, you open the box to find a beautiful diamond-encrusted flash memory stick.

Irvina explains, "It contains my findings showing how much each of our living standards will rise if we get married, move to Wyoming to avoid state income taxes, contribute 6 percent of our salary annually to regular IRA accounts, annuitize our IRA balances at age sixty-five, and wait to age seventy to start collecting Social Security."

"Darling, just tell me the truth," you say. "You know I trust your analysis, and, anyway, I'll double-check the numbers tonight. Just tell me, can we swing it?"

"*Can we swing it?*" shouts Irvina. "Our living standards will rise from $35,362 each to $46,865 each!"

"*My Lord!*" you scream. "That's almost a one-third increase. I'd have to work for an extra decade—to age seventy—to raise my living standard by that amount. Of course I'll marry you!"

Economic Magic

Where did this huge living-standard increase come from? Partly from economies in shared living (two can live more cheaply than one), partly from paying no state income taxes, partly from saving taxes on a lifetime basis by contributing to an IRA, partly from annuitizing IRA balances at retirement (buying an annuity with the IRA proceeds), and partly from waiting until age seventy to take Social Security. We'll discuss the relative importance of these different factors in part 3, but for now the key point is this: Lifestyle choices and financial planning, done right, can make a *huge* difference in your living standard.

Takeaways

- Consumption smoothing means achieving a stable living standard per person.
- Consumption smoothing entails more total spending when there are more mouths to feed.
- Financial planning can dramatically raise your living standard.
- Financial planning maps out the costs and benefits of lifestyle decisions.
- Financial planning can be fun.

3. Conventional Consumption Disruption

LOOKING BACK ON your chemical, religious, and Republican metamorphoses, you realize that your spending and saving plans changed a bunch.

"Gosh," you say, "I initially planned to spend $100K this year and save nothing. Then I decided to live life to the longest and spend $40K and save $60K. Then the kids moved in, so I decided to spend $59,759 and save $38,759. Next I went straight and learned I could spend $64,024 this year, save just $8,741, pay a bucket load of taxes, and still have a higher living standard forever. Finally, I got married and discovered that Irvina and I could jointly spend $135,763, but we need to save $3,051 over and above the $12,000 in IRA contributions we're making.

"But hang on. Now that we've joined the middle class, we're going to have to think about college tuition, buying a house, taking out a mortgage, and planning to leave the kids some money when we kick. Will these factors also change the amounts of spending and saving needed to smooth my living standard?"

They sure will.

Rules of Dumb

It turns out that what you should spend and save is *extraordinarily* sensitive to your household's economic and demographic circumstances, your housing decisions, and your special expenditure goals. Hence, rules of thumb like "Save 15 percent of your income," are, in fact, rules of *dumb*. This is true whether the rules of dumb are provided by your local financial planner or your dearest uncle.

Just consider your first four transformations. Your saving prescription changed from 0 percent of your income to 60 percent, then to 39 percent, and finally to 9 percent of your income.

The conceit of a rule of dumb is that it can tell you what to do without asking you a single question. "Save 15 percent." This same piece of advice, or one like it, is provided no matter who you are, how old you are, how much you earn, what regular and retirement account assets you own, whether you have a mortgage, whether you have kids, whether you're going to pay for their college, whether your earnings are rising, and on and on.

Giving a household financial advice without knowing its circumstances is like a doctor's dispensing medicine without examining the patient or even hearing what the patient thinks is wrong. In the medical world, doing this would get the doctor fired or sued.

Quick and Dirty Diagnoses

There are literally thousands of quick retirement saving, insurance, and investment calculators that give you a three-minute or shorter financial checkup prior to dispensing financial advice. Take Fidelity's myPlan Snapshot, which it says can determine "whether you're on track for your retirement goals," "how much you need to save for retirement," and "the action steps you need to get there." The my-

Plan calculator asks just five questions: your age, your earnings, your current savings, your monthly saving, and your investment style. TIAA-CREF's Retirement Goal Evaluator asks only six questions. So does its online insurance calculator.

As we'll show, these "advice" tools too often make wildly high saving and insurance recommendations. But that's the point. The goal, it seems, is not to provide sound advice; the goal is to move you quickly from planning to purchasing and make sure that you spend as much as possible (in other words, more than you should) on financial products.

TIAA-CREF, of all companies, should know better. If there is one investment company that should care about the quality of its financial advice, it's this one. TIAA-CREF was founded by the great industrialist and philanthropist Andrew Carnegie. At the turn of the twentieth century, Carnegie was the world's richest man. Although a tough SOB when it came to running his business and handling his workers, Carnegie was also one of the humblest and most generous people to walk the earth. He attributed much of his success to others. And he followed his dictum—"The man who dies rich dies disgraced"—by donating his entire estate to charity.

Carnegie was particularly passionate about education and educators. In 1918 he endowed the Teachers Insurance and Annuity Association, forerunner of today's TIAA-CREF, with a clear mandate: to secure the financial well-being of America's teachers. Over time TIAA-CREF has grown and opened its doors to the general public. It's now one of the nation's largest mutual funds and insurance companies.

Carnegie would be rightfully proud of TIAA-CREF's tremendous growth and sound investment practices. But we think he'd be dismayed to learn that the company seems overly focused on sales, not the real financial needs of the teachers and rest of the public it serves. If TIAA-CREF is too focused on sales to provide sound advice, what about the recommendations that come from brokerage firms like Merrill Lynch and Morgan Stanley Dean Witter or insurance companies such as Allianz Life Insurance Company of North America?

These firms are well-oiled marketing machines. Product sales are their first and second priorities. Financial planning, for them, is a marketing tool.

Consumption Smoothing Is the Target

A rule of thumb like "Save 15 percent of your income" is the dumbest type of financial advice because it's based on literally no information. Simple Web-based saving, insurance, and investment calculators at least ask a couple of questions. One question they all ask is about your retirement spending needs—specifically, how much you need to spend in retirement and how much you need your survivors to spend if you kick the bucket. These calculators are used to determine how much you should save and how much life insurance you should buy. This all sounds reasonable, unless you set the wrong target.

In writing this chapter, we thought long and hard about how much we'd need to spend in retirement. Larry decided that he needed to spend $10 million a year to achieve genuine old-age bliss. Scott settled for $500,000. Why the difference? Well, Larry needs the Learjet, the big yacht, the private island in the Caribbean, lots of attendants, and so on. Scott has more modest needs, mostly involving a vintage RV collection.

Neither of our needs (our desired targets) is remotely affordable. We both could save every penny we earn, work as hard as humanly possible, and still not retire with enough money to fund our targeted spending.

After a lot of fussing and fuming about forgoing the jet and trailers, we decided to set our targets based on our current spending. But this didn't work either. Larry's current spending is far too high to maintain. And Scott's current spending is ridiculously low.

Eventually we understood that our real target was an even, sustainable living standard. Neither of us wanted a lower living standard now and a higher one later, and neither wanted a higher living standard now and a lower one later. We realized that our proper retirement and survivor spending targets are those associated with consumption smoothing.

Life's Too Short for Target Practice

In your latest incarnation as a born-for-the-first-time Republican with a wife and four kids to support, consumption smoothing dictates that you and Irvina jointly spend $74,984 in today's dollars each year in retirement. There's no guesswork here. No wishful thinking. This figure is precise and fully determined by the mathematics of the problem. Stated differently, there is only one answer to the question, What's the most I can spend each year such that my living standard and that of others in my household is both stable and as high as possible? (This abstracts from both borrowing constraints and economic and demographic risks, which we'll discuss in subsequent chapters.)

Determining this spending path, which entails the highest constant living standard, isn't easy for mere mortals. It requires some pretty tricky math. But it takes a modern computer fewer than five seconds. Given that we have such tools, there's no reason that you have to guess your spending target. When you see a doctor for an infection, he doesn't ask you to guess which antibiotic to take or suggest that you manufacture your own penicillin. No, he's there to prescribe something he knows will work.

The Downside of Self-Medicating

When Web-based financial tools ask you to set your own retirement and survivor spending targets, they are, in fact, asking you to plan for yourself. And they are asking you to do all the hard work: Setting your own targets is the toughest part of the entire financial planning problem. But Web-based financial tools are not unique in promoting self-medication.

Go visit your local financial planner and pay $2,500 for a "professional" retirement plan. His first question will be "What's your spending target?" As your mouth hangs open and your forehead creases, he'll reach for a twenty-page form and tell you, "Take this home and record each and every purchase you made over the past year, be it on dental floss or diamond earrings. Bring this back, and we'll see how much you're spending. We'll then use your current spending to set your target."

Lots of financial planning stops right there. But filling out those forms is no better, because it leads to the wrong target. Why? Because whatever you are currently spending will almost surely differ from what you should be spending, either now or in the future, based on consumption smoothing. Consumption smoothing, as you're probably starting to see, is a very precise business, and, if you don't have several Pentium 4 or later-model chips implanted in your brain, the likelihood that you are now spending anything close to the consumption-smoothing amount is remote. Using the wrong level of current spending to set your future spending targets is not a path to the right answer.

Small Targeting Mistakes Spell Major Consumption Disruption

Even small targeting mistakes—on the order of 15 percent—in setting your retirement and survivor spending targets can lead to huge mistakes in how much you're told to save and how much life insurance you're told to buy. These misguided recommendations can lead to major disruptions—on the order of 25 percent—in your living standard! Such *consumption disruption* is the hallmark of traditional financial planning.

Take Joe and Sally Blow. They're forty-year-old perfectly PC California Democrats with two kids, a modest home, $125K in total annual salary, $200K in savings, a big mortgage, lots of future college expenses, and maximum ages of life of one hundred. The Blows plan to retire at sixty.

Given the extra mouths to feed and the mortgage payments, the couple should save $6K and spend $52K on consumption this year. In retirement the Blows should spend $37K annually on consumption.

By consumption we mean the discretionary spending we're *free* to do, not the spending we *have* to do. Consumption, as we define it, does *not* include nondiscretionary "off-the-top" expenditures on taxes, life insurance premiums, retirement account contributions, regular saving, housing, college, weddings, and other special expenditures.

Joe and Sally's consumption-smoothing plan—spend $52K on consumption when the kids are at home and $37K when they've left the nest—maintains the household's living standard through time at $23K per person per year.* This $23K is the amount that Joe and Sally would each have to spend, were they living completely alone, to achieve the same living standard they enjoy as married. Note that $23K is a lot bigger than $52K divided by four or $37K divided by two. This is due to economies of shared living—the fact that two can live a lot more cheaply than one. Achieving a steady living standard per person is consumption smoothing.

Now suppose that the Blows are spending 15 percent too much ($60K instead of $52K) when they visit their financial planner, who suggests they set their retirement spending target based on their current spending. "Sounds good," say the Blows, as they set their retirement spending target 15 percent too high as well (at $43K instead of $37K).

This seems like a small mistake. It's not. In order to follow this plan, the Blows have to save twice as much as they should this year ($12K instead of $6K) and cut their current spending by almost 25 percent (from $60K to $46K), when the right cut is only 13 percent (from $60K to $52K).

In following this advice, the Blows will no longer enjoy a stable living standard of $23K per person through time. Instead their living

---

* We assume that two people can live for the price of 1.6. So two times $23K is $46K, which is greater than $37K. But the difference represents our assumed economies of shared living; that is, 1.6 times $23K is $37K. The $23K is the amount of spending a Blow would need to do to have the same living standard as a single person as she or he has when married.

standard per person will be $20K before retirement and $26K thereafter—a 30 percent difference!

So the Blows will be told to live substantially below their means prior to age sixty in order to party big-time thereafter—if they make it to the thereafter. This is consumption disruption, not consumption smoothing.

How can such a small targeting mistake lead to such major mistakes in spending and saving recommendations? The answer is that the Blows are making a small targeting mistake not for one or two years but for forty years, since they have to plan for the possibility of living to one hundred! And all these mistakes add up. They also cost the Blows a lot in taxes. In saving too much, the Blows end up with extra taxes on their extra asset income—taxes they wouldn't have paid otherwise.

Undertargeting Is Also Bad

Most, but far from all, American households appear to be overspending compared to the consumption-smoothing standard. For those that are underspending, conventional targeting leads to retirement spending targets that are too low. For example, suppose the Blows are spending 15 percent less ($44K, not $52K) than they should this year and that, with this reference point, they also set their retirement spending target 15 percent too low (at $31K, not $37K).

In this case, traditional planning will tell the Blows to save very little this year and raise their current spending by 32 percent (from $44K to $58K). In following these recommendations, the Blows will find their living standard plunges 24 percent at retirement!

This is consumption disruption.

Transforming Misers into Spendthrifts and Spendthrifts into Misers

In using current spending to set future spending targets, conventional financial planning transforms oversavers into undersavers and undersavers into oversavers. Those spending too little (oversavers) are led to set too low a retirement spending target and end up undersaving. Those spending too much (undersavers) are led to set too high a target and end up oversaving.

This is ironic; if the Blows are oversaving, they are doing so presumably because they fear a decline in their living standard at retirement. Yet traditional planning will ensure this very outcome. And if the Blows are undersaving, they are doing so presumably because they worry about missing out on life while they're young—precisely what traditional planning will have them do.

Life Insurance Advice

When it comes to purchasing life insurance, conventional practice will also push Joe and Sally Blow to use their current spending level to set spending targets, but in this case for their survivors. If Joe and Sally are miraculously spending at the correct consumption-smoothing level, they'll need $360K in combined life insurance holdings. But if they are spending 15 percent too much and use their current unsustainable living standard as the basis for setting their survivors' spending target for all sixty years of potential survivorship, they'll be told to buy $680K in life insurance—nearly twice what they need. And if they are spending 15 percent too little and set their survivor targets 15 percent too low (again, for all sixty years of potential survivorship), conventional advice will say hold $175K in insurance—less than half the right number.

So conventional advice not only transforms oversavers into undersavers and undersavers into oversavers, it also transforms oversavers into underinsurers and undersavers into overinsurers.

Margin for Error

The really scary part is that a 15 percent targeting error is small relative to the size of the errors conventional financial Web tools and financial planning software programs are generating. TIAA-CREF's Retirement Goal Evaluator, for example, doesn't ask users to add up their purchases of underwear, ketchup, Harley-Davidsons, and so on, to determine their current spending and, thus, their future spending needs. Instead the program simply recommends a *replacement rate*—a ratio of targeted retirement spending to preretirement earnings. TIAA-CREF's recommended replacement rate is 80 percent. For the Blows, whose combined earnings are $125K, this means setting a spending target of $100K. This is more than twice the right consumption-smoothing target!

Were the Blows to set such a target, they'd have to save this year over $50K instead of the appropriate $6K. To do so, they'd have to virtually starve. To say this is nuts is an understatement. But TIAA-CREF has lots of bad company in recommending such high replacement rates.

Fidelity's online Retirement Quick Check calculator recommends a replacement rate of 60 percent of earnings. This translates into a $75K retirement spending target. Vanguard, another huge financial institution, offers Financial Engines for free to customers with over $100,000 in invested assets. The online investment-advice service, although developed by Economics Nobel laureate William F. Sharpe, engages in conventional financial planning, which means that it disrupts, rather than smooths, one's living standard. Financial Engines recommends a 70 percent replacement rate. Bank of America recommends a 70 percent to 80 percent replacement rate. And the list goes on.

We're not saying these replacement rates are ridiculously high for every household. They may, by accident, be just right for some. And they may be far too low for others. But for most households they seem stratospheric.

Hawking Life Insurance

There is an old saying that "life insurance is sold, not purchased." Life insurance agents have a well-deserved reputation for being hucksters. They hawk intentionally complex policies—whole life, universal life, permanent life, variable life—that require a PhD to master. So perhaps it's no surprise that were the Blows to land at TIAA-CREF's online insurance calculator, they'd be told to hold a combined $2 million in life insurance. That's a wee bit on the high side (and we didn't even tell the calculator about the Blows' mortgage and college expenditure needs). The right number—the one computed to maintain an even living standard throughout life for all, including survivors—is $360K.

Replacement Baits

It is no accident that the investment/insurance/retirement complex frequently recommends replacement rates that are excessively high, with little or no relationship to real needs. These replacement rates—really, replacement baits—come from a single source: an "independent" Georgia State University analysis funded by Aon Corporation. Aon Corporation just happens to be a very large insurance company that just happens to service other large insurance companies. We'll discuss the method used to determine replacement rates in chapter 8. For the moment, let's just say that it's a far cry from the method required by consumption smoothing to find the right replacement rate/spending target.

Soliciting Risk

"OK, you guys convinced me. Lots of companies and financial planners are recommending too much saving and insurance. But if their recommendations are nutty, why don't their customers simply say, 'I can't afford what you're proposing'?"

They do. But the companies and many FPs have a ready response: namely, "Let's consider having you invest in higher-return securities. This will raise the probability of your meeting your target."

What they don't say is that investing in higher-return assets greatly exacerbates your downside risk, while generally increasing the fees charged for management.

This pimping of risk is our next topic. But first, please consider these takeaways.

Takeaways

- Consumption smoothing is highly sensitive to your circumstances.
- Rules of thumb are rules of dumb.
- Life is too short for target practice.
- Consumption smoothing is the target.
- Traditional planning makes you do all the hard work.
- Setting your own spending targets is incredibly difficult.
- Small targeting mistakes produce significant consumption disruption.
- Major financial and insurance companies use high replacement rates to encourage dangerous risk taking.

4. Pimping Risk

A fool and his money are easily parted.

—THOMAS TUSSER

PROSTITUTION MAY BE the world's oldest profession, but selling risky investments is surely the most lucrative. Just ask today's college seniors, vast numbers of whom are dying to land a job on Wall Street. These jobs start in the six figures and head north from there. With the right stuff, you can pull down millions within a couple of years. What's the right stuff? Well, as far as we can tell, it's a combination of skill, balls, and luck.

Take New Jersey governor Jon Corzine, whose last private-sector job was running Goldman Sachs. In his twenty-five years with the company, he amassed close to a half billion dollars in assets! This for a guy who can't even dunk a basketball! How'd he get so rich?

You might say we all chipped in. Year after year, we, the general public, get conned into paying financial wizards like Corzine to "beat the market." Trouble is, not everyone can beat the market. Indeed, three-quarters of money managers underperform the market. And there's no telling ahead of time which investment "guru" is going to hit it right in a given year. This is why we should avoid money managers. If you really want to invest in stocks, do so only one way: by buying very low-cost, highly diversified domestic and international index funds. These funds will provide the return of their asset class.

We should also be leery of financial institutions and advisers offering to match our needs to the securities they're peddling. As we showed in chapter 3, their con begins with getting us to define our needs—our retirement spending targets—at a level far above what's appropriate. Step two is their assumption that we're going to spend this amount year after year regardless of what returns we earn on our investments. In step three they use Monte Carlo simulations* to determine the probability of plan success—of being able to spend at the targeted rate through the end of life. Step four is showing that prudent but lower-return investments won't reach the appointed goal. And step five is encouraging us to invest in higher-return securities, so "our" plan will "succeed."

Getting us to buy higher-return securities means getting us to pay additional brokerage, management, and other fees. But the bigger problem is that investing in higher-return securities, while potentially raising the chance of "success," also exposes us to much more downside risk.

Take, as an example, a sixty-year-old unmarried man named Bill, whose only economic resource is $500,000 in assets. Assume Bill's maximum age of life (the oldest age to which he could possibly live, and the only appropriate age for planning because he *could* make it that far) is ninety-five. Also assume that he faces no taxes of any kind. Suppose Bill sets his spending target at $25,000 per year. Also assume that Bill holds only TIPs—Treasury inflation-protected bonds—yielding 2 percent after inflation. This secure plan will permit Bill to consume $20,413 in today's dollars each year.† What's

* Monte Carlo simulations are used to examine possible results when events are varied and uncertain—such as the sequence of returns stocks may earn. By repeated random samples, after thousands, the distribution of long-term results can be examined.

† TIPs are issued by Uncle Sam and protected against inflation. Each year as prices rise, the government preserves the purchasing power of the bond's principal (the amount you get when the bond comes due) by raising it by a percentage equal to that year's inflation rate.

Bill's probability of meeting his target? It's zero, of course, since spending $25,000 will drive Bill broke unless he fortuitously dies early.

Now suppose that Bill invests in large-cap stocks rather than in TIPs. Large-cap stocks are the stocks of the companies whose market capitalization (market cap) is greater than $8 billion. *Market cap* refers to the market value of the company's stock—the price per share multiplied by the number of shares. Since 1926 the real return on large caps has averaged 9.2 percent on an annual basis.* Were Bill able to earn this return for sure, he'd be able to spend $48,264 per year. But large-cap stocks are risky. Nonetheless, there's a better than 50 percent chance that Bill will be able to spend $25,000 per year. So if Bill uses a standard Monte Carlo portfolio analyzer, he'll find that investing in TIPs fails completely to meet his goal, whereas investing in stocks will meet his goal two-thirds of the time. Bill may view this as a pretty good bet given the way this investment outcome information is being presented.

Say Bill does invest all his assets in large caps but then experiences in the next three years the large-cap real returns recorded in 1999, 2000, and 2001: –12.1 percent, –13.2 percent, and –23.9 percent, respectively. Will Bill continue to spend $25,000 per year and remain in the stock market, given that his wealth after three years has dropped from $500,000 to $217,583? Probably not. At that point, he may well switch to holding TIPs only. In that case, he will be forced to live from that point on only $9,469 per year. Bill of course, will be kicking himself for the rest of his life. But the real culprit is the advice he received, which focused his attention on the chance of plan success rather than on the full extent of the downside.

Which well-known financial institutions engage in this type of risk solicitation? The question is, which don't? This advice is part and parcel of the conventional targeted-spending approach to finan-

---

* This is the average of annual arithmetic real returns rather than the geometric mean. The data source is *Ibbotson 2006 Stocks, Bonds, Bills and Inflation Yearbook*.

cial planning. Consumption smoothing, in contrast, entails adjusting your spending, saving, insurance, and asset holdings on an ongoing basis to secure a relatively stable living standard—one that's only as high as your wages, current assets, and other economic resources permit.

To smooth their consumption, people need to see the range of actual living standards they may experience in sticking with a particular portfolio. Had Bill been told that by holding stocks he could quickly end up living on less than ten grand a year, most likely he'd have thought twice about doing so.

The Con within the Con

As Boston University finance professor Zvi Bodie stresses in his excellent book *Worry-free Investing,* when the investment companies assess the probability of your meeting "your" target by investing in safe assets, they typically assume that you'd choose either cash or money market funds. Money market funds are very low-yielding securities whose real returns (returns after inflation) have historically been negative, on average. Cash, by definition, has a zero nominal return and a real return equal to minus the inflation rate. So if prices are rising (if the inflation rate is positive), holding cash is a losing strategy. That money under your pillow will buy fewer and fewer real goods and services as time goes by.

In addition to bearing negative real returns, on average, neither cash nor money market funds are safe. Their real returns vary over time, thanks to unexpected changes in inflation rates and money market yields. Yes, the variability of the real return on holding cash or money market funds is less than that of holding stock. But neither is safe.

The only truly safe asset in which one can invest is TIPs. Absent the U.S. government formally defaulting on its official debt, TIPs, if held to maturity, will pay a perfectly safe real return. As we write, long-term TIPs are yielding on an annual basis close to 2.4 percent real returns. Were investment companies to use TIPs as the safe asset in comparing the probability of making retirement spending targets by using safe and risky assets, they'd be forced to show a much higher probability of success from this safe investment strategy. As a result, they would surely sell a lot fewer high-fee equity mutual funds and make a lot less money.

Takeaways

- Financial institutions aren't your friends.
- Financial institutions are pimping risk.
- Understand the living-standard risk you face when investing in the market.
- The best way to invest in stocks is to buy index funds.
- The only truly safe asset is TIPs—Treasury inflation-protected securities.

5. Financial Mind-benders

Education is the best provision for old age.

—ARISTOTLE

REMEMBER THOSE TWELVE financial mind-benders that we posed in the preface? Each of these mind-benders directly relates to how you price, maximize, and protect your living standard. We want to quickly show you the power of economic medicine over conventional financial voodoo in helping you to make the right decisions.

Setting Spending Targets Is Asking for Big Trouble

To recapitulate, conventional financial planning makes *you* set future spending targets. Even small targeting mistakes can lead to enormous mistakes in recommended saving and insurance levels and to major disruptions in your household's future living standard.

Typical Households Should Hold Relatively More Stock than the Rich

To economists, portfolio risk refers to one and only one concern: the variability of your living standard. You may have every penny of your assets invested in the riskiest possible way but still have a very safe living standard if (1) your assets are relatively small compared with your income, and (2) your income is very stable. Suppose, to go to the extreme, you're a retiree with no financial assets living solely off Social Security. The stock market can go nuts—rise to enormous heights or crash wildly—and it won't make a bit of difference to your monthly Social Security check or to your living standard, which is perfectly stable.

Most low- and middle-income households have small levels of financial assets relative to their incomes. In addition, labor earnings and government benefits provide a relatively high and safe floor to their living standard. So when they invest all their assets in stocks, they face a much smaller chance of suffering a drop in their living standard than a household that is more dependent on its investments. If this seems odd, consider this: with a typical Social Security check over $1,000 a month for an average worker, the worker would need to have about $300,000 in financial assets before the income from those assets would be as important as the income from Social Security. Above-average dual-earner households will need well over $1 million in financial assets before their portfolio income approaches their Social Security income.

Diversifying Your Portfolio Is Generally a Bad Idea

Limiting our living-standard risk requires diversifying all our economic resources, not just our financial assets. But most of our economic resources are tied up in current and future labor earnings, Social Security retirement benefits, or other nonfinancial assets. These nonfinancial resources generally are like bonds with respect to their risk properties. So diversifying our resources generally requires concentrating our financial assets in stock, since we already hold so much in bondlike resources.

Stock Holdings Should Rise, Fall, Rise, and Fall with Age

Unlike the message of life-cycle funds—that stock holdings should start high and decline as you age—economics says that your stock holdings should satisfy a roller-coaster relationship with age. If you are going to hold stocks at all, you should start with a small allocation to stock when very young, increase it dramatically through middle age, reduce it as you approach retirement, increase it in early retirement, and reduce it in late retirement.

Complicated? Yes. But it reflects our commitments and capacities throughout life.

Young households are typically asset poor. They are also unable to borrow to deal with temporary financial downturns. The reason is that they have high off-the-top expenses, such as paying off the mortgage and paying for their kids' education or possibly their own education. Consequently, any reduction in income comes right out of consumption—in other words, out of their current living standard. Hence, for the young to invest their meager savings or relatively low labor earnings in stocks is much riskier in terms of living-standard variability than it is for the middle-aged.

The middle-aged, in turn, have most of their resources tied up in labor earnings, so investing more in stock better diversifies their total resources. As workers approach retirement, they face increased earnings risk. They also face government policy risk—the risk that expected benefits, such as Social Security, will be reduced. Both militate toward holding less stock. Upon reaching retirement, they find themselves receiving a very safe stream of income from Social Security. This permits their taking more risk in the form of higher stock holding. Finally, in late retirement, increased health expenditure risk suggests reducing one's exposure to stock as a means of controlling overall risk.

Having Children May Lower Your Need for Life Insurance

If you have kids, you know they aren't cheap. You also know that the more kids you have, the lower your own living standard is. This is just arithmetic. With more mouths to feed, less can be put into any given mouth. Life insurance is meant to protect the kids' living standard when they're young, as well as the spouse's or partner's living standard throughout the rest of her/his life. But in having more kids, you're also reducing the level of the spouse's/partner's living standard that needs to be protected. This is part of the reason that life insurance needs can fall with more children. The other is that children come packaged with their own life insurance policies on their parents' lives—namely, Social Security children's survivor benefits.

Spouses/Partners with the Highest Earnings May Need the Least Life Insurance

As we've said, the goal of life insurance is to maintain your survivors' living standard. So if you're the big earner in your marriage or partnership, you'd think you'd need the most life insurance. Not necessarily so. If your spouse/partner is younger than you or expects to retire later, she may have more remaining lifetime earnings to protect than you. In this case, she'll need more life insurance. Your living standard, after all, is being financed not just by current earnings, but by *all* future earnings.

The Rich Have Bigger Saving and Insurance Problems than Others

Because of its progressive benefit formula, Social Security retirement and survivor benefits replace a much larger fraction of the preretirement or prewidow(er)hood earnings of most workers compared to the rich. Stated differently, the government is doing a lot more saving and insuring through Social Security for those who aren't rich than it is for those who are. Consequently, most households have much less need to save and insure on their own than do the rich.

Maximizing Retirement Account Contributions Is Generally Undesirable

As we've mentioned, 401(k) and other tax-deferred accounts can represent a tax trap. But apart from taxes, contributing to these accounts may require reducing your current living standard in order to raise your future living standard. This outcome occurs if you're *cash constrained,* which is also referred to as *borrowing constrained* or *liquidity constrained.* In this case, having a perfectly smooth living standard would require borrowing well beyond what any lender would allow.

To see this in stark terms, suppose that you and your partner earn the minimum wage and have very few assets to your names. But your wealthy Uncle Rich has just developed a terminal disease that will kill him inside of three years. Uncle Rich has promised to leave his entire $1 million fortune to you provided that you visit him daily before he dies. Based on this promise, you head to your local bank and try to borrow money so you can raise your living standard immediately and not have to wait three years. The bank, of course, says "Sorry." A promised inheritance won't stand up as valid loan collateral to bank regulators. So you are stuck with a low living standard until Uncle Rich expires, at which point your living standard takes a tremendous jump.

Most young and middle-aged households appear to be borrowing constrained thanks to high mortgage payments, car payments, college expenses, and other off-the-top expenditures coupled with generally rising labor earnings. Households that are borrowing constrained still seek to smooth their living standards but can't borrow enough at reasonable rates to make it happen. As a result, their consumption may actually rise in stages over time.

To understand borrowing-constrained periods, go back to the Uncle Rich example. Suppose you have an even richer aunt, Aunt Judy, who has established a trust that will pay you $20 million fifteen years from now when you hit age sixty-five. In this case, your living standard will be very low prior to Uncle Rich's demise; then it will rise and be higher through age sixty-five; and then it will be higher still after age sixty-five. The period before Uncle Rich dies is one borrowing-constrained interval. The period between Uncle Rich's death and the receipt of the gift from Aunt Judy is a second borrowing-constrained interval.

For cash-constrained households, maximizing retirement account contributions may mean cutting their current living standard to the bone in order to end up with a much higher living standard in old age, if they live that long. In this case, we're no longer in a win-win situation where maximizing contributions can raise the household's living standard each year. It's no surprise that many young households fail to maximize their retirement account contributions even when their employer is offering to match their contributions.

Waiting to Take Social Security Can Dramatically Raise Your Living Standard

Social Security provides a terrific return if you wait to collect benefits. For example, if you are between your normal retirement age and age seventy, waiting an extra year to collect benefits will permanently raise those benefits by roughly 8 percent once they are received. This return is above and beyond inflation and is extremely safe. Where else can one earn such a high and safe real return on the market? The rub is that you may not make it to age seventy to start collecting Social Security's higher benefit. But if you don't care about leaving a bequest, the fact that you may die without collecting any benefits is of no concern. You just care about what happens to you, including what you get to consume when you're alive.

Your ability to wait to collect Social Security depends on your being able to eat in the meantime. If you're retired and have very few assets, waiting until the last minute to take your Social Security benefits may not be possible—even though it gives you a much higher living standard once the Social Security payments start coming.

Oversaving and Overinsuring Are Very Risky

We go around only once, and our lifetime happiness depends on our living standard at all ages, not just in retirement. When we oversave, we risk cutting our living standard when young and, because no good deed goes unpunished, dropping dead as soon as we reach retirement. When we overinsure, we risk living to a ripe old age at a very low living standard because we wasted so much money paying for life insurance on which our spouses and children never collected.

In short, don't count on living and don't count on dying.

Mortgages Offer No Tax Advantages for Most Households

Lots of low- and middle-income households aren't able to deduct mortgage interest because they don't itemize their deductions. Many rich households find their mortgage interest deductions limited by high-income phase-out provisions. But even for those who can deduct mortgage interest, there is no real tax advantage to having a mortgage. Why? Well, suppose you can pay off your mortgage but choose instead to invest in bonds. In this case, you'll earn interest at a lower rate than you pay on your mortgage, assuming you invest in bonds that have the same risk properties as mortgages. Worse, you'll have to pay taxes on the interest earned. On balance you'll be better off paying off the mortgage.

The one caveat to this statement involves the Alternative Minimum Tax (AMT). Having a large mortgage may keep you from having to pay the AMT and thereby save you taxes. Since higher-income households are more likely to be subject to the AMT, paying off your mortgage may be the wrong move if your income is relatively high.

Eleven mind-benders later, our punch line is clear: Conventional financial advice makes little, if any, economic sense. Its application violates the Hippocratic oath: First, do no harm. And as we now show, we're not exactly the picture of financial health.

PART 2

———

Financial Pathology

Taking rounds in a hospital is a surefire way to appreciate good health. It will also reassure you that no matter how lousy you feel, you could feel worse. Taking the financial rounds, as we'll now do, offers its own educational payback. Seeing firsthand the yin of financial pathology will help you better understand the yang of financial health. It will also console you that *everyone* is financially clueless, warn you that the financial industry has your worst interests at heart, and kick you into high gear when it comes to making intelligent consumption-smoothing decisions.

6. What, Me Worry?

What you don't know can't help you.

—ANONYMOUS

COLLECTIVELY, WE LIKE to fly blind. We hop into our life, gun the engine, race to the runway, and take off without any notion of where we are going—or how we will get there. The last thing we want to think about is our finances. But when we do, it can be a chilling experience. Here are a few items from the grab bag of fear:

- The Social Security Administration, never shy to tell us how important it is to our welfare, informs us that the average retired worker's benefit is $1,007 a month. According to the SSA, its retirement benefits account for at least 50 percent of income for 54 percent of married couples and 74 percent of single people. On top of this, we have Social Security sending us annual statements with a message on the front telling us in very plain English that the system is financially underwater and that something needs to be done to keep our benefits from being cut.

55

- Fidelity Investments, the largest 401(k) plan manager in the country, offers its Retirement Index twice a year to let us know whether we are getting ahead or falling behind. In mid-2006 it announced that the average worker was on track to replace 57 percent of income compared to the 85 percent the company believes "is a reasonable starting point when planning for retirement." Fidelity also reports that over half of all recent retirees wish they had done more to prepare.

- The Center for Retirement Research at Boston College surveyed 400 employers and asked for their estimates of how many workers in their fifties would have the resources to retire at the traditional time. Answer: 1 in 4 won't retire—because they can't.

- Annamaria Lusardi, a researcher at Dartmouth College, and Olivia Mitchell, an economist at the University of Pennsylvania, surveyed 4,489 workers and found that 32 percent thought about retirement "hardly at all." Another 38 percent thought about it "some" or "little."

- In a separate study, Lusardi and Mitchell found that 1 in 3 households aged fifty and over have never engaged in retirement planning. Another 22 percent have tried but failed to formulate a retirement plan.

- The Vanguard Center for Retirement Research found that 70 percent of older working households are saving for retirement. But 30 percent are not. The mutual fund firm also reports that only 64 percent of workers participate in employer savings plans, that 25 percent of participants contribute less than 4 percent of income, and that only 14 percent of older workers are taking advantage of the new catch-up provisions that allow more saving.

- A study of federal workers by the Employee Benefit Research Institute found that 49 percent believed they were ahead of schedule with respect to retirement saving, yet, of these, only 49 percent had calculated what amount of money they would need. And even though they intended to retire earlier than private-sector workers, they felt their need for money would be no greater.

- An examination of research on baby boomer retirement preparedness done by the Congressional Budget Office in 2003 concluded that about half of all boomers were going to be OK in retirement. But the other half faced a living-standard decline that varied from modest to major.

The broad finding is very simple: Go to most workplaces, look at any three workers, and you can be sure that one of them is completely lost when it comes to his financial affairs. His financial life is an unending surprise, usually an unpleasant one.

There is a good chance that one of the two remaining workers has a lot to worry about. We're not talking about financial illiteracy here. We're talking about a large group of people—about one-third of the population—that is preliterate or just crazy. It's not that they make mistakes in thinking about their financial future; the concept of a financial future simply doesn't exist for them.

How can this be? We don't know. Nor does anyone else know. All we can do is catalog the behavior. Some of it is mildly self-destructive. Some of it is spectacularly self-destructive, the frequent subject of cover stories for supermarket checkout tabloids that regale us with Elvis and Bigfoot sightings or tragic celebrity weight gains.

We borrow too much, too often, for too long. We gamble for pure fun, collectively losing billions that could have been saved and invested. At the same time, many of us fail to buy enough life insurance to keep our survivors from cursing us for losing the game of chance we all play when we cross the street. Returning from the casino, we fail to invest enough of our income to get money that is actually being given away—one of the few free lunches in town—the free money our employers offer in 401(k) matching funds. If we do save in our employer's plan, we let our decisions be influenced by the menu of choices rather than what we actually need. This includes holding large amounts of our employer's stock, which could be down the week we leave the company—or worse, could disappear entirely, as in the case of Enron.

As rich as this cornucopia of dysfunction is, it's not big enough to hold the nutty investors who either day-trade, base their decisions on astrology, or hold cash in their retirement accounts through their entire lifetime.

If at First You Don't Succeed, Borrow

Failing to save for a distant retirement isn't the only mass evidence of financial pathology. Collectively, we continue to believe that no dollar should go unborrowed. The size of U.S. consumer debt is simply staggering: over $2.5 trillion. This figure, which includes outstanding credit card balances and car loans but excludes mortgages, translates into over $22,000 per U.S. household! (If you add in mortgage debt, we're talking $12 trillion in aggregate debt and $108,000 in debt per household.)

According to recent figures, the average American has credit card balances of over $8,500, on which he pays in excess of 18 percent interest per year, on average. That's about fifteen weeks of pre-tax income for the average earner. Households with incomes of $75,000 to $100,000 have even higher levels of credit card debt. Americans are now paying north of $50 billion per year in credit card interest.

The percentage of credit card users who pay the entire balance monthly has declined from 40 percent to 37 percent over the last few years, indicating that the magic of credit card spending continues to grow. Hardly a week goes by without someone pointing out that collectively our debt is growing faster than our income.

We've been able to do this for years because interest rates have been declining, so it costs less to make the payments on our home mortgage, credit cards, and car loans. Even the lowest interest rates in a generation, however, have not prevented the burden of debt service from increasing as a percentage of disposable income. As an exercise in euphemism, consider this 2004 statement by then Federal

Reserve Board chairman Alan Greenspan on the expansion of consumer credit:

> *In addition, improvements in lending practices driven by information technology have enabled lenders to reach out to households with previously unrecognized borrowing capacities.* *

Consumer debt figures, however, don't reflect our true debt because they don't include the ever-growing volume of leased cars to which the consumer never has title. It was recently estimated that some 21 percent of all new cars are lease sales. Although lease sales peaked in 1999 at 24.4 percent, 1 in 5 new car sales is a deal in which the driver has no equity now and never will. In fact, a growing percentage of people are upside down on their car loans. This means the balance due on the loan is greater than the car is worth—but car dealers will roll the obligation into a new car simply to make a sale.

In the spring of 2004 J. D. Power and Associates found that 38 percent of all new car buyers were upside down on their trade-ins, up from 25 percent in 2001. At the same time, the average loan period increased from 53 months to 58 months, making it likely that more car owners would be upside down in the future.

We are using our homes as credit cards, paying off credit card debt with home equity credit lines. According to the 2004 Survey of Consumer Finances from the Federal Reserve Board, 31 percent of all home equity borrowing was used to pay off credit card balances, car loans, and other consumer debt. While the case for doing this is strong—you replace high-rate, non-deductible-interest payments with low-rate, deductible-interest payments—it's another reason our national savings rate has plummeted.

In spite of the fastest home appreciation rate in decades, the per-

---

* To his credit, Greenspan has acknowledged that statements like this helped precipitate the subprime lending crisis that, as of this writing, has roiled financial markets and put the economy in recession.

centage of our homes that we own debt-free has barely changed due to cash-out refinancings and credit lines. According to Federal Reserve figures, for instance, homeowners with mortgages now own less than 50 percent of the value of their homes. And house prices are now falling fast.

But that's not all. When your favorite newspaper has a story on any of these figures, usually using government statistics and averages, it is invariably presented as though we were all one giant family. We're not. A statistician would tell us that debt in America does not have a normal distribution. It doesn't look like a steep mountain. Instead it looks more like a camel's back: two humps. One is for the savers. The other is for the debtors. Take a close look at the underlying data—or check reader mail at a newspaper—and you'll find that there are two kinds of people in America. There are people who hate all forms of debt and avoid it as though it were a deadly disease. And there are people who wait by their mailbox, hoping for a new credit card.

Did you know that 30 percent of all homes in America are owned mortgage free? Did you know that nearly 12 percent of all new automobiles in America were bought for cash?

So think about it.

If some 30 percent to 40 percent of all consumers operate on a no-debt/cash-only basis, what does that mean about the rest? It means that 60 percent to 70 percent of the households are carrying 100 percent of the loans and liabilities. The unequal distribution tells us that a large portion of U.S. households is up to its eyeballs in debt.

Lots of people are writing about this. Juliet Schor, who teaches sociology at Boston College, has chronicled the pressure on American families to keep up with the Joneses. In *The Overspent American*, she details how we spend too much and the pressures that keep us doing it. Anya Kamenetz focuses on recent college grads in *Generation Debt*, showing how much debt college kids are taking in during and after school. And Harvard Law School bankruptcy expert Professor Elizabeth Warren has penned *The Two-Income Trap:*

Why Middle-Class Mothers and Fathers Are Going Broke. Here's a sample of what Professor Warren has to say:

> *Middle-class families across America have been quietly drawn into an all-out war. Not the war on drugs, the war about creationism, or the war over sex education. Their war has received little coverage in the press and no attention from politicians, but it has profoundly altered the lives of parents everywhere, shaping every economic decision they make. Their war is a bidding war.*

The bidding war, Professor Warren explains, is for houses in neighborhoods with good schools, for second cars, and for day care. It is not consumption gone mad. Instead of being more secure because it has two incomes, the two-income household is more at risk because two earners can lose their jobs and need both incomes to service all their debt.

Parental striving, to most, sounds more admirable than pathological. But all this striving is happening in America, the land of the infinite upgrade. One result is a never-ending rise in levels of expense for everything from Dunkin' Donuts' $4.40 Coffee Coolattas to the ubiquity of hot stone spa treatments.

Another result of all this striving, as Barry Schwartz points out in *The Paradox of Choice: Why More Is Less,* is stress—the terminal overload of not knowing how to deal with two hundred varieties of jam, preserves, jellies, butters, and spreads at Whole Foods Market, or the still larger varieties of cheese at Dean and DeLuca and other luxury markets.

Somehow the perfectly natural desire to give the kids a good start has morphed into competitive consuming. The end result is, yes, luxury inflation. The cost of luxury goods is rising faster than the price of nonluxury goods. Being rich—or appearing so—costs a lot of money, more every year. This is not a new phenomenon. Scott wrote about it in 1975, explaining that his La Dolce Vita index was rising faster than the consumer price index. Today the champagne maker Moët & Chandon regularly updates its Luxury Index, which tracks the price of luxury goods. The cost of being rich, chronicled in detail by *Wall Street Journal* senior writer Robert Frank, has been rising about twice as fast as the CPI. Small wonder we're all a bit unbalanced and that many of us are buried in debt.

Banned in Las Vegas

Economists are reluctant to say so, but down deep they view both spendthrifts and skinflints as economic sickos. They feel the same about risk lovers, who never buy insurance or diversify their portfolios, and risk haters, who never risk a penny no matter how good the odds. These are all examples of folks who fail to achieve economic balance—that is to say, who fail to smooth their consumption. One way to gauge economists' views about healthy financial choices is to consider their own behavior.

The hotel and casino owners of Las Vegas, Nevada, have effectively banned the American Economic Association—the main association of academic and business economists—from holding its annual meetings there, and for good reason. The last time the convention was held in Vegas, virtually none of the attendees gambled. Indeed, the vast majority refused to spend a single quarter on a slot machine, let alone sit down at a poker game, blackjack table, or roulette wheel. Instead they stood around gawking at the host of people feeding noisy machines with their buckets of quarters.

The economists refused to gamble for a good reason. They knew that the gambling options at Las Vegas represent unfair bets. They also knew that if their colleagues caught them gambling, they'd never hear the end of it—just as doctors look askance at colleagues they catch smoking.

Kimosabe Plays the Slots

Our failure to save is a fairly pale symptom of financial pathology. To see genuine pathology—the stuff that makes us squirm and wince—we need to leave the low savers and visit the gamblers and borrowers. Let's start at the far extreme: gambling. Have you noticed that gambling has achieved ubiquity?

We can watch the side effects of gambling life on *CSI: Las Vegas*. We can pretend we live in a casino by watching James Caan on the NBC series *Las Vegas*. And if we want to watch card by card, we can check the weekly television listings on the Web site ThePokerforum .com. One recent Sunday evening, poker freaks could watch *Championship Poker at the Plaza* on the Fox Sports Network at 4:00 p.m.; *Celebrity Poker Showdown* at 5:00 p.m. on Bravo; *World Series of Poker* at 9:00 p.m. on ESPN2; or at the same time, *The Bad Boys of Poker* on the World Poker Tour, Travel Channel. Then they could watch other portions of the *World Series of Poker* through midnight on ESPN2.

That's just a Sunday night.

Can't get enough, you say? Not to worry, the Casino and Gaming Television network is on the way.

You can also play poker online at Planet Poker, Paradise Poker, and other sites. Or if you just want to read about the game, you can go to countless poker blogs, like the listings on www.liquid-swords.com.

Still not enough? No problem. There are now over six hundred casinos in America, spread over thirty-four states. Many, in what may be deemed Tonto's revenge, are on Native American reservations. Most are open twenty-four hours a day. They offer a wide variety of slot machines and table games. They vary from some of the seedy little casinos along highways in New Mexico and the byways of Nevada to over-the-top grandiosity in Las Vegas like Wynn Las Vegas, Bellagio, and Caesars Palace.

If economists won't be invited back to Las Vegas because they failed to gamble, neither will the ink-stained wretches of financial journalism. Quite a few years ago, the personal finance writers group of SABEW, the Society of Business Editors and Writers, had a meeting at the Golden Nugget in downtown Las Vegas. While many attended a performance of Cirque du Soleil's "O" at the Bellagio for $100 a ticket, few did any gambling. Those who did gamble left the casino floor after losing a hefty $20. They did it, of course, "for the experience."

What do academic economists and professional journalists have in common, beyond a lack of disposable income? They share a tough mind-set that forbids magical thinking. Even though they aren't gamblers, many can tell you the house take—"the vig"—on different games. They sneer at the foolishness of the slot players who patiently sit and give their stake to slot machines, losing 5 to 20 percent of the money risked, on average, each time they pull the handle.

They know the odds are better at the roulette table. Its vig ranges from only 2.63 percent to 7.31 percent. Move to the craps table, and you can cut the house vig to a tiny 0.8 percent. Play blackjack expertly, and you can cut the vig to 1.5 percent. Develop a photographic memory and a capacity to count cards like the Massachusetts Institute of Technology brainiacs Ben Mezrich made famous in *Bringing Down the House,* and you can have a 2 percent edge on the casino.

Unless you are a card counter, however, the only real difference between the games is the speed at which you can expect to lose your money. The higher the vig, the faster you can expect to be broke. This isn't hyperbole. It's a mathematical certainty.

In spite of these realities, gambling is the fastest-growing industry in America. Las Vegas, its capital, has been one of the country's fastest-growing cities. The annual survey from Harrah's casinos tells us that 52 million American adults—26 percent of those twenty-one and older—made 322 million casino visits during 2005. That's about one casino trip every two months! Collectively, Americans are spending about $50 billion a year at casinos.

Not impressed by a mere $50 billion in a $14 trillion economy? According to the Investment Company Institute, the mutual fund industry's statistic keeper and legislative watchdog, new cash additions to IRA plans amounted to only $37 billion in 2003. New deposits to defined-contribution plans—every 401(k) and 403(b) plan in the country—totaled only $49 billion. So the gambling of 26 percent of the adult population is on a par with the amount of money put into every defined-contribution plan in America by every participating worker in America—including employer matching funds.

Indeed, we could *double* our retirement saving simply by adding the $42 billion we spend on state lotteries (where the vig averages an incredible 50 percent) and the $48 billion we spend in casinos—a total of $90 billion—to the $86 billion we put into IRAs and defined-contribution plans.

You Tell Me

Most of us are frequent and unwitting victims of *framing*—the influencing of opinions by how information is presented. Some of these encounters can have a major impact on our lives—for example, how the option to participate in the company 401(k) plan is presented to us. The decision appears to be simple. We can participate or not participate. But what if we default? What if we just leave that little check field blank?

Until the recent Pension Protection Act of 2006, most companies assumed that you did not want to participate if you left the field blank. That means the default was "opt out," not "opt in." So for most of the two decades that 401(k) plans have existed, the indecisive were defaulted toward poverty in their old age. Without a positive decision to participate in the company 401(k) plan, no money was taken from their paycheck, and their employer didn't have to come up with the usual matching funds.

Much the same happens with default choices for funds. If you don't make a fund choice, your money goes by default to whatever investment the plan sponsor chooses. And it tends to stay there. Research has shown, for instance, that matching contributions in company stock tend to stay in company stock long after employees are free to move their money into other investments. That inertia makes for an employee-managed retirement plan that has far more risk than a defined-benefit pension plan managed by the same corporation.

Many researchers have commented on the "menu effect"—that

what we choose to do is strongly influenced by the menu of choices we are given. If 70 percent of the mutual funds offered by your 401(k) plan are fixed-income, 70 percent of the money will tend to be found in fixed-income funds. If 70 percent of the funds are equity funds, 70 percent of the money will tend to be in equities. This is diversifying over funds, but not over assets. Here again, how our choices are framed influences what we choose.

Damning the Dead

"A man who dies without life insurance doesn't die; he *absconds.*" Those, as you might suspect, are the words of an ardent life insurance salesperson. While we would like to disagree with him, almost on general principles, the sorrowful fact is that he's pretty much right. Each year thousands of widowed spouses discover that their late husband or wife left them with little or nothing in life insurance—but with a mortgage to pay, kids to educate, and a retirement to finance.

This happens at all ages and all income levels. Almost everyone knows, or knows of, someone whose life disintegrated when it was discovered that a policy had been allowed to lapse, was discussed but never purchased, or was borrowed against. The shortfall has caused many widows (widowers) to reevaluate posthumously what they'd thought was a loving, thoughtful husband (wife).

As a consequence, premature death is one of the major causes of impoverishment in America. This happens in spite of the common provision of life insurance as an employee benefit and in spite of the absolute certainly that you will be solicited for life insurance when you marry, buy a house, refinance a mortgage, buy a car, or talk to that earnest-looking guy in church. It happens in spite of the offer of life-saving life insurance that comes with our monthly checking account and credit card statements. And it happens in spite of the elder-channel advertisements offering "final expense" life insurance policies that require a check but no checkup.

Let's face it: we don't like to think about dying. So we don't.

But if we want to provide for those we love, life insurance is a great invention and a wonderful tool. Indeed, it's one of the primary tools created to mitigate financial risks and help families recover from terrible events.

The question is, why isn't it used? And what are the consequences?

Research by Larry (and many others) has shown:

- Roughly one-third of secondary-earning spouses (almost all of whom are wives) are dramatically underinsured.
- Insufficient insurance is the primary cause of poverty among widows.
- The most underinsured are secondary-earning spouses in households between the ages of twenty-two and thirty-nine.
- There is essentially no relationship between the amount of insurance coverage people have and the amount they need.

One study that Larry did with Douglas Bernheim, Katherine Carman, and Jagadeesh Gokhale, based on data from the well-known Survey of Consumer Finances, found that couples age thirty needed a median of 12.6 years of income in life insurance. But on average, they had just over 1 year. Couples with a median age of thirty-nine needed 5.6 years of household income in life insurance but had only 1.9 years. Couples with a median age of forty-seven needed 2.1 years of income in life insurance but had 1.4 years.

Ironically, couples with a median age of fifty-six had no need for life insurance but had 0.96 years of household income in insurance. So while most couples were grievously underinsured, a portion carried (and paid for) insurance they no longer needed.

Enron-itis

According to the consulting firm Hewitt Associates's 401(k) Index, a monthly report that examines the investing habits of thousands of 401(k) plan participants, nearly 20 percent of plan assets is in employer stock.

It took the Enron implosion, but most people now know that holding their employer's stock in their 401(k) plan—even if the employer is giving the stock—isn't a good idea. Why? Because it increases our risk. Since individual stocks are more volatile than broad market indices, holding a large portion of your savings in employer stock adds unnecessary risk. This is particularly true given that our employer is more likely to fire us or limit our raises when its stock goes down the tubes.

Which would you rather have for a long-term investment: a fund of stocks that reflects the market generally or an individual stock that's more than twice as risky as the market? Confused by "free" and conflicted about company loyalty, many employees have difficulty thinking about this. But if you asked any investment professional, you'd get an instant answer—eliminate the individual stock and reduce risk. We find it amazing that the same corporations that put so much effort into carefully crafting executive stock options and compensation plans can't find the time to warn employees about the risks of holding company stock in their 401(k) plans.

"I'll Starve in the Future, but I'm Safe Today"

Not long ago Scott spent a morning with a partner at a midsize CPA firm. The partner, a woman in her late fifties, enjoyed a substantial income and had a net worth over $1 million. Fear of loss, however, had caused her to keep the bulk of her savings in money market accounts.

Her low returns would make it virtually impossible for her to achieve her retirement goals. She will face a major drop in her standard of living when she retires. She knew she should do something else, but she was paralyzed.

Cash functions much like another all-or-nothing investment, gold. When anxious investors are scared out of the stock or bond market, they tend to stay out because they can never find a time to commit again. The world is an anxious place. It always has been, and it always will be.

A Dallas investment manager recently told Scott of an aging client who had kept all his assets in gold since the early 1980s, certain that economic devastation would eventually make his stocks worthless and his gold priceless. Gold forces people to think in terms of extreme events. It may have value as insurance against disaster, but it isn't a substitute for actual investing. (The circumstances that will make gold a really good investment are also the circumstances that will make ownership of a Smith & Wesson a good investment.) Gold crowds out what goes on, day in and day out.

Had the aging goldbug survived till today he'd have really profited from his anxiety. Unfortunately, he died in 2003 before gold prices started to take off.

"I Lose on Each Trade but Make It Up in Volume"

One of the by-products of falling commissions and a rising stock market is the world of day-trading. There, naïve and uninformed investors quit their day jobs to sit behind a computer and try to make a living out of statistical noise. Without the high brokerage commissions that were once a barrier to trading, day traders can flash in and out of stocks for as little as $16 round-trip, sometimes less.

The problem is that computer screens give traders what behavioral economist Terrance Odean calls illusory knowledge, and that, in turn, leads to overconfidence and losses. Studies have shown that the majority of day traders not only lose the time they could have spent working, they also lose their original investment.

Much the same happens when the investor isn't directly involved and allows others to day-trade for him, making rapid changes in risky positions. While this was once done with commodity trading pools, where the investor faced monthly expenses that often exceeded 3 percent, the fashionable vehicle today is hedge funds. Now numbering over seven thousand, there is no evidence to support the idea that really smart people can overcome the burden of 2 percent expenses and 20 percent of profits, which is what investors give up to managers of these funds. Few ponder this simple reality: if 70 percent of managers who are paid 1 percent of assets and zero percent of profits to run mutual funds can't overcome their expenses to deliver a market index return, what percent of managers who charge 2 percent of assets and 20 percent of profits will?

Greater Fool Theory

The common foundation of both the Internet/technology bubble of 1997–1999 and the residential real estate bubble that followed is the esteemed greater fool theory. That's the idea that a greater fool than you will always come along and pay still more for your no-revenue, no-profits stock than you did. Everyone knows about it, everyone sees the disaster coming, but most would rather believe that someone else will be the greater fool.

Collectibles have always offered greater fool opportunities, and no year is complete without a passing collectible (remember Beanie Babies?) or a more enduring collectible like baseball cards. Recently, a single baseball card sold for $2.35 million.

Many of us have very odd uses for money.

Dumb and Dumber

One of our favorite literary characters is Guy Grand, Terry Southern's feisty billionaire in *The Magic Christian*. Mr. Grand liked to "make it hot" for people. He baited them with improbable sums of money, sometimes causing riots as people swarmed and fought to get it. Southern, best known for his classic screenplay *Dr. Strangelove*, would have had to modify his notions of human motivation and behavior if he'd spent some time examining the habits of 401(k) participants. Instead of finding raw greed and unrelenting money seeking as the core of all human behavior, he'd have been confronted with people who appeared strangely indifferent to money.

This is not how we are supposed to behave if we are even vaguely related to *Homo economicus*. The data come from research done for the National Bureau of Economic Research by three academics, James J. Choi at the Yale School of Management, David Laibson at Harvard University, and Brigitte Madrian at the Wharton School. Working with Hewitt Associates, they examined the contribution decisions of 401(k) plan participants who were at least fifty-nine and a half years old. They wanted to see how many captured the full employer match. They set the age limit at fifty-nine and a half because that's the age when you can withdraw from your account without any penalties. As a consequence, these workers are faced with two painless options:

- They can increase their contributions to capture the full match.
- Or they can increase their contributions to capture the full match and then withdraw the employer contribution.

In the extreme case of a dollar-for-dollar match, an extra $1 contribution increases their savings by $2. They also have the option of removing $1. So if they make a contribution, they can remove an equal amount that has been contributed by their employer.

Some would call that a win-win situation. Either they double their savings, or they add to them without any effective cost in terms of immediate spending power. That's a slam dunk, a no-brainer, right?

Wrong.

Ever so deftly, the researchers noted that many employees made decisions "that are clearly precluded by normative economic theory." In other words, confronted with absolutely free money, they simply ignored it.

The amounts involved here were more than petty cash. The researchers pointed out that a sixty-year-old with a weekly salary of $1,000 and a 401(k) plan that matched dollar for dollar up to 5 percent of salary was passing up $50 a week, or $2,600 a year. That employee could contribute $2,600 and enjoy an employer match of $2,600, for a total of $5,200. Or he could contribute $2,600 and take out $2,600, increasing his savings at no expense.

So how many pass up free $50 bills?

About half.

This doesn't mean that half of all employees with 401(k) plans blow them off completely. That's the extreme. But about half fail to save enough to capture the match. On average, they throw away an amount equal to 1.3 percent of their annual salary.

Going back to the Vanguard Center for Retirement Research's study of its plans, it's clear that money is regularly left on the table. While some plan participants do more than capture the match, only 70 percent of employees participate—even in the immediate pre-retirement years (fifty-five to sixty-four). Of those 70 percent, many don't contribute enough to capture their employer match.

If 30 percent of all employees don't participate and another 20 percent, according to the study, don't participate fully, is there a countervailing group of maximum savers?

The Vanguard study indicates that 11 percent of all employees are maximum savers, and most of those are at upper income levels. While only 1 percent of those who earned less than $30,000 saved the maximum, 13 percent of those earning $75,000 to $99,999 maxed out, and a whopping 42 percent of those earning more than $100,000 maxed out.

The same pattern was found among older employees eligible for "catch-up" provision saving—the additional contribution allowed to those age fifty and older. Only 14 percent of those eligible were participating. That's 1 in 7, in a group that knows it's on the last stretch before retirement.

We have to wonder: what are they thinking?

Pinching Pennies

Charles Huffman achieved immortality, of sorts, for being found dead on a Brooklyn street, penniless. This was in the 1950s. The police discovered that he lived in a $7-a-week rented room, but the room was lined with bankbooks and stock certificates valued at more than $500,000. Today he lives on as a Wikipedia example of "less-famous misers in history."

While the vast majority of us squander our money, first in the service of youth and then trying to recover it, there are others who hoard their money and squander their youth. They don't spend. They save. Then they save some more. And still more.

They enjoy saving more than they enjoy spending. They lock their youth in a room, doing little, missing the opportunities of youth for future opportunities they don't dare think about. It's a rare condition, to be sure, but it exists. Scott, for instance, regularly gets letters from readers who have, in their late thirties, no consumer or mortgage debt and already have college funds for their kids.

So what do they write to him about? They invariably ask where they should invest their savings—now that they have reached the limit of their 401(k) plan and their IRAs.

One Minneapolis reader of Scott's column listed so much in savings and life insurance policies that analysis showed his widow's living standard would soar were he to die. That condition, as you saw when we discussed life insurance coverage, is rare enough to be considered freakish. But there is evidence that a significant percentage of all workers oversave.

Yes, you read that right: *oversave*.

One source of evidence is Vanguard's annual report on its defined-contribution plans. In "How America Saves 2006," the firm—the second-largest U.S. provider of 401(k) plans—reports that 25 percent of plan participants saved less than 3.9 percent of their income and that 50 percent saved 6 percent or less.

If that sounds familiar, it's because media reports invariably pick up on the dark side of the news—the 50 percent of plan participants who don't save enough to "capture the match" provided by their employer. They walk down the street ignoring the free money on the sidewalk.

But what about all the others?

It turns out that 16 percent of participants saved between 10 percent and 14.9 percent in 2005. Another 8 percent saved a whopping 15 percent or more. While the figures vary slightly from year to year, about 24 percent of all plan participants save at least 10 percent of their income.

We'll bet big money you never heard that before.

Of course, not all of these people are compulsive oversavers. Some are just playing late-career catch-up. Some are compensating for a spouse who doesn't save as much or has a less desirable 401(k) plan. Others may be compensating for earlier life disasters like divorce, job loss, or major illness. But the fact is that 1 in 4 plan participants may be saving more than necessary, not less than necessary.

Just as those who don't save will go from a higher standard of consumption to a lower standard of consumption when they no longer work, the oversavers will go from a lower standard of consumption while they work to a higher standard when they retire. They are depriving the present to spoil the future.

Is this rational? We don't think so. As behaviors go, we think it's almost as crazy as the better-publicized nonsaving of the clueless. For economists, the ideal path would be a virtually constant standard of living throughout life, avoiding either a late-life decline or a deprived youth. Of course, the future is uncertain, making oversaving less problematic than undersaving; but there's playing it safe and then there's playing it too safe.

Left to our own devices, without tools to figure that path, most of us err. However incomplete our catalog, you've probably seen enough to be discouraged. You may even be ready to include *Homo economicus* with the great oxymorons of our age, right up there with "airline food," "military intelligence," and "bipartisan cooperation."

Takeaways

Having cataloged financial disease, we're now going to try to explain it so that we can overcome it. But first here's a summary of the scope and depth of financial pathology:

- Most of the elderly are heavily dependent, if not entirely dependent, on Social Security.
- Most workers never think about retirement or do so rarely.
- Roughly half of older households have never developed a financial plan.
- The Congressional Budget Office expects a significant minority of baby boomers to fall off a cliff come retirement.
- The average American has a credit card balance above $8,500, accruing 18 percent or more in interest.
- Fewer than two-fifths of Americans pay off their credit card balances monthly.
- Casino revenue surpasses annual 401(k) contributions.
- A quarter of American adults average one casino trip every two months.
- Default options make a huge difference in whether employees contribute to their 401(k)s.
- Some 20 percent of 401(k) assets are invested in employers' stock.
- Half of older workers throw away, on average, 1.3 percent of their salary by not capturing a 401(k) match.
- One-third of secondary-earning wives are severely underinsured against their spouse's death.
- Penny-pinchers, goldbugs, misers, and doomsdayers are a lot more common than you think.

7. Understanding Financial Disease

A sucker is born every minute.

—Anonymous

MOST ECONOMISTS ARE reluctant to call a spade a spade when it comes to diagnosing financial disease. They tell themselves that no matter how poorly people manage their finances, there are always factors—preferences—that make it rational.

Take a middle-aged high-income earner named Jack, with a non-working wife and two young children. Jack has a top-of-the-line Lexus, a spiffy cabin cruiser, membership at an elite country club, and, well, you get the picture. But Jack also has virtually no regular assets, a small retirement account, and very little life insurance. Moreover, Jack is saving next to nothing, unless you call paying off perennially high credit card bills saving.

Now, you'd call Jack nuts, and we'd call Jack nuts. But many economists would instinctively disagree. They'd say that Jack is as rational as anyone else; he simply has unusual preferences that lead him to splurge when young and starve when old. They'd also point out that, given his preferences, forcing Jack to save more will reduce, not raise, his financial welfare.

Mind you, economists defend consumer sovereignty (technically known as *revealed preference*), no matter how bizarre, for a good reason. Admitting that people can have sick preferences would send the economics profession down a slippery slope. In particular, it would undermine a great deal of economic theory, starting with Adam Smith's proposition that a competitive economy, left to its own devices, efficiently allocates resources as if by an "invisible hand."

Economic efficiency, as first defined by Vilfredo Pareto, a twentieth-century Italian economist, means that you can't make someone better off without making someone else worse off. "Left to its own devices" means keeping the government's mitts off the economy.

But if people can't judge what they want or comprehend the implications of their decisions, the phrases "better off" and "worse off" and the notion of economic efficiency start to lose meaning. Moreover, the grounds for laissez-faire government policy start getting shaky. This is particularly the case if Jack is jeopardizing not only his own future but those of his wife and children.

Had Adam Smith, the world's first real economist, written a book entitled *The Poverty of Nations* rather than *The Wealth of Nations*, the economics profession would have gotten off on a different foot. Rather than fixate on the value of individual choice and the wonders of competitive markets in catering to that choice, the profession might have openly acknowledged economic disease and started looking for cures. As it was, the science developed based on the assumption that everyone is fundamentally healthy when it comes to knowing and satisfying his or her own desires.

Fortunately, the medical profession took a different tack. Rather than describing disease as simply an unusual manifestation of perfect health, the medical profession saw its mission as curing morbidity and preventing mortality. Imagine your doctor telling you that having cancer is perfectly natural, that your physiology is ideally suited to generating cancer, and that cancer is a very special expression of cell growth. You'd find a new doctor quick.

Economists have never viewed themselves as healers when it comes to personal financial health. And many of them would be appalled at donning that title. But an increasing number would not. Moreover, the profession is gradually moving from viewing households as comprising fully rational economic agents to viewing households as full of people who routinely make mistakes in even the simplest choice settings.

This may have something to do with the fact that most people have never been taught to read, write, or speak economese.

Financial Illiteracy

A frequently cited *National Geographic* poll tells us that 11 percent of Americans age eighteen to twenty-four can't find the United States on a map, 29 percent can't locate the Pacific Ocean, 58 percent have no clue where Japan is, 69 percent can't find England, and 85 percent can't pick out Iraq!

This is a remarkable statement about our educational system. But it also has some bearing on why so many people are lost when it comes to financial matters. Geography, history, and social studies are disciplines everyone studies in school. Most of these subjects offer a reasonably good sense of where one might encounter the Pacific Ocean. But personal finance isn't even part of the curriculum in our school systems. Small wonder most people are more clueless about personal finance than about the location of England. When personal finance does enter a school's curriculum, it's through brief examples in algebra or via an elective course in economics.

For half of high school graduates—the half that doesn't attend college—the chance to receive a formal financial education ends when they leave high school. The half that does attend college also faces no requirement to study economics or finance. Yes, lots of college students take these subjects. But the majority does not. Indeed, if you add up those who don't attend college and those who do attend but don't study economics or finance, the lion's share of Americans enter adulthood with no formal education in financial matters.

There are, of course, lots of informal ways to educate oneself in this area. You can ask your friends and relatives for advice. You can consult your employer. You can read the business section of the paper. You can purchase financial planning books and magazines. You can talk to stockbrokers, lawyers, accountants, insurance agents, and bankers. You can listen to financial planners on the radio. And you can pay financial planners for their advice and counsel.

Lots of us do these things. But the sum total of our financial knowledge is not much greater than that of high school grads. One indication of this comes from a relatively recent U.S. Department of Education study showing that 80 percent of adults can't make proper change without the help of a calculator or cash register!

In 1993, under the auspices of Stanford University economist Douglas Bernheim, Merrill Lynch administered a very short financial knowledge test to over 1,200 baby boomers. The results weren't pretty. Four out of five boomers failed, scoring 55 or less on a 100-point scale.

Here's some of what the boomers missed: Nearly 2 in 3 hadn't the slightest inkling of the value of the Dow Jones Industrial Average. A third of the sample thought investing $1,000 for thirty years at 8 percent would generate $5,000 or less, when the correct answer was $10,000 or more. Half of the boomers overstated the inflation rate by at least one-third. And 1 in 3 boomers wildly underestimated the size of the federal debt. Interestingly, older boomers preformed no better than younger ones. Males did better than females, whites did better than blacks, college grads did better than high school grads, and the rich did better than the poor. But the differences were very small.

Remarkably, a full four-fifths of the boomers described themselves as either somewhat or very financially knowledgeable. But even those who said they were very financially knowledgeable did quite poorly on the test, scoring not much higher than those claiming to be "not at all financially knowledgeable." In addition to being fairly confident about their financial knowledge, two-thirds of the boomers described their personal finances as "fairly secure or very secure," and less than one-third expected a decline in their living standard in retirement.

Unfortunately, boomers are not only kidding themselves about what they know, they are also kidding themselves about their retirement preparation. Take the quartile of boomers with the lowest ratio of wealth to earnings. Despite having saved next to nothing, over half of this group state that their finances are "fairly secure or very secure" and less than 30 percent foresee a problem in maintaining their living standard in retirement.

The fact that most of us (present authors included) think we are financially smarter than we are and that many of us (present authors included) are overly optimistic about our finances doesn't mean that nothing gets through our thick skulls. On the contrary, the same Merrill Lynch study shows that those with more financial knowledge (the highest test scores) save the highest fraction of their earnings, other things being equal. So financial knowledge matters, and accumulating more financial knowledge is very important.

The Blind Leading the Blind

One thing that we do learn when we're young is what our parents do and don't do in the financial realm. In the same Merrill Lynch study, respondents were asked if their parents were more or less thrifty than average. This information was then compared to the respondents' own saving behavior. Sure enough, boomers with particularly thrifty parents save more than those whose parents saved poorly.

So if your credit cards are maxed out and your parents were spendthrifts, hand them the bills. Tell them it's their fault you can't save. And if you can't manage to blow a few bucks on yourself, tell your parents to treat you. Explain to them that it's their fault you can't spend your own money.

The imprinting of parental preferences, experiences, and behaviors shouldn't come as any surprise. A large fraction of us vote the way our parents did. If they were Republicans, we became Republicans. If they were Democrats, we became Democrats. It's very hard to break these habits. Voting for the other party feels like betraying one's clan.

Asians are widely purported to be particularly good savers and to transmit their saving ethos to their kids. Is there any factual support for this proposition? There is. Larry and two colleagues ran an experiment in which Boston University undergraduates were asked to specify how much they would save in various hypothetical situations. It turned out that Asian and Asian-American students proposed a much higher level of saving than everyone else!

Parents' and siblings' experiences can also have an important impact on our financial planning and saving behavior. Having a close relative experience a major financial reversal appears to concentrate the mind when it comes to saving. The flip side of this is that if our relatives have had a straight glide path, we naturally assume things will work out smoothly for us as well.

The problem here is that navigating without a financial road map and simply following your parents' route doesn't generally cut it. In this regard, it's worth pointing out that over two-thirds of the boomers surveyed by Merrill Lynch said they relied on their parents, their friends, or their own judgment as their primary source of financial information and advice. Those with college degrees and higher earnings were more likely to rely on financial planners, financial software, or financial publications—but not by much. In short, when it comes to financial planning, the blind are leading the blind.

Designed Neglect

It's one thing for a person with no financial knowledge to make boneheaded financial moves. It's another for people who are financially savvy. In a recent experiment, finance students at the University of Pennsylvania's Wharton School were given a hypothetical $10,000 and the challenge to choose an optimal portfolio from a choice of four stock market index funds. They were free to invest any way they wanted, including putting all their money into just one of the funds.

An index fund, by the way, invests in particular stocks in proportion to the value of each stock relative to the value of all outstanding stocks included in the index. For example, as we write, the S&P 500 index fund has 2.84 percent of its assets invested in General Electric stock because General Electric stock accounts for 2.84 percent of the market value of all of the stock of the five hundred very large companies included in the Standard and Poor's index.*

Each student was handed the prospectus on each fund. Had they carefully read the prospectuses, they would have learned quickly that all four funds were investing in the same securities in the same proportions, yet they had dramatically different fees.

Of course, reading a prospectus is up there with eating sand. Almost none of the budding finance wizards bothered to read the prospectuses or read them carefully. Consequently, virtually all opted to invest in two or more of the funds, thinking this would garner a gold star. The right move, of course, was to invest in just one fund—the one with the lowest fee.

The research team, led by Harvard behavioral economist David Laibson, was shocked by these findings. But then Laibson realized that asking Wharton School students to read and absorb a detailed prospectus was asking too much. So he tried his experiment again with a different set of Wharton students. This time Laibson provided the subjects with a simple one-page statement for each fund indicating the funds' holdings and how much it was charging. Sure enough, these budding MBAs also goofed up. A full 80 percent chose to invest in two or more funds.

No doubt some Penn faculty member will repay Laibson's favor by repeating his experiment at Harvard Business School. But the message here is clear. Even the financially literate can *neglect* to process critically important financial cost information because the infor-

---

* Figure from Morningstar based on March 31, 2007, values.

mation is *designed* to be incomprehensible and excruciatingly dull. We call this "designed neglect."

Much of the financial industry survives on designed neglect. The sale of stock market index funds—the funds considered in Laibson's study—is a case in point. The annual cost of holding these funds ranges from less than one-tenth of 1 percent of the amount invested to a massive 2.5 percent. Paying the higher cost, which far too many people do, is, in Laibson's words, like "buying a box of Cheerios for fifty dollars when you can get it elsewhere for two dollars."

How the Securities and Exchange Commission can let this happen is a good question.

Overconfidence

Overconfidence is another factor underlying financial disease. Ask students at the beginning of a college course to raise their hands if they expect to do better than average. Almost all hands go up. If you ask people how long they expect to live, their answers will average more than their life expectancy. And if you ask people if their portfolios will outperform the market, they say yes by a wide margin.*

Apparently, we're living in Garrison Keillor's Lake Wobegon, where all the women are strong, all the men are good-looking, and all the children are above average.

People act on their inflated beliefs. Among the Merrill Lynch survey respondents, those who were sure they'd get their full Social Security benefits accumulated, on average, a year's less in earnings by middle age than those who expected their benefits to be cut.

Men seem to be particularly overconfident. Duh! In a recent study of stock trading through discount brokers, Terrance Odean and a fellow economist at the University of California, Berkeley, Brad Barber, found that both men and women trade to an excessive

---

* B. Barber and T. Odean, "Boys Will Be Boys," *The Quarterly Journal of Economics,* vol. 116, No. 1 (February 2001), pp. 261–292.

degree, but men trade 45 percent more frequently than do women. In so doing, men not only end up with lower returns than the women, they also end up underperforming the market by 2.65 percentage points—a huge price to pay for one's testosterone.

Overconfidence can be contagious. The tulip mania, the Mississippi scheme, the South Sea bubble, the South American mining mania, the railway mania, the Roaring Twenties' investment bubble, the Japanese bubble economy, the dot-com bubble—these are all examples of entire societies becoming convinced that things they know can't continue will continue. In each case, overconfident investors purchased securities at insane prices because they were convinced that prices would continue to rise.

How insane? Well, during the Dutch tulip mania of the 1630s a single tulip bulb sold for as much as an Amsterdam town house! During the Japanese bubble economy of the 1980s, the value of the three-quarter square mile of land comprising the emperor's Imperial Palace exceeded the value of all the land in *Florida* according to the January 24, 1993, *New York Times*! And during the dot-com bubble, the Nasdaq (a stock market dominated by many high-tech firms) rose from 600 to 5,000 in just four years! By 2002 it was back down to 800.

The bottom line is that we're emotional creatures. We get excited. We don't stop to think. We act on impulse.

The "we" includes economists like Irving Fisher.

Irving Fisher (1867–1947) was not any old economist. He was the leading economist of his day and surely would have won a Nobel Prize for economics had it existed at the time. The founder and first president of the Econometric Society, Fisher was keen on applying mathematics and statistics to business and economic activity.

In addition to being a prolific writer and researcher, Fisher taught at Yale and was an entrepreneurial businessman. He parlayed the sale of a small business into a $10 million fortune, the equivalent of more than $100 million today. Fully aware of risk, he borrowed money "on margin" to buy stocks and add to his fortune during the

Roaring Twenties. No one knows what caused him to take such risks, because he regularly preached prudence and caution.

Today graduate students in economics are still likely to read his *The Rate of Interest* (1907) or *The Purchasing Power of Money* (1911), but for the general public, Fisher achieved immortality with a mere ten words, spoken in 1929 to reassure nervous investors: "Stocks have reached what looks like a permanently high plateau."

Google "famous last words" and you'll find Fisher's statement keeping company with other extraordinary errors, like a Western Union memo from 1876, "This 'telephone' has too many shortcomings to be seriously considered as a means of communication. The device is inherently of no value to us," or Decca Records's explaining its decision not to sign the Beatles in 1962, "We don't like their sound, and guitar music is on the way out."

Within days of Fisher's pronouncement, the stock market crashed. This "Black Friday" ushered in the Great Depression. Fisher lost his fortune. He didn't lose a third of it or half of it. He lost every single dime. Yale, knowing his difficulties, bought his house and rented it back to him. But Fisher wasn't able to pay the rent and was eventually evicted.

Now for the rest of the story: *Fisher was the father of consumption smoothing.* He was the first economist to rigorously study how much people should consume and how much they should save. But even his deep knowledge of consumption smoothing couldn't keep him from bankruptcy.

Where did Fisher go wrong? It's hard to say. But at some point he stopped thinking like an economist and started shooting craps. His extraordinary academic and financial success was probably his downfall. If you're the smartest guy around, and everyone tells you you're the smartest guy around, and you are making money like crazy, you start believing your own PR.

Compulsive Behavior

Gambling and other compulsive spending behavior, of the kind we refered to in the last chapter, play an important role in financial pathology. So does compulsive saving behavior.

Recently Scott was asked to meet with a friend's sister. We'll call her Sophie. His task was to convince her she was rich. Sophie is divorced and has two kids in high school. She's in her late forties, well educated, and makes $65K per year as a social worker. But thanks to her brother—a terrific investor—Sophie is sitting on $10 million.

Clearly, Sophie's *very* well heeled. Yet she can't bring herself to acknowledge it. Nor can she bring herself to buy a new car, buy new clothes (she shops at Goodwill), frequent restaurants, or take a vacation.

After an hour showing Sophie that she could safely spend many times more than she did, Scott began probing Sophie's spending phobia. After another hour, the truth came out. Sophie didn't want to show up at her job with a new BMW or designer clothes because her fellow social workers weren't well off and her clients were dirt poor. She didn't want to feel out of place or make people jealous.

Sophie also didn't want her kids to know she was rich. Indeed, she had told them the opposite—that she was poor and that they were poor as well. Sophie was convinced that the knowledge their mom had money would spoil them and spoil her relationship with them.

After browbeating her a bit, Scott got Sophie to agree to buy a vacation home. Sophie bought the home but otherwise has stuck to her old spending habits. At last check, Sophie was worth $15 million and was still shopping at Goodwill.

Operating in the Dark

The interesting thing about Sophie is that before she met with Scott, she didn't even know how much money she had. She didn't want to know.

There are lots of Sophies out there. Most are married women who let their husbands manage their finances. This often leaves the wife in the dark as to what the couple can really afford. She may go on shopping sprees, redecorate the house every three years, book expensive vacations—you name it— all under the presumption that her husband is making more money than he is or that their assets are much greater than they are. Or she may scrimp and save because she's underestimating his earnings and their assets.

A recent study by Ohio State University economist Jay Zagorsky confirms that many couples either don't talk or don't talk straight about their finances. The study shows that spouses strongly disagree about how much income their partners earn and how much in assets they jointly own. In a nationwide survey of couples, half of the husbands and wives differed in their respective reports of the family's income by $5,000 or more. Ten percent differed by $15,000 or more. These are substantial amounts, given that the median pretax U.S. household income is less than $50,000. The study also shows that relative to their husbands, wives tend to understate the household's income and assets and overstate the household's debt.

What's going on? Well, some husbands may be too embarrassed to tell their wives the truth about what's happened to their earnings or to the "slam-dunk" stocks in which they invested. Others may be control freaks, save-aholics, or Chicken Littles.

Whatever explains the lack of financial communication between spouses, it can certainly undermine consumption smoothing. As we've seen, small degrees of underspending or overspending when young can lead to major disruptions in pre- and post-retirement living standards.

Economic Schizophrenia

In 2002 Princeton University psychology professor Daniel Kahneman received the Nobel Prize in economics for "having integrated insights from psychological research into economic science, especially concerning human judgment and decision making under uncertainty." Kahneman's work with the late Amos Tversky has inspired economists to develop the aforementioned field of behavioral finance, which explicitly entertains the notion that people have a variety of psychological and neurological problems in conducting their financial lives.

Some of the most interesting work in this area involves *economic schizophrenia*—the suggestion we planted earlier that our future and current selves are actually separate people fighting for dominance within a single mind. As freaky as it sounds, a growing number of economists are now writing down mathematical models in which one's current and future selves are locked in an ongoing struggle over control of the purse strings. When current self dominates, we shop 'til we drop. When future self dominates, we put away money in accounts that only our future self can access without penalty. Examples here include 401(k)s, medical savings accounts, and 529 college savings accounts.

Think about these repositories. Each locks up *our own money* for one and only one future purpose and slaps us hard on the wrists if we violate our own commitment. If we were fully rational and had full control of our impulses, why would we ever want to limit access to our own money?

The notion that economists have just discovered people's self-control problems may seem odd, given that they are in plain sight. Three in five Americans are overweight, and three in ten are obese. One in five Americans smokes. Gambling, as described, is rampant. And one in five young adults uses illegal drugs on a fairly routine basis.

Actually, economists have been thinking about self-control for fifty years. The first analysis was done by Northwestern University economist Robert Strotz. It goes under the heading "time inconsistency" because it references the problem people have of sticking to their saving game plans. In recent years, Laibson has taken up Strotz's mantle. He's shown that economic Dr. Jekylls and Mr. Hydes are time inconsistent, that they try to control themselves by locking away specific assets for specific purposes, and that they will even cover income shortfalls by borrowing at exorbitant rates to avoid tapping into targeted pools of money.

Laibson and other economists view our failure to control our current spending in part as addictive behavior. (The list includes the University of Chicago's Nobel laureate Gary Becker and Stanford University's Douglas Bernheim.) This sounds extreme, but there is a reason for all those recovery group jokes—most of us are addicted to something. Larry has a friend named Steve, who fancies himself a wine connoisseur. Over the years, Steve has spent an increasing share of his ever-declining income buying ever more expensive wines and impressing his friends with his impressions of an elite sommelier. Steve, it's fair to say, is now addicted to fine wine. Indeed, Larry recently slipped Steve a glass of Gallo and watched him gag. Talk about an acid test.

Another of Larry's friends, Bob, is into leasing fast high-end sports cars, which he too can't afford. But Bob's been driving such cars for so long that were he forced to drive a Chevy Suburban for the rest of his life, he'd likely slit his wrists.

And then there's Larry's friend Sandy, who practically salivates over fancy footwear.

In fact, human beings do react physically to spending opportunities. Economists have begun teaming up with neurologists and psychologists to study what parts of the brain light up when Steve passes a wine store, Bob walks into a Porsche dealership, and Sandy slips on a pair of Ferragamos. This research, called *neuroeconomics*, literally involves imaging people's brains with magnetic resonance imaging (MRI) scans as they are asked economic and financial questions.

The upshot of the brain-imaging studies is that there is no single central processing unit guiding us in making our spending, insurance, and investment decisions. Instead, according to Jonathan Cohen, a neuroscientist and director of Princeton University's Center for the Study of Brain, Mind, and Behavior, "There are multiple systems within the brain. Most of the time, these systems cooperate in decision making, but under some circumstances they compete with one another."

So we literally are schizoid, but not quite as Hollywood has imagined.

Interestingly, the brain treats complicated decisions as threats. Those sections of the brain that light up when we are confronted with threatening situations also light up when we are confronted with complicated decisions. Or as behavioral economist Colin Camerer of the California Institute of Technology puts it, "When [the brain] can't figure out what is happening, the amygdala transmits fear to the orbitofrontal cortex." (Not exactly something you might have heard in your intro-to-economics course.)

Another interesting finding is that the part of our brain that lights up when we're angry or distressed also lights up when we're charged an unfair price. This indicates quite conclusively that our emotions are directly involved in economic decision making.

Yet more striking evidence of the interplay among emotions, physiology, and economic decisions comes from a study by University of Zurich economist Ernst Fehr. He and his colleagues set up a controlled experiment in which participants could make more money if they trusted their co-participants. Inhaling a spray form of oxytocin, a hormone produced by the brain and associated with breast feeding, sexual intercourse, and other types of social bonding, made the subjects trust one another more, which led them to earn a lot more money.

Laibson and his collaborators have also looked at how the brain deals with instant gratification versus deferred gratification. They MRI'd subjects who were given a choice between immediate and delayed rewards. Both options lit up the lateral prefrontal cortex, but the immediate reward caused particular activity in the limbic areas, which govern our emotional lives.

These findings concerning the tug-of-war between emotions and reason operating within the brain may help us understand framing—the proposition, mentioned earlier, that how a problem is presented can often influence actions. Here is an example: enrolling someone automatically in a 401(k) plan and giving her the option to disenroll as opposed to inviting her to enroll of her own free will. The economic choice is the same in both cases, but the way it's presented is different. Presumably, the manner in which the brain is handed these options leads it to process the options differently. If, for example, the status quo elicits sensations of safety, pre-enrolling employees in a 401(k) may make them feel that remaining in the plan is the right thing to do.

Reliance on Big Brothers

If the mere thought of complicated financial decisions makes us physically anxious (and lights up our amygdala), while the thought of having someone handle our finances induces feelings of being nurtured (and lights up our limbic systems), then, by golly, why not let someone else handle our financial decisions?

Lots of us do just that. We rely on our employers and Uncle Sam to save, insure, and even invest for us. But when it comes to these players, our internal wires are definitely crossed. As we've discussed, neither our employers nor Uncle Sam necessarily has our best interests in mind.

Former Enron employees will certainly confirm this fact. As discussed earlier, eleven thousand of them lost a collective $1 billion in assets (not to mention their jobs) when Enron went down the tubes because they had invested their 401(k) assets in their company's stock. To add insult to injury, as its stock headed south, Enron prevented its employees from selling their company shares, which constituted almost two-thirds of their 401(k) holdings.

Today close to 16 percent of defined-contribution retirement account plan assets are invested in company stock. These include 401(k)s, 403(b)s, employee stock ownership plans (ESOPs), simplified employee pensions (SEPs), and profit-sharing plans. In some companies, such as Procter & Gamble, the share has, in recent years, been close to 100 percent! Despite this clear compounding of participants' labor income and investment return risk, participants often have no say in the matter. Their employers contribute stock rather than cash to their retirement accounts and then dramatically limit the participants' ability to sell these shares and thereby diversify their portfolios.

You might think that it was small employers who were breaching their ethical (if not legally binding) fiduciary responsibilities in ensuring that their workers would lose both their jobs and much of their retirement income were the company to fail. But it's primarily large employers doing this. Indeed, 43 percent of the defined-contribution assets of companies with five thousand or more workers is invested in company stock. And over five million American workers, most employed by Fortune 500 companies, have three-fifths or more of their retirement account assets invested in their own company stock.

This wouldn't be happening if either big business or Uncle Sam was concerned about our financial well-being.

Computational Limitations

Our minds are marvelously complex. But none of us is wired to solve really complicated financial problems. We probably didn't need to tell you that; many of us are reminded on a regular basis, like when we try to figure out the tip in a restaurant. Computers, of course, are fantastic at this kind of thing. IBM's BlueGene/L, the world's most powerful supercomputer, can make 280 trillion calculations per second. The typical home computer now has the power the very fastest computers had only years ago.

Most financial-planning software in current use was designed for computers (or calculators) that were outmoded decades ago. The software does simple time-value-of-money calculations, examining one life issue at a time. But, like the rest of life, in financial planning, everything is connected to everything else. Change one thing, and everything else changes with it. This reality is passionately ignored by most financial planning, which routinely offers the wrong answers.

Takeaways

Financial pathology has many causes, including:

- financial illiteracy
- the blind leading the blind
- designed neglect
- overconfidence
- compulsive behavior
- operating in the dark
- economic/neurological schizophrenia
- reliance on Big Brothers
- computational limitations
- tax and benefit complexity
- the technical challenge of developing fast consumption-smoothing programs
- the absence, until now, of publicly available consumption-smoothing software

8. Financial Snake Oil

When I see someone rich,
both my thumbs start to itch . . .

—"You've Got to Pick a Pocket or Two,"
Oliver!

HAVING SURVEYED OUR financial pathologies in chapter 6 and learned some of their causes in chapter 7, you're probably ready for a comforting hero—someone who will give us the equivalent of a financial miracle drug to rescue us from our ills.

Unfortunately, no hero is in sight. Instead we're surrounded by hard-breathing packs of financial charlatans. Some are sincere and well meaning, but that only makes it worse, because we are led astray by people we trust. If we examine this more closely, we learn that the tools they use almost always work to create and enhance their incomes.

One way to see this in action is to look closely at the retirement income replacement rate. Have you ever wondered about this widely accepted rule of thumb? It's the one that tells us that our retirement income must be 70 percent to 85 percent of our preretirement income in order to maintain our standard of living in old age. That figure, in turn, is often the basis for calculating what former *Esquire* magazine editor Lee Eisenberg called "the number" in his book of the same title—the amount of money you need to have in your retirement nest egg before you say *hasta la vista* to your employer.

The replacement rate, regularly cited in personal finance magazines and on Web sites, is so standard a fixture in financial planning that it has earned urban legend status. People assume that it's correct and reasonable because they've heard it so many times. Millions of us can recite this rule of thumb but can't cite its source. This includes financial planners who know and care as little about the rule's parentage as they do about its derivation. What they know is that using the replacement rate helps make them money.

The "Science" Behind the Replacement Rate

The replacement rate has a source. It's calculated every three years by the Center for Risk Management and Insurance Research at Georgia State University, using the Department of Labor's Consumer Expenditure Survey. As the center's Web site acknowledges, it was established in 1969 "through grants and general financial support from the insurance industry." The replacement rate study itself is, as previously mentioned, financed by AON Corporation, a major insurance brokerage, consulting, and underwriting firm headquartered in Chicago.

In other words, the replacement rate is calculated by the insurance industry.

The calculation itself is an exercise in reverse engineering. The "researchers" at Georgia State start with the preretirement income of a variety of households (married, single, different income levels) and then make adjustments until they get to the spending being done before retirement. They assume this income needs to be replaced. Then they calculate the pretax retirement income needed to cover that spending.

Let's take it step by step. Let's say that you are a sixty-five-year-old worker with a sixty-two-year-old nonworking spouse. Your salary is $70,000.

How much of that $70,000 do you actually get to spend?

Well, $5,355 comes off the top to pay FICA (Federal Insurance Contributions Act) taxes. Another $7,040 and $1,678 are estimated to be lost to federal and state income taxes. That leaves you with $55,927—your preretirement after-tax income.

Next the GSU researchers subtract your savings, estimated from survey data. In their study, it amounts to $2,421, or 4.3 percent of gross income. They also adjust for age-related work expenses, which cuts $1,975 off the required income of the $70,000 household.

That leaves $51,531 as the amount of money that's being spent before retirement and that supposedly needs to continue forever at the same level and be covered by postretirement income net of postretirement taxes. Given their estimates of $1,264 and $278 in postretirement federal and state income taxes, the Georgia Staters conclude that you need total postretirement annual income of $53,073 to net $51,531 each year.* Divide $53,073 by $70,000, and you get 0.76. So we've arrived at a 76 percent replacement rate.

Repeat these steps for a range of incomes and household compositions, and you come up with the fabled 70 percent to 85 percent replacement rate rule of thumb.

Pretty cool, right?

The Wrong Number

Sorry, it's an easily calculated number, but it will be dead wrong for most people. Let's see why.

For starters, the calculation blithely assumes that a household's spending after retirement will be precisely the same as its spending before retirement (the one exception to this rule being work-related

---

* These amounts are in 2007 dollars.

expenses). "Spending" here refers to *all* household outlays, be they on food, housing, education, medical bills, and so on.

This assumption leaves one scratching one's head. After all, mortgage payments adjusted for inflation change from year to year and stop once the mortgage is paid off. Tuition payments, whether for primary, secondary, or higher education, stop at some point. Spending on children ends when the kids grow up and move out. Special vacations taken prior to retiring may not be repeated after retiring. And the list goes on.

Let's get personal about this. One of us—Larry—is a preretiree. Larry's wife, Dayle, is younger than Larry. Indeed, for the record and to avoid future litigation, Dayle is *much* younger. This explains why their boys, Alex and David, are only seventeen and ten.

Recently, Larry was feeling a tad self-conscious about being the oldest dad in David's fourth-grade class. So he did some research. Turns out he isn't. Larry's not the oldest fourth-grade dad, nor the second oldest, nor even the third oldest. He's the fourth oldest.

Larry and his fellow geezer-dads number among the millions of preretirees who still have young children at home. Their preretirement spending involves significant outlays on children. For their part, Larry and Dayle spend a bundle each year feeding, clothing, transporting, entertaining, computerizing, summer camping, vacationing, electric guitaring, piano lessoning, iPoding, X-boxing, and Game Boying Alex and David.

The one saving grace for all this spending on kids is that it will eventually end. In Larry and Dayle's case, it will end in approximately thirteen years, when David, following Alex, graduates from college and starts earning a living. When that time comes, Larry and Dayle will be spending dramatically less than their current preretirement spending. The boys will be on their own. The mortgage will be paid off. Their life insurance needs will also be over by then. The same could well be true of their financial help to Larry's mom.

You would never know any of this from AON's replacement rate formula. It asks no questions. So it incorporates no information about children, mortgages, insurance premiums, financial assistance to parents, and a host of other temporary or short-term expenditures. Instead the formula assumes that what Larry and Dayle are spending now, they will spend in retirement. This mistake leads, in Larry and Dayle's case, to a roughly 40 percent overstatement of their replacement rate—the key number that is supposed to tell them how much to save.

You might think that research-oriented companies like TIAA-CREF and Fidelity would try to adjust for the brain-dead nature of the AON replacement rate formula by asking questions about children, mortgages, and so on before using the replacement rate to tell you what to save. But, no, they accept the whole idea. TIAA-CREF's Retirement Goal Evaluator and Fidelity's myPlan ask just six and five questions, respectively, before using an 80 percent replacement rate to pronounce you a savings disaster.

The second mistake in the replacement rate method is the assumption that there will be no new spending needs in retirement. Examples here include taking care of parents who live longer than expected, paying for a country club membership, paying Medicare Part B premiums (which are slated to soar), and paying for home health care and nursing home care. Of course, by omitting these and other retirement-specific expenditures, the replacement rate method *understates* the household's future spending needs and, therefore, what it needs to save.

Could it be that these two huge blunders in determining replacement rates cancel each other? Well, anything's possible. But this is akin to suggesting that we can get a good estimate of the Ford Motor Company's annual sales by leaving out the sales of its truck division but adding in the sales of Boeing jumbo jets.

The third mistake with the replacement rate is its presumption that the household's demographic composition will remain constant throughout retirement. Because of the age difference between Larry and Dayle, even if Larry makes it to his maximum age of life, Dayle will still have many years left before she maxes out on her potential life span. So Larry and Dayle's postretirement spending will eventually entail spending on just one person—Dayle. This is not unusual.

In most marriages, the wife will typically survive her spouse by five or six years. So if there is any logic to calculating replacement rates, this argument indicates that one needs a different replacement rate for each period for which there is a different demographic composition of the household.

The fourth fundamental mistake with the replacement rate approach is that it assumes that retirees use none of the principal of their assets to finance their retirement consumption. Instead, retirees are assumed to be able to spend only the income earned on the assets.

Apparently the replacement rate researchers believe, contrary to all experience, that retirees would choose to starve rather than invade their principal in order to pay for consumption.

This is ridiculous. Retirees, whether poor or rich, will spend their assets (their principal), as well as asset income, to pay for consumption in retirement.

To get an idea of the importance of using principal as well as income earned on principal to pay for old-age consumption, let's ask how much a sixty-year-old with $500K in assets who earns no income on these assets (his real return is $0) can safely consume each year if his maximum age of life is one hundred. The answer is $12,244 on an inflation-adjusted basis. (It would be $500K divided by 40, or $12,500, were it not for taxes.) Now suppose the person can invest in inflation-indexed bonds yielding 3 percent above inflation. In this case, his sustainable level of consumption expenditure rises to $19,488. So being able to spend principal as well as income on one's assets can account for almost two-thirds of one's total retirement spending. Clearly, if you spend principal, you won't need to save nearly as much.

The fifth and most damning error with the replacement rate method is that it assumes that the household's current saving behavior is consistent with consumption smoothing—in other words, with maintaining the household's underlying living standard per person through time. There is no reason to believe this is the case. Ironically, if households are already saving the consumption-smoothing amounts, they have no need for a replacement rate target. But if they are not, the replacement rate methodology will produce the wrong replacement rate because it will use actual savings (the wrong savings amount) in calculating the rate!

To see this point in the starkest terms, take Sebastian, a single, fifty-year-old man earning $100K, with no children, no regular assets, no retirement accounts, no house (he rents), no pensions, and no work-related expenses. We'll assume that Sebastian neither pays taxes to, nor receives benefits from, the government. Now suppose that Sebastian is currently saving the wrong amount. Indeed, suppose he's saving absolutely nothing. Then the replacement rate method will subtract nothing from his $100K in earnings, deduce that Sebastian is spending $100K, presume that Sebastian's $100K living standard should be maintained through the end of his life, and conclude that Sebastian needs to target for a replacement rate of 100 percent.

But here's the rub. For Sebastian to "maintain" his current $100K living standard *before* as well as after retirement, he'll have to keep spending $100K each year right through retirement. But this means he'll have no money left over to save and no hope whatsoever of doing anything other than starving once he retires. On the other hand, if Sebastian tries to save enough before age sixty-five to hit the $100K spending target for people age sixty-five and older, he'll be forced to save virtually every dollar he earns and, in effect, starve before he retires. In fairness, the AON/GSU study does acknowledge that there is a feedback loop between savings and replacement rate, but it's in the fine print of the exercise.

What's patently obvious is that Sebastian can't afford to spend $100K annually from age fifty through age one hundred, given that he has saved nothing until now, earns only $100K per year, and has only fifteen more years to work. But the suspension of logic and arithmetic is inherent in the replacement rate method. Upon reflection, it should also be clear that the replacement rate method is telling undersavers (those whose saving is less than the consumption-smoothing amount) to oversave and oversavers (those saving more than the consumption-smoothing amount) to undersave. This is doing neither group a service. Undersavers have a hard enough time getting their act together. They should not be told to save far beyond what's appropriate, when they are having a hard time getting started. And those who are oversaving shouldn't be told to undersave, when this is most likely the thing they fear most about their future finances.

The Ripper-Offers

Once the financial services industry has conned you into replacing an impossibly high share of your preretirement income, its real sales job begins. Specifically, it wants you to buy into at least one of over 23,000 mutual funds, each of which intimates that it will beat the market for its particular category and provide you with above-average returns.

This is a highly improbable event, akin to using lottery tickets as a savings vehicle. Not everyone can perform above the average. And given the efficiency of the capital markets, there is also no reason to believe that any one of the 23,000 funds can systematically (year after year) and legally (without the benefit of inside information) perform above the average.

The ones making the strongest pitch to beat the street are equity funds. Why? Because they stand to earn 1.41 percentage points of your return compared with the 1.10 percentage points that the typical bond fund extracts. The 1.41 percent fee is the average amount charged by equity funds. Some charge fees above 2.50 percent! Such fees are grossly higher than the 10 or 20 basis point fees (.10 or .20 percent) you'll pay if you follow our advice and invest in equities only via index funds.

Follow the Money

In 2002 mutual fund investors paid a whopping $39 billion in fees to brokers selling the 23,000 different funds. These fees went to pay

$3.6 billion in front-end sales commissions, $2.8 billion in back-end sales commissions, $8.8 billion in 12b-1 marketing fees, and another $23.8 billion in fund operating expenses.

That's a lot of money for America's households to shell out on financial services that have no clear value. It's difficult to overestimate the impact the added investment costs have on what working Americans accumulate for retirement. While annual expenses of, say, 1.4 percent for a mutual fund may seem reasonable, paying them is equivalent to being hit with a tax that exceeds 35 percent—the highest marginal federal income tax rate.

This is not obvious. Wall Street tells us the cost is modest because common stocks can be expected to return an inflation-adjusted 9.1 percent a year, and 1.40 percent in fees is only 14.6 percent of this expected return. And if our manager is worth what we pay her, she'll make a higher return.

The reality is different. First, most managers fail to beat their appointed benchmark. And they tend to trail it by an amount equal to their expenses. The greater the expenses, the greater the investors' loss of return. Worse, one year of simple loss compounds over many years.

Suppose you have the good fortune to be a federal employee and participate in the federal Thrift Savings Plan, which offers an index of U.S. stocks at a cost of only 0.03 percent (3 basis points). Over thirty years, a $10,000 investment would grow to $248,171, losing only 2 percent of the potential return to expenses.

The same investment made by a worker in a typical 401(k) plan would lose 1.41 percent (141 basis points) to expenses and would grow to only $172,106, losing 33.7 percent of its potential gain. Worse still, hundreds of thousands of schoolteachers invest in variable annuity insurance products in their 403(b) plans and pay expenses of 2.4 percent (240 basis points). This reduces their accumulation to only $130,815. They lose an incredible 50.9 percent of their return to the costs of management and marketing.

Most teachers—indeed, most households—are in the 15 percent federal income tax bracket or lower. So the long-term burden of industry standard fees is far worse than what the taxman takes. Afflu-ent readers will find that hard to believe, but that's the case. A couple filing a joint income tax return in 2007 can have taxable income of $63,700 before entering the 25 percent tax bracket. Since that $63,700 is after adjustments such as 401(k) and IRA contributions, not to mention a standard deduction of $10,700 and a personal ex-emption of $3,400 per household member, a family of four can have a gross income well over $90,000 before starting to pay taxes at 25 percent. According to IRS data, about two-thirds of all taxpayers pay at the 15 percent rate or less.

It Can Be Worse

Sadly, the mutual fund hype that does so much for the financial services industry and so little for people who actually invest and take risks is minor when measured against some of the financial products being sold under the banner of good retirement planning. The most egregious example is a popular product called the equity index annuity, with recent annual sales approaching $30 billion a year.

Rather than owning equities directly, the investor owns an insur-ance product that provides a portion of the rise in price of a major index, usually the S&P 500. In exchange for giving up dividends and a portion of the capital appreciation, the investor gains the assur-ance of never having a losing year. This "no loss" feature caused EIA sales to soar when the market crashed in 2000–2002 and investors sought safety at any price.

While equity index annuity products don't have explicit expenses as mutual funds do, financial economists have calculated that the cost of this safety is extraordinary. Economists have shown that investors would be better off in a simple portfolio of Treasury securi-ties and large-cap stocks 97 percent of the time. They've also calcu-lated that the typical equity index annuity purchase amounted to a transfer of 15 percent to 20 percent of wealth from the investor to insurance companies and their sales forces.

Charity Begins at Home, Not at Your Broker-Dealer's

As now practiced, the financial planning offered by the financial services industry gives us two unpleasant choices. We can follow their prescriptions and help them build their 10,000-square-foot cabins in Jackson Hole, Wyoming, while we suppress our consumption during our most vital years; or we can live in anxiety created by the constant barrage of studies and surveys telling us that we're on the road to retirement disaster because we're not saving as much as we should or getting a high enough return on what we do save.

We think there is a better way, one that does not rest on patently ridiculous assumptions about future spending needs and equally unlikely investment returns to finance that spending. The better way is our mantra, consumption smoothing. It looks at all your current and future economic resources, all your committed expenditures (housing, tuition, taxes, weddings, and so on), ends up with your lifetime spending power, and allocates that spending power to generate the smoothest (most consistent) path of living standard *per person* for your evolving household without exceeding your ability or willingness to borrow.

Takeaways

- Replacement rates come to you courtesy of people who have their very best interests at heart.
- Replacement rates assume that spending on children continues after they leave the house.
- Replacement rates assume that spending on mortgages continues after they're paid off.
- Replacement rates assume that spending on tuition continues after children are out of school.
- Replacement rates assume no change ever in the household's demographic composition.
- Replacement rates assume that assets are accumulated but never spent.

- Replacement rates are calculated using actual saving rates. If actual saving rates are appropriate, end of story—forget about replacement rates. If they aren't, the replacement rates will promote consumption disruption, not consumption smoothing.
- Replacement rates are con jobs—pure and simple.

PART 3

Raising Your Living Standard

And now for what you have been waiting for: how to achieve a higher living standard! Note that not a single example in this part and the next involves actual investment decisions, portfolio management, or anything requiring possession of an MBA. Both of these parts, from start to finish, deal with decisions in daily living.

Let's start with choosing your career and then consider whether it makes sense to have a career at all. If you, our reader, are no longer able to work, don't feel left out of the next few chapters. What you'll learn will be surprising and may be worth imparting to your friends and relatives. And there are lots of examples coming of direct relevance to you.

9. My Son the Plumber

"WHO MAKES MORE, a doctor or a plumber?" Larry asked his family over dinner.

"The doctor," they all chimed.

"OK, who has the higher living standard?"

Silence, interrupted quickly by Dayle, Larry's wife.

"The plumber, *duh!* The doctor has to take on a mountain of debt to attend college and med school and needs to repay it. Plus, he doesn't start working for years. The plumber can start work right after high school, and there's no malpractice insurance. It's obvious.

"Maybe to you, but it sure wasn't obvious to me," said Larry. "After all, general practitioners in Ohio—the docs I'm considering—average $146K a year once they finish their residency. Ohio plumbers also have to train, although they earn money along the way. It takes them four years to get to the top plumbing class—class 3—at which point they make only $50K. There's a big distance between $146K and $50K."

"Right," said Dayle. "But let's talk tuition. What are you figuring for tuition?"

"About $33K for each year of college and $41K for each of four years in med school. These are Boston University rates; I figured

they should get the best training. I'm also assuming a three-year residency paying $44K a year, after which the doctor's regular salary
kicks in."

"OK, and how high did you set the borrowing rate?"

"Good question. I assumed 9 percent after checking several Web
sites and calling Chase's student lending department. This seems
high, but it's actually fairly low relative to what typical lenders are
charging students who take on tons of debt."

"Gee," offered Alex, Larry's sixteen-year-old, "maybe I should
be a plumber?"

"Good choice," said Larry. "The doctor's living standard is
actually 15 percent below the plumber's."

"I don't believe it," said Alex.

"Don't move, Alex," said Larry. "I'll explain why it's true. After
you factor in the costs of medical malpractice insurance, the doctor
earns only 2.4 times more than the plumber. But that's just looking
at their gross incomes. If you subtract all the interest payments
the doctor has to make, the doctor's net income is only two times the
plumber's, or lower, for most of their working years."

"Next you are going to tell me about taxes, right?" asked Alex,
who had gotten up and begun edging toward the door.

"Exactly," said Larry, brimming with pride. "The doctor pays
disproportionately more taxes for two reasons. First, the federal income tax and Ohio state income tax are progressive. Second, the
feds and Ohio tax the doctor's gross income, not his net income—his
income net of the interest payments he's forced to make in paying off
his debts.* You can deduct up to $2,500 of interest paid on student
loans, but that's a small portion of the total interest payments the
doctor makes in most of his working years.

"Once you factor in taxes, malpractice insurance premiums, and
interest payments, the doctor's and the plumber's net incomes are

---

* Given the ceiling on taxable earnings, FICA taxes are regressive. But for almost all his
career, the doctor's earnings fall below the ceiling once one takes into account the fact
that the taxable ceiling is indexed to economy-wide real wage growth.

very similar in many of their prime working years. For example, at age forty, the doctor nets $41,992, while the plumber nets $40,817.

"But don't forget, the plumber's net income is much higher than the doctor's for eleven years, between ages nineteen and twenty-nine. The doctor's in school for eight years and then does his internship and residency for three. During the eight years of college and med school, he earns nothing and has to borrow not only to pay tuition but also to sustain his living standard. And when he's an intern and resident, he earns less than the plumber on a gross basis and dramatically less on a net basis."

"Hmm," said Alex, "plumbing's looking pretty good. Guess I can skip my homework."

"And I didn't mention Social Security benefits. They're provided on a progressive basis. So the doctor gets more, but not that much more. Throughout retirement, the doctor's Social Security income is only 50.2 percent higher than the plumber's even though his gross earnings are 180 percent higher. Moreover, a larger share of the doctor's benefits gets hit by federal and state income taxation because the thresholds beyond which benefits are taxed aren't indexed for inflation!"

Flabbergasted

Both of us (Scott and Larry) were flabbergasted by the comparison of the living standards of plumbers and doctors. We had intended to point out that the doctor's living standard was higher than the plumber's, but not that much higher. We had no idea that the plumber would come out ahead.

In running the comparison, we had the doctor and plumber borrow as much as needed to smooth their living standards. As indicated, we assumed a 9 percent borrowing rate. Our assumed investment rate was lower: 6 percent, in keeping with the reality that borrowing rates exceed lending (investing) rates. Since we assumed a 3 percent rate of inflation, the assumed real borrowing and investment returns were 6 percent and 3 percent, respectively. When we assumed a 9 percent rather than 6 percent investing rate (in other words, a 6 percent real rate), the doctor's living standard was 21 percent lower than the plumber's. For the plumber, there was actually no need to borrow, since he made money from the get-go. The doctor, on the other hand, went deeply into debt and spent much of his working life paying it off.

Now, we realize that many budding doctors get help from their parents, receive financial aid, and attend less expensive educational institutions. These factors would obviously limit the amount they need to borrow and would change our analysis.

We also realize that many would-be doctors choose to limit their borrowing by cutting their living standard when young. They do so for a good reason. No medical student knows for sure whether she'll be able to stomach gross anatomy or what she'll earn if she actually gets through the med school, internship, and residency gauntlet. Given this, prospective docs are naturally reluctant to begin their careers with a mountain of debt—debt they may never be able to repay. Consequently, many choose to have a very low living standard while in school and while training. Then, if things work out, they can enjoy a much higher living standard thereafter. (This strategy mitigates the risk of the doctor's going bankrupt down the road, but it raises the risk of the doctor's dying before she has fully enjoyed the fruits of her hard-won income.)

To consider this behavior, we reran the doctor's profile but specified that he wanted to triple his living standard after he finished his residency. Doing so generated a post-age-thirty living standard for the doctor that was 35.4 percent higher than the plumber's.

Does this mean that being a doctor really pays more than being a plumber? The answer is no. If you properly add up the *lifetime* consumption of the doctor and the plumber, the plumber still comes out ahead. By that, we mean forming the present values of the doctor's and the plumber's annual consumption paths, including the very low levels of consumption the doctor experiences when young.

The fact that so many older docs have higher living standards than older plumbers makes it easy to conclude that the material rewards of diagnosing and treating disease exceed and, indeed, greatly exceed those of stopping leaks. But as we've seen, such conclusions ignore the major sacrifices in living standards that doctors make early on in their careers, not to mention the enormous number of hours they spend studying and working as interns and residents. We haven't even considered the many hours doctors work relative to plumbers. If we adjusted for this, the case would favor plumbing still more because the hourly wage of the doctors would be significantly lower.

The Moral of This Story

Becoming a doctor is not solely an economic decision. The profession offers tremendous psychological rewards that go beyond dollars and cents. Saving someone's life, limiting someone's pain, delivering a baby—these are gratifications that can't be valued in absolute terms. But they can be valued (priced out) in relative terms. Would-be doctors need to decide whether these rewards make it worth going into medicine rather than into plumbing, given that plumbing offers higher lifetime consumption and many fewer 3:00 a.m. emergency calls!

Specifically, in choosing between medicine and plumbing, would-be doctors should compare their psychological benefits with their loss in lifetime consumption. There is certainly some *cutoff* loss in living standard—a point at which they are just indifferent between being a plumber and becoming a doctor. The dollar value of this cutoff loss tells us in dollars and cents the value of the psychological rewards.

Our guess is that most of today's premed college students think they'll be consuming a lot more than plumbers on a lifetime basis and would be shocked to learn they will not. Yet, given the other rewards, the vast majority would, no doubt, still prefer medicine over plumbing. But if they don't know what medicine and plumbing are really paying, chances are they don't know what other professions are really paying.

Web sites such as PayScale (www.payscale.com) can show you what different careers pay, on average, in particular cities, regions, and even countries. But, as we've seen, what you'll earn in a given career, once you've done all your training, is only part of the story. In order to really determine which job delivers the most spending power, you need to consider not just what you'll ultimately earn but how long it will take to train, how much it will cost to train, how much you'll need to borrow, what it will cost to borrow, how long you'll work, what taxes you'll pay, and what Social Security retirement benefits you'll receive.

Again, this is impossible to figure out on your hand calculator. But with ESPlanner you can compare your living standard from pursuing different careers in a matter of seconds.

So what's the moral of this story? It's this: *don't take your career for granted*. Knowing for sure that you've made the right career move is different from *hoping* for sure. Indeed, the first thing to decide is whether *no career* is actually your best career—in other words, whether it pays not to work, something that we discuss in chapter 11.

10. Does College Really Pay?

THE COLLEGE BOARD, which administers the Scholastic Aptitude Test, or SAT, claims that college pays *by a lot,* with the median annual earnings of college grads exceeding those of high school grads by $22,600. But the board's focus is entirely on the income gains from college. It ignores the expenses associated with attending college—four years of tuition plus room and board and four years spent learning, not earning. It also ignores the relatively high interest rates charged on student loans. Finally, the board ignores the progressivity of our tax-transfer system, which places a relatively higher burden on those with higher incomes. The federal government as well as many state governments tax income on a progressive basis. Social Security benefits are provided on a progressive basis. Even Medicare premiums are now collected on a progressive basis.

The real question is not whether college grads earn more once they get to work. The real question is whether they can achieve a higher living standard over their lifetimes given the costs of attending college. So the fact that the College Board says that college pays doesn't necessarily make it so. The College Board, bear in mind, is in the business of getting people to go to college, and to get into most colleges, you need to take the SAT—the College Board's sales product.

Take eighteen-year-old Rebecca, who is considering attending a four-year college at $40K per year. She expects to earn at each age the median college-grad earnings level stated in the report "Education Pays" (posted online at www.collegeboard.com). Rebecca's parents can't offer any financial help, so she's looking to borrow all her college costs and start repaying the loans once she graduates. Rebecca's alternative, she figures, is earning the age-specific median earnings of high school grads also reported by the board.

Comparing the two options shows that college does pay, but not by much. If Rebecca attends college, her living standard will total $21,033 per year (in 2007 dollars). If she skips college and goes right to work, her annual living standard is $19,068. So college delivers a higher *expected* living standard, but only 10 percent higher.

These results assume that Rebecca borrows enough after college to smooth her living standard. If, as is likely, she looks at her $183K in college loans and vows never to borrow another penny, her living standard from age twenty-three through thirty-five will average only $15,416—27 percent less during these years than her living standard would be were she not to attend college. After thirty-five, when Rebecca's paid off the bulk of her college loans, her living standard rises to a permanent $23,638.

Sacrificing one's youth is one consideration. Another is risk. If, having borrowed heavily, Rebecca ends up earning below the median (and there's a 50 percent chance this will happen), her college loans will loom even larger. Indeed, borrowing to raise your future labor earnings is not much different from borrowing to invest in the stock market. It's risky business.

Aren't the median earnings of college grads higher for those attending more expensive schools? They may well be. We aren't aware of such data, or we'd have used them to make this comparison. But there are, no doubt, many students attending expensive private colleges who will earn, at most, the median amounts the College Board is advertising.

What if Rebecca's parents were able to foot the bill? Would that change the story? It would change the story for Rebecca, but it wouldn't change the basic economics at all. Regardless of who pays the bill, we're talking about a highly risky investment that has a pretty good chance of not paying off.

And if it doesn't pay off for Rebecca, what does that mean, exactly? Well, if she's signed the loan documents, it potentially means a lifetime of loan repayments with no ability to discharge the debts by declaring bankruptcy. This inability to default on student loans comes courtesy of Uncle Sam, who also actively helps loan collectors go after delinquents. The government even goes so far as garnishing Social Security checks to repay past-due student loans! So this is really *very* nasty business if things don't turn out as planned in terms of your future labor earnings.

There's more to college than just making money, of course. Rebecca will have lots of fun and will, no doubt, make lifelong friends. She also should learn a lot. But on pure economic grounds, going to college, at least an expensive one, is far less beneficial than most people believe.

11. Fire Your Job

MANY PEOPLE LOVE their jobs, find them truly fulfilling, and, truth be told, would pay to keep them. Others can't stand working, hate their boss, barely tolerate their coworkers, and would be much happier unemployed, provided that it didn't mean a much lower living standard.

If you fall into the "work sucks" category, make sure you're actually making money by going to work.

There are, in fact, hundreds of thousands of Americans for whom working is a financial mistake; for whom earning more money means *less, not more,* spending power. For these Americans, earning more not only means paying more taxes, it means losing tax credits and various government benefits such that, on balance, their overall spending power declines.

We're speaking here primarily of married couples earning less than $40K and singles earning less than $30K. Like everyone else, these folks are forced to pay the FICA tax. They also face state and federal income taxes. But earning more may also cost them some or all of the federal earned-income tax credit (EITC) and savers credit, both formally part of the federal personal income tax, state tax breaks of various kinds for low earners, plus other benefits such as food stamps, Transitional Aid to Families with Dependent Children,

Medicaid, housing assistance, Low Income Home Energy Assistance, Supplemental Security Income, and the Special Supplemental Nutrition Program for Women, Infants, and Children.

Understanding the provisions of any one of these fiscal programs is no small feat.* Understanding the provisions of all of them as well as their interactions is worthy of a PhD in accounting. The details of these programs that are of most concern in making job decisions are income and asset tests. These provisions reduce a recipient's benefits when her income or assets exceed certain thresholds.

Take Medicaid, for example. In many states, if your income or assets are a dollar more than the allowable values, poof, that's it. You're kicked off of Medicaid, which, incidentally, provides its participants, on average, some $6,000 a year in free medical benefits. Or consider the earned-income tax credit. This feature of the federal income tax pays you to work. But once your earnings are sufficiently high, the EITC is reduced by as much as 22 cents for every dollar you earn, depending on your marital status and number of children.

Unfortunately, anyone with low income really needs to sweat the details of these programs to determine if working at all, or working as much as she is now, actually raises her bottom line—her spending power. Say, for example, you're married, and both you and your wife earn $17,500, which is a bit above current minimum-wage pay scales. According to a 2003 study by yours truly, Larry, and Dr. Jagadeesh Gokhale, if either you or your wife stopped working, you'd likely *raise* your spending power. The reason is that your combined $35,000 household income probably disqualifies you for most, if not all, of the aforementioned tax credits and benefit programs. Reducing your household's earnings by half will likely qualify you for the tax credits and benefits, as well as reduce your taxes by a combined amount that more than equals $17,500!

So if you and your wife are making $17,500 each, and one of

---

* For older households, the government has recently added an income test to determine the size of Medicare Part B premiums.

you is hooked on *The Young and the Restless, General Hospital,* or *The Bold and the Beautiful,* or just craves *Seinfeld* reruns, staring at the tube all day rather than working may make financial as well as psychological sense. Do not, however, take our word for this. Look before you leap, and check which tax credits and benefits would actually be available were one of you to "fire your job."

If either you or your wife can make money by *not* making money while the other one works full-time, having each of you work *half-time* will leave you in the same boat. So the Solomonic solution for deciding who should fire his/her job is for you both to fire half your jobs; i.e., you should both switch from working full-time to working half-time.

Larry and his grad student David Rapson recently updated the Kotlikoff-Gokhale study in a way that lets you eyeball the gains or losses from earning more money. (You can find it online at http://people.bu.edu/rapson/DIPW_METR_1006.pdf.) The paper has graphs like figure 1 below, which shows how much a forty-five-year-old couple earning a given amount each year affects the couple's lifetime spending power (the amount it can spend over time measured in present value).

Figure 1. Lifetime Spending Including Transfers ($'000s)
45-Year-Old Couples

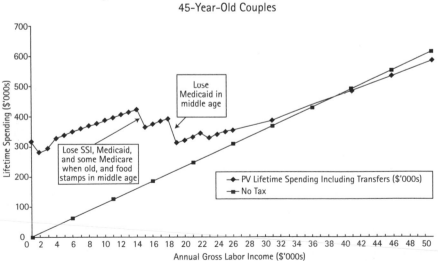

As you can see, if the forty-five-year-old couple are initially earning around $14,000 per year, earning more money actually means *less* lifetime spending power until the couple's earnings exceed about $38,000 per year. If the couple's choice is between not working and earning close to $30,000 per year, they'd have more spending power by not working.

How screwed up is this?

Don't ask.

Why would our government want to induce people to earn less or even stay *out* of the workforce? The answer is malign neglect. The government simply hasn't bothered to ask what all of its complex and interacting tax and benefit systems/provisions mean for different Americans' work incentives.* So don't expect the government to tell you if it's put you into a sky-high tax bracket that can easily exceed 100 percent. It doesn't know and apparently doesn't care to know. You have to check for yourself.

That's the moral of this story: know thy effective tax bracket.

This dictum applies to moderate-income as well as high-income workers. As the study shows, when you consider the entire fiscal system, almost all households earning $50K or more are in the 35 percent to 45 percent bracket; in other words, out of every extra dollar they earn, Uncle Sam grabs between 35 and 45 cents.

Whoever said the U.S. was a low-tax country?

It's not. We should all understand this before we choose to work ourselves to death. If you don't know your effective tax bracket, you may end up working a lot more than you would were the financial rewards really clear.

---

* These studies appear to represent the first truly comprehensive analyses of the total net return to work. The Congressional Budget Office has studied total effective marginal federal taxes but ignored state taxes as well as all the benefit programs.

12. Location, Location

HAVE WE GOT a house for you! It's a three-bedroom, two-car-garage beauty on a lovely tree-lined street in a middle-class neighborhood with great schools and easy access to downtown shopping and cultural attractions. It's in the Midwest, in a great town: Cedar Rapids, Iowa.

Ever hear of Cedar Rapids? It's named after the Cedar River that runs through the town and around Mays Island, the center of municipal governance. (Think Île de la Cité in Paris.)

The town's many famous sons, daughters, or short-term residents include the Wright Brothers, Paul Tibbets (pilot of the *Enola Gay,* which dropped the atomic bomb on Hiroshima), and former Ms. Czech-Slovak USA beauty queens Lisa Volesky and Stasia Krivanek.

The town boasts several colleges, a symphony orchestra, a number of museums, and a handful of cultural exhibits, the most important of which is the Czech Village, where you can buy Czech crystal and Royal Dux porcelain and dine on pierogies, dumpling soup, liver sausage, cabbage rolls, and for dessert, babovka, houska, rohliky, and kolaches.

Best yet, Cedar Rapids has polka! It's the home of the sensational Czech Plus Polka Band, which performs throughout the year at the Kosek Band Stand and various churches around town.

Excited?

You should be. As far as we can see, there's only one downside to living in Cedar Rapids: the city is smack dab in the middle of Tornado Alley, the nation's area of highest tornado activity. So, big deal, you'll learn to duck and outrun the damn things! Sure beats the hurricanes in Tampa, Florida, and the rain in Seattle, Washington.

The main thing going for Cedar Rapids, though, is this: it's a really cheap place to live. The price for the home we've found for you in suburban Marion is only $174,950. The same house in Safety Harbor, Florida, or Bellevue, Washington—comparable suburbs of Tampa and Seattle—will cost you $309,000 and $525,000, respectively. Those are big chunks of change when it comes to your living standard.*

Care to venture a guess how big? If so, jot down how much higher you think Donald and Ivana Trumpinski's living standard would be were they to live in Cedar Rapids rather than in Tampa or Seattle.

Donald and Ivana, by the way, are married and both are age thirty-five. Donald makes $40K a year and Ivana, $30K. The couple have a seven-year-old son (Donaldesque) and a three-year-old daughter (Ivanaesque) on whom they plan to spend $30K per year for four years of college each. Their assets total $45K, of which they plan to use $30K for a down payment to buy a home.

To keep things simple, assume that Donald and Ivana can get a thirty-year fixed, 7 percent mortgage in all three cities and that Donald and Ivana plan to live in their house until the last of them croaks, which could happen as late as age one hundred.

Ticktock, ticktock—game-show music.

And the answer is?

Living in Cedar Rapids provides a 33.5 percent higher living standard than Tampa and a 78.4 percent higher living standard than Seattle!

---

* All three prices are median 2007 home values in the suburbs in question.

These are really big differences, much bigger than we expected. But they make sense when you compare housing costs. In Seattle, Donald and Ivana pay (in today's dollars) $42,312 in housing costs at age thirty-five; $29,556 at age fifty; and $6,696 from age sixty-five on. In Tampa, where homeowners insurance and property taxes are particularly high, these figures are $26,435, $19,638, and $7,456, respectively. But in Cedar Rapids, the respective costs are just $14,936, $11,435, and $5,161.

The advantage of living in Cedar Rapids arises in spite of considerable tax savings from living in Seattle or Tampa. Neither Washington State nor Florida has a state income tax. That fact plus the higher mortgage interest deductions under the federal personal income tax mean that Donald and Ivana pay at age thirty-five only $2,384 in taxes (excluding FICA taxes) in Seattle and only $4,669 in Tampa. By comparison, their age-thirty-five tax bill in Iowa is $8,787, of which $3,275 represents state income taxes.

Living in Iowa does provide one tax advantage, however. The state sales tax rate is 5 percent, as against 6 percent in Florida and 6.5 percent in Washington State. This means Iowa's living-standard advantage is somewhat greater than just indicated.

The bottom line?

Learn to polka.

The Devil's Advocate (Himself)

No doubt a short-horned, long-tailed, tiny red creature sporting a trident is right now perched inside your brain, screaming "It will be a cold day in heaven before I let you move to Cedar Rapids. The weather, which these guys just happened to forget to mention, is terrible. You'll blow up like a blimp eating that food. And I'll be damned (oops, praised) if I let you do the polka.

"Furthermore, these jokers are overstating the financial gain of Cedar Rapids by a mile. First, they are ignoring the fact that Donald and Ivana will have a much more valuable house to leave to their kids when it's time for them to move into my own special village, and if they ever need to sell their house to buy into a nursing home, they'll get a much higher price in Tampa or Seattle.

"What's more, when Donald and Ivana retire, they can take out a reverse mortgage to unlock all the equity—all the money—they have trapped in their home. They can use this income from their reverse mortgage to pay for long-term care insurance or, hell forbid, polka lessons."

Rebuttal

The devil, bless his heart, has made some valid points. Cedar Rapids' cold winters do help explain its low housing prices. But we'd take cold, crisp, snowy winters over wet, damp, foggy ones. And Cedar Rapids' weather is only half bad. Its summers are mild (average high of eighty-five, average low of sixty) compared with Tampa's (average high of ninety, average low of seventy-five).

Certainly Donald and Ivana will end up leaving a much more expensive house to Donaldesque and Ivanaesque if they live in Tampa or Seattle. But their kids are likely to end up earning more money—a lot more money—than Donald and Ivana earn. Donald and Ivana, after all, make less than the median level of earnings, and U.S. wage rates, adjusted for inflation, can be expected to grow over time. So for Donald and Ivana to move to Seattle or Tampa, forgoing a much higher living standard in Cedar Rapids may make little sense even to their kids.

Having a more valuable house does mean a bigger security blanket to help cover unexpected expenditures, particularly unexpected health-care costs. But given Medicare and the major medical health insurance policies now available to retirees, the real expenditure risk is not cancer or some other major illness. The real risk is catastrophic nursing home expenses. Or at least so it seems until one thinks about Uncle Sam.

Nursing home costs are so out of sight, averaging over $70,000 per year, that Uncle Sam has long directed Medicaid to cover these costs for those who can't afford them. That's the good news. The bad news is that to qualify for Medicaid, you can't have more than a few thousand dollars in assets. Mind you, Medicaid won't count the equity in your house in applying this asset test. But once you die, watch out. Medicaid will go after your estate and demand to be reimbursed for all the money it laid out on your behalf.

So if Donald or Ivana or both end up in a nursing home, they'll surely end up in one covered by Medicaid, meaning that when the last of them dies, much if not all of their home equity will go straight to Uncle Sam, leaving Donaldesque and Ivanaesque with little or nothing.

In short, the devil's got this one wrong. Low- to moderate-income households like Donald and Ivana's should not try to save up for more than the amount needed to buy into one of the nicer nursing homes that take Medicaid. And since nursing home costs are lower in Cedar Rapids than in either Seattle or Tampa, owning the Cedar Rapids house free and clear may provide as much equity as is needed to pay the up-front nursing home entrance fee. A third option they should consider is buying a long-term care policy.

The devil's point about reverse mortgages is more telling. Reverse mortgages represent an interesting way to simultaneously spend the equity in one's home and also ensure against living too long (outliving your money). But, as we'll detail in chapter 17, the reverse mortgage market is in its infancy, and the reverse mortgages now on the market entail significant up-front costs. So, at least at this point, there is every reason to believe that Donald and Ivana would not take out a reverse mortgage at retirement. But when we get to chapter 17, we'll revisit the idea of reverse mortgages.

Takeaways

- Where you choose to live can make a huge difference in your living standard.
- Don't break your back paying off a house that you can't afford and will never sell.
- Learn to polka.

13. Whether 'Tis Wiser

ECONOMISTS CALL THEM "superstar cities"—urban areas where house prices are seemingly out of sight. The *median* home price in San Diego, for instance, was $579,800 at the close of 2006!

To someone living in Fargo, Kansas City, or Cincinnati, where the corresponding median prices were $136,600, $153,100, and $138,700, respectively, San Diego's prices are beyond belief and have just one way to go: down!

But for those living in San Francisco, with its $733,400 median price, house prices in San Diego look cheap.

Rents in the twenty or so superstar cities are also seemingly insane, but much less crazy than house prices. San Diego's house prices are 4.2 times Fargo's. But its rents are far more reasonable. As a consequence, it is possible to buy a starter house in Fargo and pay about the same as rent. In the superstar cities, however, ownership comes at a massive premium over renting.

For people with ordinary incomes, living in a superstar city is now virtually impossible. That's one reason it will cost you $2,600 to rent a Budget truck to move from San Diego to Dallas, but only $299 to rent the same truck to move from Dallas to San Diego. More people are leaving San Diego than are moving in, and the net exodus is depressing San Diego housing prices. In 2006 San Diego real house values (house values adjusted for inflation) fell by 7 percent.

Sounds like the wrong time to move to San Diego, let alone buy a house there, doesn't it?

Maybe. Maybe not.

First you'd have to decide if you can afford San Diego, period. But if your income is high enough to live there and you expect to do so for the long term, buying rather than renting and doing so sooner rather than later may actually be the best policy.

Take Andrew, a thirty-five-year-old corporate attorney starting a new job with a prestigious law firm, Howe Duey Cheatum Best, LLP, in San Diego. His starting salary is $200,000—a handsome sum by most measures—and it will rise at 1 percent above inflation each year. Andrew is married to the lovely and quasi-talented country-and-eastern singer Jessica Volksanger, who delights her audiences but clears nothing after expenses. Jessica is pregnant with the couple's first and only child, Andi Jess.

Should Andrew and Jessica buy a house or rent in San Diego, given that prices could keep falling and the immediate costs of owning—mortgage payment, homeowners insurance, property tax, and maintenance—are almost twice the cost of renting?

Good question.

San Diego's house prices have been falling, but they could start rising tomorrow. Indeed, when it comes to housing prices as well as all other asset prices, economics defies gravity: what goes up doesn't necessarily come down.

In fact, if asset markets are working right, asset prices will follow what's called a random walk, and no one will be able to say for sure that a given asset price will rise or fall. The reason is that if any of us knew for sure what would happen to any given asset price, we'd immediately buy or sell the asset until its price rose or fell to the point that there was no longer a sure profit opportunity. This immediate price movement ensures that where the price goes next is anyone's guess.

Andrew and Jessica may suspect that San Diego house prices will continue to fall, but they can't be certain. And waiting to buy has a potentially big downside. Rather than keep falling, house prices might start to rise—and do so sharply. The same is true of mortgage interest rates. So unless Andrew and Jessica know something no one else knows about San Diego's housing market, the move with the smallest downside risk is to buy right away rather than to wait. The important caveat here is that you must be highly confident that you will live in the house for a long time—like the rest of your life. If you move or are transferred every three years, this isn't a risk to take.

As for the second major issue—whether buying is more expensive than renting—given the immediate cost differences between owning and renting, renting would seem to offer the couple a much higher living standard. But surprisingly, it doesn't. Buying rather than renting a median-price San Diego house or condo leaves Andrew and Jessica with a 4.6 percent higher living standard every year of their lives despite paying much higher housing costs early on when they buy. Indeed, their first-year housing expenses are $55,942 when they buy versus $30,000 when they rent.*

Buying not only raises their living standard, it also leaves Andrew and Jessica in a position to leave Andi Jess a huge bequest: a $579,800 house free and clear of any mortgage if, as we assume, Andrew and Jessica hold on to the property until they die, and it neither appreciates nor depreciates in real terms.

So why does buying beat renting? Taxes and time.

Taxes

By buying their home, Andrew and Jessica save a ton of taxes each year of their lives. For example, in the first year, they pay $49,099 in total federal and state income and payroll taxes. That's a big tax hit,

---

* Calculations assume a starting salary of $200,000 that rises 1 percent faster than inflation of 3 percent a year, and real investment returns of 5 percent a year. We also assume a home price of $600,000 versus rent of $2,500 a month and that the house is taxed at 1 percent of value; a $600,000 mortgage at 6 percent for thirty years; and insurance of $2,000 a year. We also assume that both Andrew and Jessica will die at age ninety.

but it's $14,336 less than the $63,435 in taxes they'd pay the first year were they to rent.

This 23 percent first-year tax advantage comes courtesy of hefty federal and state income tax deductions for mortgages and property taxes. It also permits Andrew and Jessica to itemize their deductions rather than take the standard deduction. This, in turn, lets them deduct their state income taxes.

Years later, when Andrew and Jessica have paid off their mortgage, the absolute tax advantage from home ownership declines. But it's still impressive. At age seventy, for example, it's $5,147. (This reflects taxes of $19,431 when buying versus $24,578 when renting.)

Of course, by age seventy they've paid off their mortgage. So why does buying the home save taxes at that age?

The answer is that when they buy, Andrew and Jessica have less taxable financial-asset income at age seventy. They have less taxable financial-asset income at seventy because they have fewer financial assets. And they have fewer financial assets at seventy because they did most of their overall saving when young in the form of paying off their mortgage. This leaves them with an asset at age seventy that yields a special form of income—housing services—that is in-kind and, thus, tax free.

In contrast, when Andrew and Jessica rent, they accumulate more financial assets—about $200K more by age sixty-five—to help pay the $30K per year in rent that they face throughout retirement. (We'll explain this in more detail on page 139.)

Time

To repeat, Andrew and Jessica face much higher housing costs when young due to their mortgage payments. But over time the real value of their mortgage payments falls.

How come?

Because the number of dollars Andrew and Jessica pay each year stays fixed, while the rise in prices—inflation—makes those dollars worth less and less each year in terms of the real goods and services they can buy.

Of course, once the couple pay off their mortgage at age sixty-five, their mortgage payments drop to zero. At this point their housing costs, consisting of property taxes, maintenance, and homeowners insurance premiums, fall to $14K—far below the $30K they'd pay as renters. So time matters here—the time spent paying more on housing versus the time spent paying less.

The Bottom Line

To summarize, buying conveys lifetime tax breaks. It also entails higher short-term but lower long-term housing costs. Only consumption smoothing can tell us how these time-varying advantages and disadvantages balance out in terms of what living standard they permit.

Bonus Time

OK, let's say we actually talk Andrew and Jessica into buying. What happens if their house loses value? Do they sue us?

No, they thank us even more.

If the house loses value at a 2 percent real (inflation-adjusted) annual rate, Andrew and Jessica will enjoy a living standard *increase* of 2.4 percent. The reason is that Andrew and Jessica aren't moving. They are living in their sunny castle until they die. And every year their house value declines, so do, presumably, their property taxes and homeowners insurance premiums. This liberates income for consumption! Their home equity and ultimate bequest to Andi Jess will be smaller, as will be their net worth. But their lifetime consumption—the money they can spend on things other than shelter—will rise. Note the subtle shift: when you focus on maximizing lifetime consumption rather than maximizing assets because you think that will maximize consumption, you get some counterintuitive answers.

On the other hand, if the value of their home rises at a 2 percent real annual rate, a feat that would amount to a continuation of the California bubble, their living standard will suffer. It will decline by about 4.5 percent—to about what they'd experience by renting—because of the need to pay ever-higher property taxes and homeowners insurance premiums. Their net worth, on the other hand, will exceed $2 million at retirement. This is good for Andi Jess but not for Andrew and Jessica.

So here's how it plays out. If San Diego home values rise at the rate of inflation or decline, Andrew and Jessica will enjoy a higher lifetime standard of living than if they rented. If the real estate market continues to appreciate faster than inflation, their lifetime standard of living could be reduced to that of a renter, but their estate will be larger because their home equity will be greater.

Postscript

Would you have thought that Andrew and Jessica would save taxes even in old age by becoming homeowners? Or that they'd have a higher living standard if their house depreciated rather than appreciated given their decision never to sell? We didn't. We were as surprised as we imagine you are when we saw these counterintuitive results. But that's what you learn when you start focusing on what you get to spend rather than targeting your assets, income, or some other variable that relates only indirectly to your living standard.

Takeaways

- Whether you rent or buy your home changes the level and timing of your housing expenses.
- Whether you rent or buy changes the level and timing of your tax payments.
- Determining which option offers the highest living standard requires careful analysis.

14. Pay It Down, Way Down

WHAT DO AKRON, Pittsburgh, and Wichita have in common?

They all share a dirty little financial secret. Fewer than half of their resident homeowners have ever benefited from mortgage tax deductions. Their only solace is that millions of other Americans—in places like Tulsa, El Paso, Peoria, Bangor, and Cedar Rapids—live under the same cloud of tax-break deprivation. Indeed, if you visit the National Association of Realtors Web site (www.realtor.org/Research.nsf/Pages/MetroPrice), you'll find that median home buyers in one-third of all U.S. cities don't enjoy any tax savings whatsoever from holding a mortgage because their mortgage interest payments are too low to justify itemizing deductions on their tax returns. This happens because low housing prices beget small mortgages and small mortgage interest payments.*

For these home buyers and roughly half of their new neighbors, the amount of itemizable deductions, including mortgage interest

---

* These figures are updated quarterly and now distinguish between single-family homes and condos.

deductions, falls below the level of their standard deduction. This means that it's better for them to take the standard deduction; so paying mortgage interest, property taxes, and state income taxes makes no difference to their federal income taxes.

The fact that so many people get no tax benefit from paying mortgage interest is hard to square with the widespread support for the mortgage interest deduction. If Social Security is the "third rail of politics," the deduction for home mortgage interest is its electric chair. Few deductions are more treasured—especially by those who don't get them. Few are more heartily defended. The strongest defenders, of course, are real estate agents and lenders. They've convinced themselves that the deduction makes home ownership nearly free, and they routinely inform their clients of this myth.

Common knowledge to the contrary, the real beneficiaries of the mortgage interest deduction are, in fact, the rich, particularly the McMansion improvers who load an equity line of credit on top of a hefty home mortgage to install the Viking range, Sub-Zero refrigerator, and a quantity of marble countertops that would cause Michelangelo to weep.

To see the mortgage-tax-break winners and losers in higher relief, please follow Armand, Bart, and Chuck as they graduate from college and head out to change their worlds by making money and acquiring all manner of possessions, including their own homes.

Armand is the least ambitious and financially successful of the three. (He's also the happiest.) At age thirty-five he's married, making $60,000 a year, and has modest savings. He isn't quite sure how he managed to make this much money, but he thinks it has a good deal to do with luck.

Armand wants to buy a house. More important, his wife, Alice, wants to buy a house. She has been clipping pictures from magazines for three years. She thinks the right combination of country-French-soft-modern-Tuscan-Tudor is being built nearby.

So they buy a $180,000 house with 20 percent down and move into their San Antonio palace. Readers in the pricey parts of the country would be surprised to find a house with indoor plumbing for that little money, but those who dare to admit there is habitable land between New York and Los Angeles know that $180,000 gets you pretty far up the housing ladder in the hinterlands. Although $180,000 is less than the recent national median price of $212,000, it's higher than the median house price in eighty American cities. It's well over the $148,300 median price in laid-back San Antonio.

After moving in, Armand accidentally surfs over to Scott's online home ownership benefits calculator (www.dallasnews.com/shared content/dws/bus/scottScott/calculators/mortgage_cal.html). There, to his disgust, he learns that his and Alice's total tax saving in the first year from deducting mortgage interest is a piddling $224. Armand also learns that this tax benefit will disappear after the fifth year, with a cumulative five-year benefit of only $616.

Again, the mortgage interest tax break is small because you get it only if you itemize your deductions. Most low-income households don't itemize or, as in Armand and Alice's case, don't itemize for very long. Bear in mind that mortgage interest payments generally decline over time and aren't adjusted upward for inflation. In contrast, the size of the standard deduction is indexed for inflation and rises (in nominal dollars) each year. As the standard deduction rises, more and more households find that itemizing their deductions is a loser compared with taking the standard deduction.

How much does the ability to deduct mortgage interest raise Armand and Alice's living standard? Not much. Armand and Alice enjoy an annual living standard per adult of $21,364. If mortgage interest weren't deductible, their annual living standard would be $21,203. The $161 difference between these living standards is only 0.75 percent—small potatoes.

Armand's friend Bart, who went on to get an MBA at Texas A&M University, is no slacker even though he lives in Austin. Compared with Armand, Bart lives higher on the hog, pulling down $150,000 a year selling real estate. This puts his household among the top 7 percent highest-earning households in America. Most households get there by having more than one earner. If you're

136 ■ SPEND 'TIL THE END

among the nation's superrich, $150,000 probably seems like peanuts. But it's serious money in most parts of the country.

Bart's wife, Beverly, has had her eye on a $400,000 house in the community of Steiner Ranch, not far from Lake Travis. Bart is a little fearful of the move, given that virtually all of their prospective neighbors are pregnant or getting pregnant. Then again, if they can have margaritas at the nearby Oasis restaurant and applaud the sunset, as everyone does, he thinks it might be worth it.

For Bart and Beverly, the interest deduction means a $4,098 tax saving in the first year. And this tax saving keeps coming for twenty-five years. The total tax savings over the years come to $64,092, or 16 percent of the purchase price of their house. Bart and Beverly enjoy a $46,663 living standard per adult, which is 3.8 percent more than they'd experience if mortgage interest were not deductible.

Chuck, the third of our graduates, has hit the big time. His wife, Corinna-Corinna (her dad was an early Bob Dylan fan), earns $400,000 a year, a sum that puts the couple in the top 1 percent of all households. They are, in other words, fat cats. They live in a $1 million house in Houston and pay property taxes of $20,000 a year for the privilege. Chuck and Corinna-Corinna enjoy a first-year tax saving of $18,821 on their house because they have a lot of deductions and are in the 33 percent tax bracket. They'll also enjoy a full thirty years of tax savings, with a cumulative total of $451,823, or 45.1 percent of the purchase price of their house!*

Each year Chuck and Corinna-Corinna enjoy a living standard of $96,503. This would drop to $91,449 were interest not deductible—a 5.5 percent difference, all thanks to a generous Congress that looks out for the poor and needy.

Our short Armand, Bart, and Chuck trilogy can be summarized as follows: however you cut it—lifetime tax savings or increase in long-term living standard—most Americans get little or no benefit

---

* See http://ideas.repec.org/p/nbr/nberwo/9284.html for an analysis of who benefits from the home mortgage interest deduction.

from being able to itemize and deduct home mortgage interest. Those who really gain from deducting mortgage interest are members of the upper class.*

Pay It Down, Way Down!

You might think, from what you've just read in this chapter and the previous one, that Bart, to some extent, and Chuck, to a large extent, would be nuts to pay down their mortgages were they in a position to do so. Not so. They'd be nuts *not* to.

Let's take Chuck. When he and Corinna-Corinna are fifty-five, they still have a $300K mortgage outstanding, on which they are paying 7 percent annual interest. They borrowed initially to buy the house to avoid being severely liquidity constrained. And they'd still be in no position to pay off the $300K immediately were it not for a fortuitous event.

Corinna-Corinna's least favorite aunt, Ethel, just happened to be run over by a tractor-trailer while riding on one of those new motorized scooters. It was a horrible mess. After several minutes of mourning, Corinna-Corinna realized that as Ethel's sole surviving relative, she'd be in a position to get a big recovery from the tractor-trailer's insurance company. The insurer was happy to pay up right away to avoid adverse publicity, and Corinna-Corinna walked off with a check for $500,000.

Chuck called Bart for advice. Bart said, "Pay it down, way down."

"Pay what down?" asked Chuck.

---

* The Tax Foundation offers figures on the distribution of home mortgage interest deduction claims at www.taxfoundation.org/news/show/1341.html. This book is about consumption smoothing, not tax policy, so we won't go into an extended rant here. But this regressive and wacky policy, like so many others, is one of the reasons both of us advocate the "fair tax"—the notion that we should junk the entire current tax system, including the employment tax, and replace it with a national sales tax plus a rebate, which makes the tax progressive. To learn more about this, visit Larry's Web site (http://people.bu.edu/Kotlikoff/). It contains several papers on the proposal and its benefits. For a quick summary of the reasons we should favor it, read Scott's column on the subject at http://assetbuilder.com/?p=66.

"Your mortgage, knucklehead," said Bart.

"But what about all the tax breaks on the mortgage?"

"Listen," said Bart. "You are paying a higher interest rate on the mortgage than you can earn by investing in bonds that have the same risk properties as the mortgage. The rate you're paying on your mortgage is 7 percent, right? And you can earn only about 4.5 percent by investing in bonds. So by paying off the mortgage, you save yourself 2.5 percent. And, yes, you will no longer have any interest payments to deduct, but by paying off the mortgage, you won't have as much taxable asset income either. So tax-wise it's close to a wash. There is one advantage of having a large mortgage interest deduction. It can keep one from having to pay the alternative minimum tax. But I doubt this applies to you given your income."

"Hmm, sounds right," said Chuck. "Will it save me much money?"

"Gee," replied Bart, "give me a couple seconds and I'll tell you. OK, I've got the answer. Doing this will raise your living standard by 0.7 percent every year for the rest of your life."

"Not huge, but certainly worth doing," said Chuck, "since all it takes is writing a single check. But I do have one question. I was thinking about investing the money from Aunt Ethel in a new stock I heard about over at the club. Wouldn't that be a smarter use of the money than paying off the mortgage?"

"Good question," answered Bart. "But doing that would be like borrowing to invest in that particular stock. To see this, let's suppose you follow my advice and pay off the mortgage. Once you've done so, you'll have only $200K left of the original $500K in dead-Ethel money to invest. So put yourself in that situation. You no longer have a mortgage, and you have only $200K, not $500K, to invest. Would it make sense from that spot to borrow another $300K and put it in the overall equity market, let alone in some golfing buddy's pet stock? No, that's far too risky. I know Corinna-Corinna. I also know that she'll send a tractor-trailer your way if you blow poor Aunt Ethel's money."

Chuck took Bart's advice. He also spent some of Ethel's money on a night-school course in economics, his second passion after golf. There he learned the source of the real tax break from home ownership.

The Real Tax Break from Home Ownership

The real tax advantage of home ownership actually has nothing to do with whether or not you take out a mortgage to buy your home. The real advantage comes from receiving income on your home in the form of housing services (*implicit rent* is the economics term) and not having to pay taxes on this income.

To see what's going on, take two private detectives, Frank Hardy and Nancy Drew. Frank and Nancy live next door to each other in identical homes worth $1 million, which they own outright. If they wanted to, Frank and Nancy could rent their homes for $100K a year—the going rental rate on the market.

Now suppose Frank and Nancy actually do rent out their homes—*to each other*. Frank moves into Nancy's house, and Nancy moves into Frank's. After the move, both are in precisely the same housing situation as before. Since their houses are identical, both are enjoying exactly the same housing services. But now Frank will have to report $100K in rental income (the rent he receives from Nancy) to the IRS as part of his taxable income. Nancy will have to do the same. This will mean paying higher taxes.

To make the system neutral with respect to renting and owning, the IRS would have to tell homeowners each year: "Gee, we see you are living in a home you own. How nice for you. But what you are really doing is renting the home to yourself, and this implicit rent that you are receiving from yourself amounts to X dollars, and you need to add X dollars more to your taxable income in filling out this year's tax return."

The IRS doesn't do this, but don't think it hasn't considered it.

Takeaways

- The tax advantage from home ownership is not related to borrowing or paying interest on a mortgage.
- The tax advantage is from not having to pay taxes on the rental income/services you earn/receive on your asset—your house.
- Hence, even those with no mortgage or no itemizable mortgage enjoy a tax break from home ownership.
- Paying off your mortgage is one of the smartest and safest investments you can make.

15. Does It Pay to Play?

ANOTHER NO-SWEAT WAY to raise your living standard is to decide when to pay your taxes and how much taxes to pay.

"Decide when to pay my taxes and how much to pay? What are you smoking? The IRS will be all over me if I don't pay all my taxes on time."

Actually, the government provides us with perfectly legal ways of choosing when to pay taxes and, as a consequence, how much to pay. They're called retirement accounts. In choosing which account to use, how much to contribute, when to contribute, and when to withdraw, you change not only the timing of your tax payments but also their levels.

The most familiar retirement accounts are tax-deferred 401(k) and IRA plans.* By putting money into these plans, you lower your taxes now but raise them later. The reason, as you probably know, is that contributions to these plans are tax deductible, whereas withdrawals from these plans are taxable. If you're currently in a high tax bracket but will subsequently be in a low bracket, contributing

---

* The 403(b) is a close cousin of the 401(k) except that it applies to employees in non-profits. Other relatives of the 401(k) include SEPs, Keogh accounts, and profit-sharing plans.

more will lower your lifetime taxes and let you enjoy a higher living standard, potentially in the present as well as in the future.

We say "potentially" because of the point made in chapter 5: Borrowing constraints may require you to reduce your current spending at the benefit of higher future spending. Of course, there are ways to get around borrowing limits. If you have equity in your house, you may be able to refinance your mortgage or use an equity line of credit to come up with the cash flow to contribute more to a retirement account and thereby raise your future living standard without reducing your current living standard. We're not necessarily recommending this. You may want to preserve your borrowing capacity for emergencies. Also, borrowing at interest rates that aren't fixed is a risky business. Plus, there are no guarantees on what you'll earn in your retirement account. Also, bear in mind that Uncle Sam is virtually guaranteed to raise tax rates in the future (more on this later). So your future tax rates may be a lot higher than you think.

Contributing to 401(k)s and IRAs lets you postpone your taxes. Contributing to Roth 401(k)s and Roth IRAs does not. But a Roth retirement account has a different and truly beautiful feature: You pay no taxes *ever* on your withdrawals. This includes all the interest, dividends, and capital gains you earn on your Roth investments—no taxation ever, no matter how high Uncle Sam sets future tax rates. (Unless, of course, Uncle Sam changes his mind.) This definitely beats investing in regular assets (if you don't need the money in the short term). It may beat investing in a regular IRA and even a regular 401(k), depending on the size of your employer's matching contribution. (At this point, employers aren't allowed to contribute to their employees' Roth 401(k) plans.)

An Economics Paradox

Retirement accounts are supposed to be the greatest tax-saving device since taxes were invented—a surefire no-sweat way to raise your future living standard. Yet up to a third of eligible employees don't participate, and of those who do, many contribute too little to receive their employer's match.

Employers have cajoled their workers with free beach toys, lottery tickets, T-shirts, parties, you name it, and still some of them won't play ball. More and more employers are now automatically enrolling new hires and forcing them to opt out. This is raising over-all 401(k) participation, but many new hires are still saying no thanks.

Given the tax breaks, why do workers opt out of their 401(k)s? Are they just plain loco?

Maybe not. They may just be borrowing constrained. Contributing to a 401((k) would save them taxes and raise their future living standard, but it would also require cutting their current living standard, which they aren't prepared to do. If this sounds like your situation, you're in good company.

Roughly two-thirds of American workers are liquidity constrained—in other words, they have trouble making ends meet, let alone contributing to a 401(k).

The Bang for the Buck

If you're a typical worker, what's the precise pleasure-pain trade-off from contributing to a 401(k)? That is, what's the short-term reduction and long-term increase in your living standard if you contribute on a regular basis?* The tables that follow give the answer for single and married households who are initially ages thirty, forty-five, and sixty.

We'll spare you most of the details, but each of these households has two kids, a mortgage and other housing expenses, and college

---

* Feel free to substitute 403(b), regular IRA, Keogh account, SEP, or other tax-deferred accounts whenever we reference "401(k)." And feel free to substitute Roth 403(b) or Roth IRA whenever we reference "Roth 401(k)."

expenses. The thirty-year-olds have zero initial regular or retirement account assets. The forty-five- and sixty-year-olds have regular assets and 401(k) account balances that correspond to what the thirty-year-old households would accumulate by those ages were they to contribute to a regular 401(k) starting at age thirty.

Because they are borrowing constrained, the thirty- and forty-five-year-old households face a reduction in consumption until they reach age fifty-one but are rewarded with an increase after age fifty-one. The sixty-year-old households aren't borrowing constrained, so their living standard is smooth.

The earnings listed in the far left column of the tables are annual and keep up with inflation through age sixty-five, when each household retires. In the case of married households, each spouse makes the same money. Everyone lives in Pennsylvania and pays federal and Pennsylvania state income taxes, the FICA tax, and Medicare Part B premiums (starting at sixty-five). Everyone receives all available Social Security retirement benefits.

May I Have the Question, Please?

Table 1 answers the following questions: Given where the listed households are at with respect to initial regular assets and regular 401(k) holdings, what happens to their living standards if they either (1) contribute 6 percent of their earnings each year through age sixty-five to a regular 401(k) or (2) make equivalent contributions to a Roth 401(k)?

In columns 3 and 4 ("No Match"), we're also assuming that the entire contribution is made by the worker, with no employer match. Since employers aren't permitted to make Roth 401(k) contributions, assuming that only employees contribute lets us compare the two 401(k)s on an apples-to-apples basis. In columns 5 and 6 ("Match"), we're assuming that there is an employer match.

TABLE 1. LIVING STANDARD GAINS FROM 401(K) CONTRIBUTIONS

Single, Age 30

Earnings	401(k)	Percentage Living Standard Change			
		No Match		Match	
		Before 51	After 51	Before 51	After 51
$15,000	Regular	0.4	4.5	4.2	6.4
	Roth	0.4	4.5	NA	NA
$25,000	Regular	−5.1	15.0	−1.0	17.1
	Roth	−5.1	15.1	NA	NA
$50,000	Regular	−9.8	20.8	−4.8	23.2
	Roth	−9.8	19.8	NA	NA
$100,000	Regular	−9.9	23.2	−4.9	25.6
	Roth	−9.9	21.3	NA	NA
$250,000	Regular	−3.1	20.8	1.7	23.5
	Roth	−3.1	16.3	NA	NA

Table assumes 6% contribution to 401(k) with Roth contributions set to achieve same pre-age-51 living standard change.

Married, Age 30

Earnings	401(k)	Percentage Living Standard Change			
		No Match		Match	
		Before 51	After 51	Before 51	After 51
$30,000	Regular	−0.2	10.7	4.6	13.1
	Roth	−0.2	9.3	NA	NA
$50,000	Regular	−8.3	17.2	−3.2	19.8
	Roth	−8.3	16.2	NA	NA
$100,000	Regular	−10.2	20.8	−4.8	23.3
	Roth	−10.2	19.4	NA	NA
$200,000	Regular	−5.9	20.1	−0.6	22.3
	Roth	−5.9	16.3	NA	NA
$500,000	Regular	9.9	9.9	13.6	13.6
	Roth	8.4	8.4	NA	NA

Table assumes 6% contribution to 401(k) with Roth contributions set to achieve same pre-age-51 living standard change.

Single, Age 45

| Earnings | 401(k) | Percentage Living Standard Change | | | |
| | | No Match | | Match | |
		Before 51	After 51	Before 51	After 51
$15,000	Regular	−9.2	5.8	−3.7	7.4
	Roth	−9.2	4.5	NA	NA
$25,000	Regular	−11.5	4.8	−5.0	6.5
	Roth	−11.5	4.4	NA	NA
$50,000	Regular	−17.4	5.1	−8.6	7.0
	Roth	−17.4	5.5	NA	NA
$100,000	Regular	−18.3	6.5	−9.0	8.6
	Roth	−18.3	5.6	NA	NA
$250,000	Regular	−15.4	9.1	−7.7	11.5
	Roth	−15.4	7.3	NA	NA

Table assumes 6% contribution to 401(k) with Roth contributions set to achieve same pre-age-51 living standard change.

Married, Age 45

| Earnings | 401(k) | Percentage Living Standard Change | | | |
| | | No Match | | Match | |
		Before 51	After 51	Before 51	After 51
$30,000	Regular	−10.0	5.7	−4.0	7.3
	Roth	−10.0	4.1	NA	NA
$50,000	Regular	−15.2	4.9	−7.6	6.7
	Roth	−15.2	4.7	NA	NA
$100,000	Regular	−17.2	6.1	−8.6	8.4
	Roth	−17.2	5.7	NA	NA
$200,000	Regular	−18.0	7.3	−9.0	9.4
	Roth	−18.0	5.7	NA	NA
$500,000	Regular	−13.7	8.2	−6.9	11.0
	Roth	−13.7	6.1	NA	NA

Table assumes 6% contribution to 401(k) with Roth contributions set to achieve same pre-age-51 living standard change.

Single, Age 60

Earnings	401(k)	Percentage Living Standard Change	
		No Match	Match
$15,000	Regular	0.4	0.9
	Roth	0.4	NA
$25,000	Regular	0.2	0.8
	Roth	0.2	NA
$50,000	Regular	0.4	0.9
	Roth	0.4	NA
$100,000	Regular	0.7	1.2
	Roth	0.7	NA
$250,000	Regular	0.9	1.6
	Roth	0.9	NA

Table assumes 6% contribution to 401(k) with Roth contributions set to achieve same pre-age-51 living standard change

Married, Age 60

Earnings	401(k)	Percentage Living Standard Change	
		No Match	Match
$30,000	Regular	0.4	1.1
	Roth	0.4	NA
$50,000	Regular	0.3	0.9
	Roth	0.3	NA
$100,000	Regular	0.6	1.2
	Roth	0.6	NA
$200,000	Regular	0.9	1.6
	Roth	0.9	NA
$500,000	Regular	0.9	1.8
	Roth	0.9	NA

Table assumes 6% contribution to 401(k) with Roth contributions set to achieve same pre-age-51 living standard change.

And the Loser/Winner Is . . .

There is nothing duller than tables full of numbers. So we'll make this quick. First, please check out the columns labeled "No Match." These are our results assuming just the aforementioned 6 percent employee contribution. We also made the assumption that the employer match earned the same return, even though it may be in employer stock.

Note that in the age-thirty and age-forty-five tables, all the living standard changes except for one are negative prior to age fifty-one— when the kids graduate from college and tuition payments stop. After age fifty-one, all the living-standard changes are positive. This is the borrowing constraint at work. The households need to cut their living standard in the short run to make their contributions.

Here's the interesting thing: *the short-run pain from contributing to a 401(k) or Roth 401(k) can be huge!*

Here's the other interesting thing: *the long-run gain from contributing to a 401(k) or Roth 401(k) can be huge!*

Take the married thirty-year-olds earning $100K. Contributing 6 percent for the rest of their working days to a regular 401(k) means a 10.2 percent cut in their living standard before age fifty-one but a 20.8 percent increase thereafter. Making the equivalent contribution to a Roth 401(k) entails the same pre-age-fifty-one sacrifice and a quite similar gain—namely 19.4 percent.

For sixty-year-olds, the borrowing constraints no longer bind, so contributing to either type of 401(k) produces an immediate and ongoing living-standard boost. For single sixty-year-olds earning $50,000 a year, there's a 0.4 percent permanent living-standard gain associated with contributing 6 percent of earnings through age sixty-five. This is all upside and ready for the taking.

What Do We Mean by an Equivalent Roth Contribution?

As you know, contributing to a regular 401(k) comes with an immediate tax break. Contributing to a Roth 401(k) comes with a future tax break. To make the two contributions comparable, we simply tried different Roth contribution rates until we found one that produced the same living-standard reduction before age fifty-one as arises from contributing 6 percent to the regular 401(k).

Since the short-run living-standard changes are set up to be the same for both types of contributions, the way to compare them is by examining their long-run living-standard impacts.* Here's the interesting conclusion that emerges for all three sets of households: generally speaking, contributing to the regular 401(k) beats contributing to the Roth 401(k), but not by much. There are some exceptions. Take, for example, thirty-year-old singles earning $250K. Whichever way they contribute, they suffer a 2 percent short-term living-standard cut. But after age fifty-one, their living standard is 21.3 percent higher if they go traditional 401(k), but only 15.8 percent if they go Roth.

Why the Differences?

What explains the huge differences in living-standard changes by age, marital status, and earnings? Many factors, including:

- your earnings and regular assets
- the low-income savers credit and whether you pay enough taxes to benefit from it
- the difference between pre- and post-retirement tax brackets
- age, because it matters to how much will be contributed by sixty-five
- Social Security taxation, which may be triggered by regular 401(k) withdrawals
- birth year, since Social Security benefit taxation isn't inflation indexed
- the degree to which you are borrowing constrained

---

* Note that for the sixty-year-olds who aren't borrowing constrained, there is no difference between the traditional 401(k) and the Roth 401(k) living-standard gains. After determining the gain from the traditional 401(k), we found that the Roth contribution delivers the same gain.

These and other relevant factors interact, making it devilishly hard to ascribe particular results to particular factors.

Is Contributing Worth It?

If, like our stylized sixty-year-olds, you're not borrowing constrained and the tax rules don't change in the future, contributing to either a regular 401(k) or a Roth 401(k) is a free lunch. Your consumption will rise now and in the future, provided that you smooth your living standard.

For those who are liquidity constrained, the decision to contribute can be a tough call. Take, for instance, the forty-five-year-old couples earning $50K. Contributing 6 percent to a regular 401(k) means taking a 15.2 percent living-standard hit for the next six years in order to reap a 4.9 percent living-standard boost for the remaining forty-nine years. The living standard hit is large because most of the young couple's income is committed to "off-the-top" expenses. Here are the actual figures: Six percent of $50,000 is $3,000. For this to constitute a 15.4 percent living-standard cut, the household's initial consumption expenditure has to be $17,045. This is far below $50,000. Where'd all the money go? The answer is taxes, housing expenses, and tuition payments. At age forty-five, the couple pay close to $6,000 in taxes, have $12,500 in tuition payments (soon to double when the second child goes to college), have almost $20,000 in housing expenses, and pay close to $1,000 in life insurance premiums. But they also have some assets saved to help defray the college expenses.

Long-Run Gain versus Short-Run Pain

One way to trade off the long-run gain against the short-run pain is to consider their *net* present values. Recall, *present value* refers to the value today of money that you either receive or pay in the future. The next two tables show the net change in the present value of consumption from contributing to either regular or Roth 401(k)s. The term *net* refers to the fact that we're subtracting the short-term consumption reductions from the long-term consumption increases.

TABLE 2. NET CHANGE IN PRESENT VALUE OF CONSUMPTION

Single Households

Earnings	Regular			Roth			Match		
	Age 30	Age 45	Age 60	Age 30	Age 45	Age 60	Age 30	Age 45	Age 60
$15,000	$5,048	$4,503	$1,051	$5,092	$2,624	$1,051	$13,844	$10,280	$2,347
$25,000	$7,628	$5,415	$880	$7,821	$4,378	$880	$20,929	$13,790	$3,007
$50,000	$11,790	$9,810	$2,689	$9,302	$11,710	$2,689	$37,275	$25,569	$5,891
$100,000	$27,289	$24,500	$6,453	$19,566	$17,338	$6,453	$72,372	$52,472	$11,660
$250,000	$138,430	$71,339	$14,960	$98,596	$46,132	$14,960	$233,051	$130,959	$27,892

Married Households

Earnings	Regular			Roth			Match		
	Age 30	Age 45	Age 60	Age 30	Age 45	Age 60	Age 30	Age 45	Age 60
$30,000	$18,930	$9,134	$2,273	$16,306	$4,887	$2,273	$35,852	$20,133	$5,476
$50,000	$12,840	$8,887	$2,078	$10,041	$8,240	$2,078	$39,969	$26,383	$6,918
$100,000	$27,815	$22,395	$7,260	$21,081	$19,041	$7,260	$79,469	$55,486	$15,498
$200,000	$98,541	$59,883	$17,796	$65,936	$36,290	$17,771	$186,256	$114,790	$30,556
$500,000	$437,693	$159,971	$30,434	$373,932	$105,114	$30,434	$601,110	$281,457	$61,943

Notice first that none of the numbers is negative; no one is worse off on a net present value basis from contributing at any of the indicated ages to either a regular 401(k) or a Roth 401(k). Next compare the entries with the size of the associated annual earnings. They're big, particularly for the rich. For thirty-year-old couples making $500K, contributing to a regular 401(k) is worth almost a year's salary! For single thirty-year-olds making $15K, the lifetime gain from contributing to a regular 401(k) is a third of a year's earnings.

The net gains from contributing are much larger when the employer puts in half the money. For example, thirty-year-old couples with $100K in annual earnings net $27,815 from contributing to a regular 401(k) without the match, but $79,469 with it.

When the Tax Man Cometh

In general, if tax rates remain unchanged, contributing to the 401(k) beats contributing to the Roth. But this assumes future tax rates won't change. What if tax hikes are coming? We believe that is just a matter of time. Do the same analysis and assume a 30 percent increase in federal and state income taxes when the households hit age sixty-five, and the results change.

For withdrawals from regular 401(k)s, this is as nasty a bit of timing as we can consider. Here you spend years contributing to your regular 401(k) expecting to pay taxes at lower rates when you start withdrawing. But then just as you start withdrawing, the government raises tax rates. Since the money in your Roth comes out tax free, the tax hikes don't affect its spending power. So which is better when the tax man cometh?

The answer is that except for those with low incomes, the Roth is a better deal. Take a forty-five-year-old married couple with $70,000 in annual earnings and assume the aforementioned 30 percent tax hike occurs when the couple hits age sixty-five. The couple's present-value gain from contributing to the Roth 401(k) is $15,767—

almost 50 percent higher than their $10,799 gain from contributing to the regular 401(k). As a second example, consider a single forty-five-year-old earning $35,000 a year. Her present-value net gain from contributing to the Roth is $8,803—far above her $3,277 net gain from contributing to a regular 401(k). But if the couple and single person earn $30,000 and $15,000, respectively, the story is different. Now the present-value gain from the regular 401(k) exceeds that of Roth by about 70 percent.

Our bottom line: Unless your income is low, contributing to a Roth 401(k) or a Roth IRA generally beats contributing to a regular 401(k) or a regular IRA if major tax hikes are in the offing.

Taking the Employer Match

A 6 percent employee contribution to a 401(k) account is pretty high. In many companies a contribution that large would be split 50-50 with the employer.* To examine the living standard impacts of contributing to a regular 401(k) in the presence of a 50-50 match based on a 6 percent total employee plus employer contribution, we consider the same households in the tables and continue to calculate their no-contribution living standard as we did. But now, in calculating how they'd fare contributing, we have them contribute 3 percent and their employers contribute 3 percent.

In Table 1, the columns labeled "Match" show there's a much better pain-gain trade-off for younger liquidity-constrained households in the presence of the employers' match. Indeed, our take on these numbers is that you have to be nuts not to take the employer match. Scrimp, starve, whatever it takes, but take the match. It's just too good a deal to pass up.

---

* Mind you, the money employers contribute to their workers' accounts is really being earned by the workers. Employers aren't contributing out of the goodness of their hearts. They are contributing to retain the services of their workers. So the employer's match is really the worker's money except that it's being paid to the worker in a curious manner, coming as it does with a catch—the worker can't get it unless she contributes as well.

Which Way Should I Go? Which Way Should I Go?

Elmer Fudd is forever asking this question when chasing his neme-sis, Bugs Bunny.* Every time Elmer lines up Bugs for a clean shot, bingo, Bugs comes up with some distraction and escapes, driving Elmer nuts.

Figuring out whether to contribute to a regular 401(k) or IRA or their Roth counterparts can make us equally crazy. Ignoring future tax hikes, the regular route seems best, particularly for high earners. But if tax hikes are coming, the Roth makes more sense.

OK, which way should I go? Which way should I go?

Here's the way: *we advise contributing to regular and Roth 401(k)s with a 40-60 split, but only after you've maximized your employer's match.*

We're pretty sure tax hikes are coming, and this strategy will at least hedge your bets. If you are close to retirement, have never been in a Roth, and are worried that there is no time to do so, make sure to read the next chapter.

Takeaways

- For young and middle-aged workers, contributing to a retire-ment account generally provides a long-term living-standard gain at the price of a short-term living-standard loss.
- For older workers, contributing to a retirement account gen-erally permits a higher current and future living standard.
- The present-value net gains from contributing can be sub-stantial.
- When employers make significant matching contributions, contributing is a no-brainer.
- Assuming no future tax hikes, contributing to a regular rather than a Roth retirement account is the better option—but not by much—for most households.

---

* Actually, it was "Which way did he go?"

- Assuming significant future tax hikes, contributing to the Roth generally beats contributing to regular retirement accounts.
- Our advice is to allocate your contributions 60 percent to Roth and 40 percent to regular retirement accounts.

16. Converting

"SCOTT, YOU'RE NOT going to believe this," said Larry.

"Believe what?" said Scott.

"I'm going to convert!"

"You found Jesus?"

"Not quite. I'm going to convert all of my 403(b) money to a Roth IRA to save taxes."

"But this will cost you taxes," Scott replied. "You're in a high tax bracket now. If you convert all of your qualified plan money to a Roth, you'll have to pay taxes on all of your plan balances immediately. Conventional wisdom says this is nuts, that it's better to pay your taxes as late as possible so that you can earn interest on Uncle Sam's money while he waits to collect. Plus, when you do pay your taxes, you'll be in a lower tax bracket. Conventional wisdom makes sense, at least in this case. Maybe you need to think this over? Consult with someone. See an economist."

"I *am* an economist."

"Apparently not much of one if you're going to convert whole hog to a Roth without thinking through the tax and living-standard implications."

"But I have," Larry protested "or at least ESPlanner has. I ran it through the program, and it shows a 5 percent permanent gain in my

156

family's living standard. It makes sense. Remember, I make a pretty good income, so like millions of other upper-income Americans, I have to pay the alternative minimum tax. Indeed, by the end of this decade, unless the law is changed, one in five taxpayers will be hit by the AMT because the threshold beyond which it kicks in isn't indexed for inflation."

"I know the problem."

"Now, here's the thing: The top marginal rate under the AMT is 28 percent. The top marginal rate under the regular income tax schedule is 35 percent. So by converting all of my 403(b) money at a time that I'm still working and being hit by the AMT, I can ensure that the 401(k) money will all be taxed at a 28 percent rate. If I don't do this, I'll end up in my retirement years withdrawing too little income to get hit by the AMT but enough to be in the top regular federal income tax bracket. So by converting, I get my 403(b) money out at a 28 percent rate rather than at a 35 percent rate. This does, of course, mean foregoing the deferral of taxes. But deferring taxes isn't a big enough factor to offset saving 7 percent (35 percent minus 28 percent) of my 403(b) balances."

"Gee," Scott admitted, "this *does* make sense."

"It sure does. But wait, there's a second factor. By converting all my plan money to a Roth prior to collecting Social Security, I'll reduce my future taxable income and thus limit how much federal and state income taxes I have to pay on my Social Security benefits."

"Good point. The taxation of Social Security benefits is a nasty surprise. It's great to have a strategy that gets around it either completely or in large part."

"I also ran the program assuming 30 percent and 50 percent permanent hikes in federal taxes starting in ten years," Larry added. "Under those assumptions, the Roth conversion raises my household's living standard by 12 percent and 17.4 percent, respectively, compared to the alternative. Why is the gain so much higher? Take the assumption that tax rates rise by 50 percent. In this case, we're talking about paying a 28 percent tax rate now versus a 52.5 percent tax rate later. And, as you know, once you pay taxes on the money you place in the Roth, the money coming out is completely tax free, no matter how large the withdrawals and when you make them."

"Listen, Larry, I hate to burst your bubble, but you're not eligible to convert your 401(k). You can't convert your 403(b) or any other tax-deferred assets to a Roth if your adjusted gross income exceeds $100K. And yours does by a mile."

"True, but I am eligible. Just not right now."

"Meaning?"

"Starting in 2010, anyone can convert as much of their 401(k), regular IRA, SEP, Keogh, and similar tax-deferred retirement account money as they want into a Roth IRA. Congress passed this provision in 2006, when it cut taxes by $70 billion. The idea was to make sure that its ten-year tax revenue projections wouldn't look so bad. The Roth conversions are clearly a long-term tax revenue loser, but they'll raise taxes over Congress's short-term horizon, which is all it cares about."

Scott surrendered. "OK, I'm persuaded. But is it really necessary to convert? What if you just withdraw your 401(k) money before you withdraw the money in your Roth?"

"Well, this is pretty similar to converting everything at once," Larry explained, "and the living-standard gain is pretty close to that from immediate conversion."

"Is converting to a Roth a good idea for everyone?"

"No. Take a low-income household in their late fifties. They can anticipate paying no federal taxes in retirement regardless of whether federal tax rates are raised in the future. For such a household, converting means an almost 2 percent drop in their living standard. Middle-middle- and upper-middle-income households, with regular federal income tax rates below the AMT rate, also see a small drop in their living standards from converting, but only if tax rates stay fixed. Were they to rise by 50 percent in ten years, converting would mean a living-standard gain ranging from about 1.5 percent to 6 percent."

Takeaways

- Upper-middle- and high-income workers stand to reap huge living-standard gains by converting their regular retirement account assets to Roth accounts in 2010.
- For lower-income households, converting may lower their living standard.
- The gains or losses from conversion depend critically on future tax policy.

17. Cashing Out

UNCLE SAM IS a generous fellow. He gives us lots of leeway in determining the size and timing of our taxes and government benefits. A prime example is collecting Social Security retirement benefits. Between age sixty-two (the early retirement age) and your normal retirement age, waiting to collect can have a big payoff. Each year you wait raises by about 7 percent the real (inflation-adjusted) benefit that you can collect annually starting in the following year.* The increase in real benefits from delaying collection beyond normal retirement age is even greater: 8 percent per year up through age seventy. After that there is no bonus for waiting.

Receiving a safe, inflation-adjusted return of 7 percent or 8 percent is a very good deal, given that inflation-indexed bonds typically yield between 2 percent and 3 percent. However, waiting does mean collecting for fewer years. Suppose your maximum age of life is one hundred and you actually make it that far. Collecting benefits starting at age seventy rather than at age sixty-two means you will receive a roughly 60 percent higher benefit for eight fewer years. Waiting will raise the present value of your benefits by about 25

---

* The rate of increase depends on your birth year. Figures are on the Social Security Administration Web site at www.ssa.gov/retire2/delayret.htm.

percent.* (A present value is the value now—in the present—of money received or paid in the future. If the interest rate is 10 percent, the present value of $110 paid or received a year from now is $100, since one can invest $100 now and have $110 in a year.)

Despite this big incentive to wait, three-quarters of the elderly take Social Security before their normal retirement age. This probably reflects borrowing constraints—the fact that many elderly can't borrow against their future benefits and need the money as soon as possible to smooth (that is, raise) their living standards. In some cases, "smooth their living standards" is a euphemism for continuing to eat food.

But many retirees may simply have made the wrong decision in electing to collect early. They probably made the mistake of asking the people working at their local Social Security office for advice. These folks are quite adamant that collecting early is the only choice that makes sense. It's not, and you should think hard and long before taking Social Security early. We understand that you may not live to your maximum age of life and that your life expectancy is likely much shorter than the maximum number of years a person can live. But for this analysis, it's really the maximum age of life that matters, since you may indeed live that long!

Another consideration is the income taxation of your Social Security retirement benefits. Recall that the thresholds for taxable income beyond which Social Security retirement benefits are taxed aren't adjusted for inflation. This means that in retirement you may find that an ever larger share of your benefits becomes subject to taxation. This argues for taking benefits early. On the other hand, waiting to collect and spending your retirement and regular assets early may be the best way to limit taxation of your benefits.

Being benefit savvy applies to more than just Social Security.

---

* This comparison uses straight discounting rather than actuarial discounting. With actuarial discounting, the two options would have the same present value. But actuarial discounting is inappropriate in this context because households do not have access, at the margin, to inflation-indexed annuities either through commercial or intrafamilial risk-sharing arrangements.

When to take Medicare Parts B and D is an additional big decision. So is taking advantage of the savers credit—Uncle Sam's huge, new subsidy to low-income households that contribute to retirement accounts. This tax credit ranges from 10 percent to 50 percent of each $1 you contribute, up to the first $2,000 you put in your retirement plan. And if your earnings potential is particularly low, you face numerous moneymaking decisions in deciding whether to qualify for Medicaid, Transitional Aid to Families with Dependent Children, food stamps, Low Income Home Energy Assistance, Low Income Housing Assistance, Supplemental Security Income, and several other government freebies. The way to quality for these programs is to earn next to nothing. This may sound self-defeating, but, as we've discussed, for some people it's income maximizing—they literally earn more staying home than working.

Steven and Bertha—A Case Study

Meet Steven and Bertha Lindal, a sixty-two-year-old, retired, childless North Carolina couple. Steven and Bertha have $500K in regular assets and $250K each in 401(k) accounts. All of these assets are invested in very safe financial securities yielding 3 percent after inflation. Steven and Bertha's only other source of old-age support is Social Security. Fortunately, both were big earners when young. So both can look forward to generous Social Security retirement benefits.

Steven and Bertha have carefully designed their retirement around their four passions: eating, golfing, shopping, and philosophical inquiry. The two devote their mornings to eating and golfing, their afternoons to eating and shopping, their evenings to eating and drinking, and their nights to eating and debating.

Their current topic of debate concerns one of life's most profound and existential questions: when should we take our 401(k) and Social Security?

Steven, who majored in philosophy at Harvard, claims, through a mouthful of nachos, that they should follow conventional wisdom and take their 401(k) as late as possible to continue deferring taxes and take Social Security as early as possible so they don't die before collecting.

Bertha, who majored in economics at Boston University (she met Steven at a BU mixer), tells Steven that their 401(k) money is meant to be spent, not hoarded, and the only desideratum to consider is achieving the highest living standard while alive.

Bertha is right. What she and Steven really care about is eating, golfing, and so on while they are still alive. They don't care about the size of their assets, per se, or whether they will be happy when they're dead. To get Steven to focus on what really matters, Bertha shows him the following table indicating what the two can spend each year on consumption under five alternative choices of how to cash out.

The first row obeys conventional wisdom and entails taking Social Security immediately and waiting until age seventy to start 401(k) withdrawals. (The oldest age one can legally begin withdrawals from 401(k)s is seventy and a half. We use seventy here because ESPlanner takes only whole ages as the input for this variable.) To Steven's consternation, this turns out to be the *worst* of the five options. Their best option is given in the last row: waiting until sixty-seven to begin withdrawing from the 401(k) and until age seventy to begin taking Social Security.

TABLE 3. CASHING OUT—FINDING THE BEST STRATEGY

Age of Initial 401(k) Withdrawal	Age of Last 401(k) Withdrawal	Age of Initial Social Security Benefit Receipt	Annual Consumption	Increase in Consumption from Ignoring Conventional Wisdom
70	100	62	$70,007	This is the CW.
65	100	65	$72,744	3.9%
62	100	70	$78,438	12.0%
65	100	70	$78,746	12.5%
67	100	70	$78,851	12.6%

Compared with obeying conventional wisdom, the best option offers Steven and Bertha a 12.6 percent higher living standard! This is a whopping big increase.

Mind you, Steven and Bertha have two difficult things they'll need to do to effect this marvelous rise in their living standard. First, they have to wait until age seventy to drive over to their local Social Security office and apply for benefits. Second, when they hit age sixty-seven, they have to remember to call their 401(k) provider to initiate withdrawals. They'll likely want to sign up for Medicare at age sixty-five, however.

Get the message?

This is free money!

Indeed, it's equivalent to Steven and Bertha's finding $262,000 on the sidewalk were they forced to follow conventional wisdom. In other words, it takes $262,000 more in regular assets to get Steven and Bertha's sustainable consumption up to $78,851 if they take Social Security at sixty-two and their 401(k) at seventy.

How'd we pull this $262,000 rabbit out of the hat?

By having Steven and Bertha take Uncle Sam's best offer, not his first offer.

As we've related, Social Security provides a tremendous return from waiting to collect. Think of delaying Social Security collection as a very cheap way of buying longevity insurance—insurance against living longer than you'd expect and possibly like. Measured in today's dollars, Steven and Bertha each receive $19,180 per year from Social Security if they start collecting at age sixty-two. But if they wait till age seventy, their annual benefit, also measured in today's dollars, becomes $33,570—precisely 75 percent higher!

Under this strategy, Steven and Bertha use their regular assets and, starting at age sixty-seven, their retirement accounts, to cover the $78,851 in annual spending and make requisite tax payments. If, as in the last row of table 3, Steven and Bertha start their retirement account withdrawals earlier than age sixty-seven, they end up paying more in taxes and are worse off. Steven and Bertha lose out on tax deferral and also kick themselves into a higher tax bracket because during their early sixties, their taxable regular-asset income is at its highest levels.

So conventional wisdom is partly correct: deferring 401(k) withdrawals, at least for some period of time, can help. On the other hand, at some point you'll likely need to access these funds in order to maintain your living standard. In Steven's and Bertha's case, were they to set about spending $78,851 per year starting at age sixty-two but waiting until age sixty-eight or later to start their 401(k) withdrawals, they'd run out of money at age sixty-seven. Here again we see that borrowing constraints matter.

To see these constraints in higher relief, suppose that Steven and Bertha choose seventy as the age to start taking both their 401(k)s and Social Security. In this case, the smoothest living-standard path for the couple entails spending $70,965 between ages sixty and sixty-nine and $81,456 starting at age seventy.

This alternative is still better than following conventional advice, which provides only $70,007. But does it beat spending a constant $78,851?

Not if Steven and Bertha are consumption smoothers.

"Bertha, We've Got a Problem"

Just when Bertha is starting to feel good about her family's finances, in walks Steven with an announcement:

"Bertha, we've got a problem—a big one."

Turns out that unbeknownst to Bertha, Steven has been sneaking out of bed at four in the morning to grab a snack and do night-trading with the couple's $500K. Everything was going great until it wasn't. To make a short story shorter, Steven lost all $500K.

Now Steven and Bertha are back to their nightly "When should we cash out?" debate, only it's become a lot more existential.

With no other resources besides their 401(k) and their Social Security, Steven and Bertha need to tap into one or the other right away to keep eating.

Bertha heads back to the computer den. There she tries the same trick of taking the 401(k) early and Social Security late. But now she stares with horror at the screen. Under this strategy, they get to spend only $20,090 annually before age seventy. After that, things aren't so bad. Consumption in those years is $74,596, which is pretty close to what it would had been had Steven stayed in bed.

Steven walks into the den and gasps at the figures on the screen. *"No way! We can't live on $20,090 until age seventy!"*

Bertha, concerned about Steven's blowing an artery, says, "Hold on. Let me see what I can do here."

Her next attempt at smoothing their living standard is to have them take Social Security early and the 401(k) late; in other words, go back to conventional advice. This run generates a living standard of $36,681 up to age seventy and $57,040 thereafter. This is certainly smoother, but not *that* smooth, and a far cry from spending $78,851 starting at age sixty-two.

Steven starts turning blue.

"Calm yourself, Steven, I'm not done yet," Bertha says.

Next she tries having them take both Social Security and their 401(k)s starting at sixty-two. This delivers a smooth living standard. That's the good news. But their annual consumption is only $50,911—miles below $78,851.

Now Bertha's turning colors.

Steven thinks fast.

"Bertha, try withdrawing all the 401(k) money from age sixty-two to age sixty-nine and taking Social Security at seventy," he suggests.

Five seconds later Bertha and Steven see their new life flash before their eyes. The plan lets them spend $56,027 per year, which is 10 percent more than $50,911.

Steven is pleased. He turns to Bertha and says, "See? I didn't go to Harvard for nothing!"

Bertha, now pale, reaches for her chest, screaming: "Yes, you idiot! Our living standard is now smooth. And, yes, it's higher than if we take Social Security early. But thanks to your blowing a half million bucks, our living standard is 35.4 percent lower forever!"

Epilogue

Bertha decides that life with Steven is too all-consuming. She moves to no-state-income-tax Texas, takes her 401(k) from ages sixty-two to sixty-nine and her Social Security at seventy, and thereby avoids the Social Security retirement benefit marriage tax, ending up with 85 percent of the living standard she would have enjoyed had she stayed married.

Commentary

Does it always make sense to take Social Security late? No. It depends on your maximum age of life. Steven's and Bertha's maximum age of life is one hundred. If it were seventy-five, waiting until seventy to start collecting Social Security would cost the couple a lot of spending power.

Your maximum age of life is different from your *expected age of death*—the age at which you will die on average. Your maximum age of life is the oldest possible age to which you could live. You may have diabetes and come from a family of diabetics, all of whom died by eighty-five. But if you think you might just make it to one hundred, you need to plan for that possibility because, hey, it could happen. Since almost all of us, regardless of our current health and family health background, have a very high maximum age of life, almost all of us should consider waiting to collect Social Security.

How long you can wait to collect depends on what regular and retirement account assets you can use to tide yourself over prior to collecting Social Security. If those assets are very limited, you'll have to take Social Security early in order to smooth your living standard. But as the above example indicates, it may make sense to use up most of these assets prior to collecting Social Security if that's what's required for a smooth ride. The one caveat here is holding some assets in reserve for an emergency, including paying for entrance into a decent nursing home that accepts Medicaid.

How about taking one's 401(k)? Is there a general rule that applies? The answer, as we've seen, is no. When Steven and Bertha had significant regular assets, starting 401(k) withdrawals at sixty-seven and ending the withdrawals at one hundred was the best move. When they had no such assets, taking out their 401(k) money between ages sixty-two and sixty-nine was the best move (ignoring the point just made to hold some back as a reserve).

What if I have nontaxable retirement account assets (Roth IRAs) as well as taxable ones (401[k]s, regular IRAs, Keogh accounts, and so on)? In what order should I withdraw these funds? This is a good question, which we addressed in the last chapter.

What if I have kids? Shouldn't I take Social Security early to ensure that my kids get some money from it in case I die quickly? No. If you want to leave money to your kids, it's probably best to give it to them now or to buy life insurance to ensure that you make them the size bequest you want.

Takeaways

- Waiting until age seventy to collect Social Security is the right move for most households.
- If you need to withdraw all or most of your 401(k) to tide you over until Social Security kicks in, so be it.

18. Double Dip on Social Security

ONE REMARKABLE WAY to raise your living standard is to "double dip" on Social Security by arranging to have Uncle Sam pay you more than one type of Social Security benefit or have him pay you the same benefit more than once. Legally. In chapter 17, we discussed when to take Social Security retirement benefits, pointing out that waiting to collect can be a powerful way to raise your living standard. But in that chapter we assumed that each spouse was a high earner prior to retiring and was not therefore eligible to receive extra benefits based on the other spouse's earnings record. We also ignored the ability of Social Security recipients to reapply for benefits. Let's look at each of these options.

Take Spousal Benefits Early

Bill and Hillary are a sporadically happily married sixty-two-year-old couple. Hillary wears the pants. She's made most of the couple's money in the past through her lucrative marriage counseling practice. This has permitted Bill to focus on his primary passion—word games.

Given their ages, Bill and Hillary are eligible to receive reduced early retirement Social Security benefits starting immediately. But they realize that there is a terrific return—a close to 60 percent higher, real retirement benefit—from waiting to collect retirement benefits until age seventy.

For her part, Hillary has decided to keep working until her normal retirement age, which is sixty-six, and to start collecting retirement benefits at age seventy. Bill, on the other hand, has had it with work. He's decided to retire immediately but isn't sure that waiting to collect until age seventy or even age sixty-six makes sense. A stickler when it comes to legalese, Bill's been staying up late studying *The Social Security Handbook*. The handbook, with its 2,728 rules, is a bureaucrat's dream and everyone else's nightmare. It's full of provisions like:

> *You are also entitled to a smaller retirement insurance or disability insurance benefit (only the difference between the larger widow(er)'s insurance benefit and the other benefit is payable as the widow(er)'s insurance benefit; however, this amount is payable in addition to the other benefit).* *

Bill's been focusing on the handbook's spousal and survivor benefits. He's correctly surmised that he's eligible to collect such benefits based on Hillary's earnings record and that the amount of these benefits won't be affected by his decision to collect his own retirement benefits *provided* he's not trying to collect a spousal or survivor benefit at the same time. If he tries to collect both at once, Social Security will give him the larger of the two.†

---

* *The Social Security Handbook*, provision 407.2.B; http://ssa.gov/OP_Home/handbook/handbook.04/handbook-0407.html.

† To make life really confusing, Social Security redefines the spousal and survivor benefits, when they exceed retirement benefits, as (a) the retirement benefit plus (b) the difference between the spousal or survivor benefit and the retirement benefit. The spousal or survivor benefit is initially calculated as A plus B, but then it is redefined as B. Consequently, recipients in this situation are given the misleading impression that they are receiving their own retirement benefit, when, in fact, their total benefit (A plus B) is determined by their spousal or survivor benefit.

So when should Bill collect? Well, Bill's own retirement benefit, if he takes it early (at age 62), comes to $7,000 a year. Were he to wait until age seventy, he'd be able to collect a retirement benefit of $12,250 each year, valued in today's dollars, from that point on. But when Bill hits sixty-six, he can collect a spousal benefit based on Hillary's earnings record *even though she hasn't yet started to collect her own retirement benefit.** This benefit comes to $13,305. And since Bill can receive only the larger of his retirement benefit and the spousal benefit, he does better taking the $13,305 spousal benefit each year starting at sixty-six.

But what about the next four years, until Bill turns 66? Well, here's the beauty of Bill's situation. For the next four years, Bill can collect his $7,000 retirement benefit each year, and doing so won't affect his $13,305 spousal benefits whatsoever. So Bill can collect retirement benefits first, spousal and, potentially, survivor benefits later, and thereby pocket an extra $28K between ages sixty-two and sixty-six. Were Bill to mistakenly wait to apply for Social Security retirement benefits until age sixty-six, the $28K would be lost. There is nothing in the handbook that says that people who could have received more benefits by applying early will receive them retroactively.

Reapply for Social Security

Dick and Jennifer Munroe just turned age seventy. They met in law school, got married, opened up a joint family law practice in Chicago, and made a killing helping their friends get divorced. Dick and Jennifer called it quits at age sixty-two, moved to Tucson, and immediately applied for Social Security retirement benefits. As a consequence, their retirement benefits were reduced, leaving each of them collecting only $11,556 per year. We say *only* because had they waited until now to apply for benefits, they'd each be eligible for

* To make this happen, Hillary will need to apply for her retirement benefit at sixty-six and also to *suspend* its collection. If Hillary wasn't working, she could collect spousal benefits until at least sixty-six on Bill's account.

$20,000 per year—their full retirement benefit adjusted by Social Security's delayed retirement credit.

Recently, Dick read an article in *Forbes' Retirement Guide* ("The 62/70 Solution," November 11, 2007). The article, written by Janet Novack, mentioned Social Security form 521, titled "Request for Withdrawal of Application." As Novack relates, the form permits one to repay past Social Security retirement benefits received, *with no interest required or adjustment for inflation or survival,* and then reapply from scratch. The Social Security Administration has to approve the application and requires applicants to provide a reason for the request. The form lets you check off one of two boxes as the reason. The first is "I intend to continue working." The second is "Other." If you check "Other," you must provide a reason in the space below the box.

Dick talked this over with Jennifer. "Gee, let's give this a shot. I've had it with retirement." He winked. "So have you. We both intend to continue working, right?

"I've done some calculations and figure that if our application is approved, we'll have to pay Social Security back $71,414 each. That's a bundle, but we can afford it. After all, we have $400K in regular assets and $400K in our 401(k)s. And if we are accepted, we'll immediately reapply for Social Security and our new Social Security benefits will be $20,000 each per year."

"But is it worth it?" Jennifer asked. "In effect, you are saying that we can pay Social Security $71,414 to receive an annual inflation-indexed annuity of $8,444 ($20,000 less the $11,556 they are currently receiving). How does that compare with the market price of inflation-indexed annuities?"

"I've been looking into that. The best-priced inflation-indexed annuity I've found is offered by the Principal Insurance Co. at elmannuity.com. Buying an $8,444 annuity from them would cost about 40 percent more. So this is a real bargain!"

"I'm tingling all over!" shouted Jennifer. "But what does it really mean for our living standard?"

"Glad you asked. ESPlanner shows a 14 percent higher living standard every year for the rest of our lives. That's big bucks!"

"Sure is!" screamed Jennifer. "Grab your coat. We've got to repay and reapply before all the other retirees who took Social Security early figure this out and Uncle Sam starts denying applications."

Is This for Real?

There are some eight million retirees now in their mid-sixties to mid-seventies who, we wager, can raise their sustainable living standards significantly by repaying their Social Security retirement benefits and reapplying. For some potential retirees, the living standard increase is huge. If Dick and Jennifer, for example, had only $400K in regular assets, their potential increase would be 25 percent! What's more, the higher the rate of inflation, the better this option will be. The reason is that the repayment will be done in ever-less-valuable dollars. So if inflation takes off, as now seems likely, this option will make more and more sense to more and more people.

Can Social Security deny form 521 applications? It's hard to see how they can. Form 521, which can be downloaded at www.social security.gov/online/ssa-521.pdf, lets you simply specify "I intend to continue working" as your reason. Clearly, it has granted applications for people in the past who have simply checked this box. So on what basis could Social Security deny the same treatment to someone else?

The option to withdraw appears to have been implemented in order to assist applicants who thought they were going to stop working and then decided to continue working and who would otherwise have lost all or most of their benefits thanks to Social Security's earnings test. But Social Security may view other reasons for wanting to withdraw an application as valid. Examples here include "I didn't think I'd live this long"; "I didn't understand the actuarial reduction and delayed retirement credit formulas"; or "I was pressured by the Social Security office worker to apply for early benefits."

Should One Plan to Reapply?

If Dick and Jennifer can raise their living standard at age seventy by repaying and reapplying, did they do the right thing in signing up for benefits at age sixty-two? Yes, true, they had to pay federal income taxes on their benefits. But as discussed in the double dip case study posted at esplanner.com, the IRS lets you recover these taxes by taking a deduction or a credit. So contrary to the last chapter, should everyone take benefits early and then at, say, age seventy, repay and reapply? Yes, assuming Social Security retains this option.

Social Security's Reaction

We checked with top as well as bottom officials at Social Security about the double dipping option. Their uniform reaction was that they are happy to approve 521 applications of any social security beneficiary who feels he or she would be better off by repaying and reapplying. They also indicated that they've never heard of anyone being turned down on a 521 application and have no basis for turning anyone down.

Takeaways

- Consider all the combinations of your own and your spouse's Social Security benefit collection dates to avoid leaving money on the table.
- If you are married and your dependent spousal benefit exceeds your own retirement benefit, taking your own retirement benefits early and having your spouse take his or her retirement benefits late may be the best option.
- If you've taken Social Security early, consider paying back what you received and reapplying.
- If Social Security doesn't change its rules and you can swing the repayment, taking early and then repaying and reapplying seems the best option of all.

19. Russian Roulette for Keeps

BEEN TO FLORIDA lately? If you have, you've probably seen the bumper stickers saying "I'm Spending My Kids' Inheritance." Such declarations of selfishness notwithstanding, most of America's elderly are doing just the opposite; they are arranging their financial affairs to leave a bequest to their kids. The reason for this is that very few of America's elderly are fully annuitized, meaning that very few have all their spending power coming in the form of income streams that die when they die. Instead the elderly are collectively holding some $25 trillion in private assets. So if all 33 million geezers were to die this very instant, their children would be—how can we put this delicately?—comforted, at least financially.

Now, not all 33 million elderly are going to die at the same time. But most will die before they have spent all their assets. Consequently, a decent chunk of today's oldsters' $25 trillion will eventually make its way to their offspring.

The elderly's failure to annuitize their assets (sell their assets and use the proceeds to buy annuities—income streams that continue as long as they live) is a big puzzle to economists. The elderly, as a group, seem to have little interest in making bequests and generally provide little financial help to their kids even when they can easily do so, and even when their kids could really use the help. The standard explanations for the puzzle are that the elderly want to keep their assets liquid (in chunky form) to deal with financial emergencies and that they worry whether annuities are really safe bets. There's a third reason that we'll mention in a while.

Both of the standard concerns are significant. The biggest potential financial emergency is nursing home care. For most low- and middle-income households, saving for an extended nursing home stay is prohibitively expensive. Buying long-term care insurance to cover these potential expenses is pretty pricey as well, particularly given the alternative: letting Uncle Sam pay your nursing home bill if you end up in one. As we've indicated, the strategy that most low- and middle-income households follow when it comes to dealing with nursing home expenses is to plan to use up their assets except enough to buy admission into a nice nursing home that takes Medicaid. And, once they've paid this up-front fee, they apply for coverage under Medicaid based on the fact that they are broke.

Unfortunately, you can't sign over your future annuity income as an up-front fee. Once you go onto Medicaid, the program will confiscate essentially all of your annual income (including your annual annuity income) before you can hand it over to the nursing home. So you need to keep some money up front to get through the door of a first-rate nursing home.

"OK," you're thinking. "I'm with you on this point. But what makes annuities risky?"

First, the insurance company may expire before you do and renege on its promised annuity payments. Major insurance companies with reassuring-sounding names like Executive Life, Mutual Benefit, First Capital, and Fidelity Bankers have gone broke over the years. If you're sixty years old and might make it to a hundred, buying an annuity requires believing the insurance company will be around to make payments to you forty years from now. Moreover, if the annuity is fixed in dollars (for example, it pays a fixed $10,000 per year), there is a major risk that its real value will be eaten up by inflation.

Needing to pay the entrance fee to a decent nursing home explains why retirees don't fully annuitize their assets. But it doesn't explain why they don't annuitize at least some, if not the bulk, of their assets. What's more, concern about insurance company solvency and inflation, while very important in the past, is less of an issue today. Today Vanguard—the giant and highly secure mutual fund/insurance company—offers reasonably priced annuities that are fully protected against inflation. So do other companies, such as The Principal Insurance Corporation, through www.elmannuity .com. Moreover, a number of highly reputable companies are getting into the reverse mortgage business. A reverse mortgage allows you to spend some or all of the equity in your home and has some annuity-type properties.

To get a sense of how much you can raise your living standard by using annuities, consider the case of Sue Sanguine, a happy-go-lucky sixty-five-year-old Minnesota woman with $300K in regular assets, $300K in a regular IRA, and $300K in home equity. Sue knows nothing about annuities, although she reports getting one—namely Social Security—to the tune of $1,000 a month. A careful investor, Sue put all her regular and retirement account assets in TIPs a couple of years back, when they were yielding 3 percent after inflation.

What else can we tell you about Sue? Well, she paid off her mortgage last year, so her only remaining housing expenses are $6K a year for property taxes, homeowners insurance, and maintenance. Apart from these costs, Sue's other expense, at least so far, is paying her Medicare Part B premium, which equals $1,122 this year but is projected to equal $5,348 in today's dollars thirty-five years from now. (More on this later.)

Sue has correctly determined that by spending over time the principal and interest on her TIPs, she can consume $28,643 each year through age one hundred, her maximum age of life. But by not annuitizing, Sue is potentially leaving lots of money on the table. For example, if Sue dies at age eighty, she'll leave an estate, including her house, worth $729,635. And if she makes it to one hundred, she'll leave $300K—the equity in her home, which we're assuming she never sells.

What if Sue annuitizes her retirement account assets, which are now throwing off $13,969 a year measured in today's dollars? How much more will she get to spend?

Well, if Sue were to purchase an actuarially fair, inflation-indexed annuity, she'd be able to count on $19,156 per year in today's dollars, which is 37.1 percent more than $13,969! (An actuarially fair annuity is one in which the insurer just breaks even on average and doesn't charge any fee or commission on the annuity contract.)

That's a tremendous difference—a magical difference. Where's it coming from? It's coming from the fact that when Sue Sanguine buys an annuity, she is, in effect, joining lots of other people who agree to put their assets in a collective pot with the principal and income to be withdrawn over time by those who continue to live. This is like playing Russian roulette for keeps. When your fellow players shoot themselves, you and the other survivors get to confiscate the decedents' money.

Unfortunately, the insurance industry isn't offering actuarially fair deals, at least not at the moment. Think of them as organizing what might be deemed "confiscatory Russian roulette," by taking a hefty cut of the pot before handing out what's left to the survivors. The only actuarially fair seller of annuities turns out to be the Social Security Administration. When you choose to delay receiving your Social Security retirement benefits or choose to repay and reapply for higher benefits, you are, in fact, choosing to buy additional annuities from Social Security. You are choosing to hand some current money over to Social Security in exchange for more money in the future *if you survive*.

The best Sue can do in the current market environment appears to be to buy, via elmannuity.com, the Principal Insurance Company's inflation-indexed annuity, which provides $17,568 per year in today's dollars. This is a far cry from $19,156, but it's still 25.8 percent higher than $13,969. Taking this route provides Sue with a $32,366 annual living standard (level of sustainable consumption), which is 13 percent higher than she'd enjoy otherwise.

What if Sue annuitizes some more of her assets, say two-thirds of the $300,000 she has in regular assets, reserving the rest for an emergency? Doing so pushes her living standard up to $35,053—22.4 percent above its initial value.

Reverse Mortgage

Can Sue do better still? Yes. She can take out a reverse mortgage on her home. A reverse mortgage is an interesting financial arrangement that has some annuity-like features. If Sue takes out a reverse mortgage, the lender (typically a bank) will pay her a fixed amount of money each year for as long as she lives in the house. Once Sue dies or otherwise vacates the house, the bank gets back either (1) all the past payments it made to Sue, accumulated at a pretty high rate of interest, or (2) the value of the house—whichever is less.

If Sue lives a very long time, the bank will lose money on the deal. Accounting for lost interest, it will pay more to Sue than it recovers from the house. If Sue dies soon after signing the deal, the bank will get repaid on the loan based on the higher than normal interest rate. This is the sense in which the reverse mortgage is an annuity contract.

According to an online reverse mortgage calculator, Sue can garner $11,328 per year (not adjusted for inflation) as long as she lives in her house. When Sue passes away, her estate may or may not receive any of the proceeds from the sale of the house, depending on her age at death. But this is of no matter to Sue, since she has no children or anyone else to whom she wants to leave either money or the house.

If Sue annuitizes her assets as previously described and also takes this reverse mortgage deal, and if inflation runs at 3 percent, Sue's living standard will be $42,947. This is 50 percent higher than the $28,643 living standard she started with!

Better Yet

After telling Sue that we could raise her living standard by 50 percent and that we could have done even better had she not already started taking Social Security, she told us she hadn't actually begun to collect Social Security. She'd only asked how much her benefits would be were she to start collecting immediately.

"This is good news," said Scott. "Listen, Sue, if you wait until age seventy to apply, you'll be able to spend not $42,947 a year but $44,625 each year through age one hundred. This is 55.8 percent more than the $28,643 you were initially planning to spend!"

All in the Family

"Wow!" Sue exclaimed. "You've just raised my living standard by two-fifths. But how can I trust you? Maybe you're working for the annuity company or getting a piece of the backward mortgage action? You look honest enough, and whoever heard of an economics professor or a financial journalist conning a little old lady? I'm going to trust you. But now that I trust you, I've got a little confession. I'm not childless. I actually have three grown kids, all with OK jobs. And I'd like to leave them something when I go. I didn't want to tell you about them before I knew who I was dealing with. I didn't want you to go selling them any of your annuities, or whatever you call them."

"Gee, Sue, thanks for telling us about the kids. This changes the picture a bit, maybe even a lot," said Larry. "You see, in the plan we've outlined, the Principal Insurance Company and the reverse mortgage bank are providing you with a lot of longevity insurance—that is, insurance against living too long. And just as it's a lot more economical to buy homeowners insurance than it is to self-insure against your house burning down—which would require saving a ton of money—it's a lot cheaper to buy annuities to insure against living too long.

"But the Principal Insurance Company and the bank aren't providing this longevity insurance out of the goodness of their hearts. They are collecting a lot of money on these insurance deals in the form of commissions, fees, loads, and so on. They don't make this money for sure; they make it if you die at a young age. Although they are paying you and their other annuity customers to live, they're really hoping that you and their other annuity customers will die young or at least on time.

"Still, there's another insurance company, apart from the Principal Insurance Company and this bank, which may be able to give you an even better deal. It's called your family. When you make risk-sharing deals with your family, there are no commissions, fees, or loads. On the other hand, there are fewer people with whom to share the risk, so you and they end up with more risk exposure."

"You mean my kids will sell me an annuity?" asked Sue, incredulous.

"Precisely," said Larry. "Although neither you nor they may call it this. Here's how it would work. You'd tell your kids, either explicitly or implicitly (by retaining assets that can be bequeathed and by including them in your will), that when you die, they are going to inherit. And your kids tell you, either explicitly (by giving you money along the way) or implicitly, that if you live longer than expected, they're going to help you out financially.

"With three kids, you can form a nice little insurance pool, and if you're confident that the arrangement won't break down in an intrafamily holy war, it might be best for both you and them to self-insure. This way you'll keep all the money inside the family and enrich neither the Principal Insurance Company nor any other third parties.

"But think about this carefully. Your kids may run into financial difficulties down the pike. They may lose their jobs, get divorced, or get sick. Or they may renege on their part of the longevity risk-pooling deal. Asking your kids to insure you against living into your eighties and nineties may be asking them to take on more risk than they can or should really handle. So you may decide, after thinking things over, that it's best to (1) give your kids right now whatever money you want to leave them as a freebie, (2) hold some money in reserve, in case you need to buy your way into a fancy nursing home, (3) use the rest of your regular and retirement account assets to buy the annuities we've discussed, and (4) go for the reverse mortgage."

"Well, Scott and Larry," said Sue, "you've given me a lot to mull over. And I surely do like the idea of getting paid to live. I never realized that financial planning could be so much fun—or could increase my standard of living so much."

Takeaways

- We can easily outlive our money.
- Annuities can dramatically raise our sustainable living standards.
- There are now inflation-indexed annuities and reverse mortgages that can mitigate longevity risk.
- All retirees should carefully consider buying inflation-indexed annuities.
- Relying on our kids to bail us out, and their relying on us to die, is risky and can get pretty messy.

20. Learning Your Bs and Ds

PARTICIPATING IN MEDICARE Parts B and D is another example of controlling your net benefits from the government and thus raising your living standard. Medicare charges premiums for its Part B (outpatient) and Part D (prescription drug) coverage. These premiums rise the longer one waits beyond age sixty-five to enroll, with one exception: if you're sixty-five or older and work for an employer with one hundred or more employees, and the employer provides you with health insurance, you can escape the Part B (but not the Part D) late-enrollment penalty.

The Part B premium rises by 10 percent a year for each year you wait to enroll, and the Part D premium rises by 1 percent a month for each month you wait to enroll. These are stiff penalties, and one wonders what our fearless leaders could possibly have had in mind in establishing them. Medicare, after all, is going broke because the benefits it pays out far exceed the premiums it collects. So penalizing people who don't join Medicare at the earliest possible moment is hard to rationalize.

If you're over sixty-five and don't have health insurance coverage from your current or prior employer, enrolling in all parts of Medicare immediately is the smart move. If you do have coverage from a past employer, including prescription drug coverage, and are really, *really* sure it will last, staying clear of Medicare is the way to go.

A third possibility is that you have *very* reliable basic coverage from a prior employer, but the coverage doesn't include prescription drugs. In this case, you should enroll at sixty-five in Medicare Parts A and D, but not B.

A fourth case is that you're still working for either a large (100-plus employees) company or a small company that will cover you, but only as long as you remain its employee. Now the decision gets tricky. The Medicare Part B premium is slated to rise dramatically, particularly for upper-income households. The Part D premium is pretty large as well and also growing like crazy. So say you're sixty-five, and you're going to work for two more years for an employer with a great plan that covers everything. It still may make sense to enroll in both Medicare Parts B and D at age sixty-five. Yes, you'll have to pay quite large premiums for two years and get nothing back from Medicare. But after two years, your annual premium payments will be more than one-fifth smaller in that year and *for the rest of your life* than they would be otherwise. (Elderly workers who have basic coverage but no drug coverage will surely want to enroll in Parts A and D when they hit sixty-five.)

Remember, we've already shown that deferring Social Security retirement benefits and reaping a 7 to 8 percent real increase in your initial benefit for each year you defer is a really good investment, worth far more than the benefits you forgo. Well, the same thing works in reverse: it's a really bad idea to defer paying Medicare premiums when the penalty for deferring will rise by 10 to 12 percent, real, per year.

Takeaways

- Whether and when to take Medicare Parts B and D is an important decision.
- There are significant lifetime penalties for signing up late for Medicare Parts B and D.
- Waiting to enroll makes sense only if you have *very* secure alternative coverage.

21. Holding Your Nuts

SQUIRRELS ARE GOOD savers. They spend much of their time gathering and hiding nuts for the winter. They're also smart investors. They don't hide all their nuts in one spot. They store them in different places so that if one stash is stolen, all won't be lost.

Ask any squirrel, and she'll tell you: find your nuts and hold them carefully.

We humans also store our nuts. Our main storage places are regular and retirement asset accounts. And we too have to worry about a hungry predator grabbing them. His name is Uncle Sam.

Keeping our nuts (assets) away from Uncle Sam isn't easy. We have to decide when to gather them, where to save them, and when to collect them. We also have to hold our nuts the right way.

There are two main options. You can hold them in equities, or you can hold them in bonds, by which we refer to standard taxable bonds.* Which decision you make affects how much Uncle Sam can grab.

---

* For purposes of this discussion, we include REITs (real estate investment trusts) in bonds because of their tax treatment.

Equities pay their returns in the form of capital gains and dividends, both of which are taxed by the feds at a rate of 15 percent or lower, depending on the level of your income. Many state income taxes also tax capital gains and dividends at preferential rates. Bonds, on the other hand, pay their return in the form of interest—and interest is taxed by the feds at ordinary rates, which run as high as 35 percent.

Worst yet, the government taxes nominal, not real, interest income (interest income adjusted for inflation), which makes the effective tax rate on real income potentially much higher than the statutory rate. And, households may be in the range where their deductions and exemptions are being reduced (see www.cbo.gov/ftpdocs/68). State governments also provide no state income tax break for interest income earned on standard taxable bonds. Their top marginal rates range from 3 percent to 9.9 percent.

Now, here's the key point. If you hold stock in your 401(k), 403(b), traditional IRA, or other tax-deferred retirement accounts, all returns on your assets—whether they come in the form of capital gains, dividends, or interest payments—will be taxed at ordinary rates when you make retirement account withdrawals. Uncle Sam doesn't care how much of the money in your 401(k) is principal, interest, capital gains, or dividends. He just cares about the total amount being withdrawn, because he taxes every dollar that comes out as ordinary income. In contrast, how you hold your regular assets will affect your taxes. The same regular-asset income will generally be taxed at a lower rate if it represents income from capital gains or dividends than if it represents interest income.

Consequently, if you have both regular assets and retirement accounts, and you are investing in both stocks and bonds, you should hold stocks in your regular-asset accounts and bonds in your retirement accounts. This way, you'll actually benefit from the tax break on the return on your stock.

How big a deal is this?

Just ask Dan Gruenberg, a self-employed forty-year-old engineer making $200K a year with $300K in regular assets and $300K in his Keogh account. Dan intends to add $10K to his Keogh account each year through retirement at age sixty-five. Dan, by the way, is a confirmed bachelor. He lives in his paid-off condo in Stratford, Connecticut, with his two dogs.

Dan went to MIT for both his BA and PhD. Nonetheless, when we caught up with him, he was investing his Keogh account in diversified stocks and his regular assets in TIPs. This act of fiscal masochism was costing him dearly. His expected annual living standard (assuming he received the historical return on stock) was $92,906. By going online for fifteen minutes and switching his regular assets to diversified stock and his Keogh account to TIPs, Dan was able to raise his expected annual living standard to $99,341!

The difference between these two numbers is 6.9 percent, meaning that Dan's fifteen minutes of effort raised his expected living standard for each one of his sixty potential remaining years of life by 6.9 percent! Not a bad use of fifteen minutes.

Investing in a tax-efficient manner is more important the higher your tax rate. Were Dan half his economic self—were he to earn half of what he now earns and have half of the regular and retirement account assets—his expected living standard would be $54,490 from holding his stocks and bonds in the wrong place and $56,234 from holding them in the right place. This 3.2 percent difference is less than half of the 6.9 percent gain but still major.

Were Dan a quarter of his economic self, the two expected living standards would be $36,854 and $37,270, which differ by only 1 percent. This is still huge when you think about it. These days, most middle-income workers spend a whole year working before they see their real wages rise by 1 percent.

A But

We need to raise a "but."

Dan doesn't need to spend his regular assets in the short run. Nor does Half Dan or Quarter Dan. But if they did, holding all their regular assets in stock might entail too much living-standard risk. Suppose, for example, that Dan has older parents who may need financial help in the next few years. If Dan is holding some of his regular assets in reserve to help them in this eventuality, investing all of these funds in stock may overly jeopardize both his parents' and his own living standards.

When this was discussed with Dan, he claimed that this concern didn't really make sense. "If I go back to my initial allocation of stocks in the Keogh account and bonds in the regular-asset accounts, I end up paying a lot more in taxes, as you guys correctly taught me. But doing so doesn't change the share of my *total* [regular plus retirement account] assets allocated to stock. It just changes the location of the stock. So doing this doesn't reduce my living-standard risk one iota."

"Dan," we said, "we're with you entirely except for one thing. Taking money out of your Keogh account before age fifty nine and a half—which you may have to do if your regular assets are invested in stock and your stocks drop in value—potentially means paying a 10 percent penalty to the IRS. We say 'potentially' because one can withdraw funds from a tax-deferred retirement account prior to age fifty-nine and a half penalty free if the withdrawals are set up to occur on a steady basis. This illiquidity of your retirement account funds needs to be factored into your thinking as well. We still think you should hold all of your regular assets in stock, because your parents are well heeled and can take care of themselves. But if they weren't and they were relying on you, you'd probably want to keep at least some of your regular assets in TIPs because of the early retirement account withdrawal penalty."

Municipal Bonds

So far we've ignored Dan's or anyone else's investing in tax-free municipal bonds. Since such assets are tax favored if held outside retirement accounts, but not if held inside (where all assets are tax favored), they, like stock, should be held outside.

Takeaways

- Hold your nuts carefully. Doing anything else would be, well, nuts.
- In general, hold stock and other tax-favored assets outside your retirement accounts and totally taxable assets inside your retirement accounts.

22. Fire Your Broker

THERE IS NO scientific basis for the "advice" offered by investment companies and stockbrokers. But this hasn't kept them from charging heavily for it. The typical brokerage investment account, including the fast-growing "wrap" accounts, which eliminate commissions in favor of an annual fee, costs about 200 basis points, or 2 percent, a year. That may not sound like a lot, but if your portfolio is yielding, say, 5 percent after inflation, paying the money manager 2 percent will reduce your annual return by 40 percent.

That's why we think you should fire your broker and manage your own investments in the simplest, least expensive way possible. Your employer should fire your expensive 401(k) plan manager for the same reason. The difference, as you will soon see, is a choice between their Mercedes SL550 Roadster (MSRP $95,000) and yours.

Ernest and Eleanor Earner are a remarkably well-matched couple. They live in Seattle. They went to the same college, have the same degree, are both thirty, work for the same small company, and have the same salary, $50,000 a year. They see eye to eye on everything. They're delighted to have two young children. They don't intend to have any more. They bought a house a few years ago and now have twenty-eight years to pay back the $225,000 balance on their mortgage.

They know they'll never make the Forbes 400 list, but that doesn't keep them up at night. They are confident their earnings will rise about 1 percent faster than inflation until they retire at age sixty-seven. They participate in their company 401(k) plan, saving 6 percent of their income. That's enough to capture the 50 percent match from their employer. The mutual fund company that provides the plan also offers a smooth transition to IRA rollover accounts at retirement, so the Earners could have seventy years of investing with the same firm.

The Earners worry about the gigantic menu of choices in their 401(k) plan. It's tougher than choosing at Baskin-Robbins and a lot more expensive. All the options have expenses of 2 percent a year. Ernest wonders how much those expenses are really costing and what they are getting in return.

Ernest thinks that 2 percent in annual expenses is a lot. "Do you realize," he says to Eleanor, "that's more than the S&P 500 pays in dividends? Surely that has to have some effect on results."

"Yes, but don't they earn it?" Eleanor asks.

"Hardly. Three-quarters of the people managing mutual funds underperform the market. These money managers are the only people I know who can systematically fail to do their jobs, make a bundle, and spend an inordinate amount of time playing golf with, guess who? Our corporate-benefits people, that's who! These folks are essentially being bribed to agree to such astronomical fees. The benefits people don't really give a damn about us working stiffs. Instead of doing any hard work and making good choices for our plan, they offer us an expensive smorgasbord. They put a lot more effort into executive comp and the corporate pension plan—the one they froze just before we joined the company."

"How do you know that?"

"I compared the Form 5500s they file. The average return for all participants in the 401(k) plan was more than 2 percentage points lower than the return earned by the investments in the pension fund.

When it comes to the execs and their own money, our benefits officers watch expenses with the devotion of judges in a wet T-shirt contest."

"So? Two percent doesn't sound like a big deal. Maybe that's just the price we pay to be small investors."

In fact, it's a big price. If Ernest and Eleanor invest in a typical 60-40 split between equities and fixed income, their expected return before expenses will be about 8 percent, compounded annually. That's about 5 percentage points better than the current rate of inflation. Were they fortunate enough to be in a hyper-low-expense plan like the federal Thrift Savings Plan, which has an annual cost of only 0.03 percent, their 401(k) accounts would hit a maximum value of $505,474 each when they were sixty-six years old, just before retiring.

They would retire with a tad over $1 million, and all they did was save 6 percent of their income a year from age thirty—and capture the match. Because of that accumulation, they would each enjoy a lifetime living standard equivalent to $27,790 from a combination of their earnings, Social Security, and their tax-deferred investments. In addition, they'd have the money to pay all their shelter expenses, their substantial Medicare Part B premiums, and the life insurance they would need to carry until they were about sixty years old. Not to mention their state and federal taxes.

We mention their "substantial" Medicare Part B premiums because these premiums will have a major effect on the retirement of young workers like Ernie and Eleanor. While current retirees pay about $1,200 a year each, the young Earners can expect to pay $10,830—in today's dollars!—when they start paying premiums at sixty-five. Their lifetime standard of living would be much higher if those premiums didn't grow at the historical rate, which is 4.6 percent more than inflation. (More on this shortly.)

But Ernie and Eleanor aren't in a hyper-low-expense plan. They're in a hyper-high one, which pays, on average, only 6 percent, net of the 2 percentage point expenses, on their investments. This is before inflation. After inflation, we're talking 3 percent. In this, their actual employer-provided and employer-blessed plan, they accumulate, on average, only $340,653 each as of age sixty-six. Together they have $329,642 less at age sixty-six than they would have had without the fees considered normal in the industry. And their actual *lifetime* living standard is only $26,371—5.4 percent lower than it would be in a no-cost plan.

"Wow, 5.4 percent!" screamed Eleanor, when she learned these facts. "That's absolutely enormous. We have 100 percent of our living standard to begin with and a lot less than that after Uncle Sam's take, and here we are blowing 5.4 percent of it on someone we hardly know and, for that matter, can't even trust to beat the low-cost index alternative!"

"You're so right," said Ernie. "The difference in net returns is huge. If we go the high-fee route, we're going to have about $330,000 less at retirement. That $330,000, in effect, went to the financial services industry.* Had we been able to invest inexpensively, we would have had that much more."

"Can we do anything about it?" asked Eleanor. "I mean, how much money would we have to add today to our regular investments to offset these higher expenses? Maybe we should suggest to our employer that the company make us whole because they've been so sloppy about plan choices."

"Lawyers could have fun with that! Well, our employer could look at it this way: they could offer us a no-expense plan and cut their current 50 percent match to zero and leave us better off. If they just cut the expenses by 1 percentage point, they could cut their match from 50 percent to 12 percent and leave us in the same boat. A different way to think about it is that eliminating the 2 percent fee is equivalent to the benefits office handing us a combined check for $90,500.

"The top dogs at our company aren't dumb. They must know about this. Surely they can fix it."

---

* This figure includes the benefits of compounding, so the brokerage industry never actually gets that much of our money to spend. The actual cash received, however, does go a long way toward buying that Mercedes.

"They may know about it," said Eleanor. "They may not. But it isn't part of their compensation plan. They don't get their stock options and bonus checks for improving our retirement; they get them for cutting payroll costs and squeezing benefits."

"Right, but if they were really smart, they'd know that in saving their workers money, they could cut back what they are paying them and thereby pass the savings back to the company."

Takeaways

- Fire your broker.
- Get your boss to offer hyper-low-cost index funds.

23. Downsize

ANOTHER WAY TO raise your living standard, albeit a sometimes painful way, is to reduce your off-the-top expenditures: housing expenses; college and private school tuition; weddings; special vacations; purchases of expensive cars, boats, furniture, and artwork; and all other nonroutine expenditures. The more you spend on these items, the less you have to spend on your regular everyday lifestyle.

The term *house poor* applies to lots of people. One retired physician whom we'll call Dr. Michael Jansen recently called Larry with the following problem. He's seventy. His wife, Carolyn, is sixty-two. They live in a huge $3.5 million house in River Oaks, the exclusive section of Houston. Apart from their mansion, they have $1.5 million in regular assets plus $40K in Social Security retirement benefits. These regular assets and Social Security retirement benefits have to cover all their living expenses as well as housing. Their mortgage is paid off, but their other housing costs come to $60K a year, thanks primarily to Houston's sky-high property taxes.

If the Jansens invest in safe assets, they can reasonably expect to earn a 3 percent annual return after inflation. In this case, after paying their housing expenses and taxes, the Jansens can spend only

$41,502 annually on consumption. This is far less than the Jansens are used to spending and explains why Michael called to ask Larry his opinion on investing in derivatives.

Larry told Dr. Jansen to forget the derivatives and sell the house. He proposed that they rent a luxury condo for $3K a month. Doing so would let them spend $171,522 annually! The plan entails Carolyn's spending $107,201 after Michael reaches one hundred—his assumed maximum age of life. Note that $177,522 is 1.6 times $107,201, consistent with ESPlanner's assumption that two can live as cheaply as 1.6.

Dr. Jansen seemed sure of his ability to beat the market, so who knows if he took Larry's advice? But think about it: by sitting in their huge house, the Jansens are forgoing the opportunity to more than quadruple their nonhousing living standard! They are staying awake at night because the only way they can maintain their level of spending is to consistently outperform the market—no mean feat.

Actually, it's the good doctor who's not sleeping. Carolyn, Larry learned, has no idea that Michael has been investing all $1.5 million of their assets in risky securities that could vaporize at any moment, creating a homemade Enron. Selling their house and leaving their neighbors won't be easy for the Jansens. But it's the sensible thing to do. Another option is for the Jansens to take out a reverse mortgage, whereby an insurance company or a bank will give them money right now for the rights to all or part of their house when they both have passed away.

The same people who tend to be house poor also tend to be car poor, college poor, vacation poor, and so on. They overspend on everything.

We can all manage to live in a smaller house, forgo buying a new car every three years, take two vacations a year rather than three, and do without this season's Boston Red Sox tickets. (On second thought, keep the Sox tickets.)

Before making any of these "get the albatross off my back" decisions, which will raise your disposable income, make sure you understand what they really mean for your living standard. Stated differently, you need to price out these expenses in terms of your living standard by calculating your sustainable living standard with and without them.

24. Equitable Alimony

ONE WAY TO raise your living standard if you are getting divorced is to make sure that you end up with a fair deal. By a fair deal, we mean a deal that leaves you with a living standard that's pretty close to that of your ex. Economics, per se, can't really say what's fair, but it can help you see what you and your spouse will end up with. It can also help you and your ex make the best of a bad situation.

Take Frank and Stacy Loveless. Frank is forty-five; Stacy, thirty-eight. He's a dentist; she's a dietitian. They live in St. Louis with their two kids, age seven and three. The couple met in Frank's dentist's chair a decade ago. Stacy asked him out, and boy, what a wedding and what a great marriage until, well, things changed. Their main goal now is settling their affairs without declaring war.

Not easy. Stacy's good with numbers. She's also nobody's lunch meat and thinks that Frank's offer is screwing her over. Frank is the big earner, netting $150K a year. Stacy earns $30K. The practice, were Frank to sell, is worth $300K. The couple have $500K in regular assets and a $500K house with a $200K mortgage. Frank has $200K in his retirement plan.

Frank is offering Stacy the house and all their regular assets. He'd keep his practice and his retirement plan money. He'd also pay $15K per year per child in child support but nothing in alimony. Frank claims this is more than fair.

Let's listen to their exchange:

Look, Stacy, I'm giving you assets worth $1 million and retaining only $500,000.

Whoa, fella! Aren't you forgetting the mortgage?

Well, OK. But there are only fifteen years left, and the interest is deductible.

I may not have enough deductions to itemize.

Well, all the money in my 401(k) is taxable on withdrawal.

Yes, Frank, but you're making five times my salary.

Right, and paying ten times your taxes.

I'm a lot younger. My money has to last longer.

You have more years to earn.

You're paying $1,250 a month to rent an identical house, while I have all the housing expenses.

You can sell when the kids leave and rent the same type of place.

Your Social Security is going to be much larger than mine.

Well, dear, let's not forget Social Security divorcée benefits.

Don't patronize me.

Stop calling me a cheap SOB.

Is Frank being generous? Or is he setting himself up to have a much higher living standard than Stacy?

Well, why should Stacy guess? Today she can readily calculate her and Frank's living standards as single individuals based on the proposed deal, taking all factors into account: demographics, child support, earnings, asset, alimony, housing, taxes, and Social Security benefits.

Turns out that Stacy's right. Based on what he's proposing, Frank's living standard will be $45,075 a year. He can spend this amount annually and still cover his taxes, child support, and rent. Stacy's living standard will be roughly half of Frank's—only $23,659.

Of course, a lot depends on Frank's being able to work until sixty-five. If his aching back ends his career at sixty, his sustainable living standard falls to $35,214. But this is still almost 50 percent higher than Stacy's.

Once Stacy runs these figures, she starts lobbying for $10,000 per year in alimony until Frank turns sixty—the retirement age assumption Stacy reluctantly accepts. This lowers Frank's living standard to $32,689, thanks in part to Frank's ability to write off the payments. But the alimony is taxable, so it raises Stacy's living standard to only $25,553.

Stacy is still 28 percent behind Frank, but this is the most she can get from her ex without going to court and facing a judge, who may split the assets 50-50 and award zero alimony.

After reaching this agreement, Frank and Stacy start helping each other tweak their plans. They find they can each do better by contributing to retirement accounts, having Frank buy a condo, having Stacy keep the house into retirement, and waiting until age seventy to start collecting Social Security.

The moral to this story is this: when it comes to reaching divorce agreements, it's easy to go to war with your ex because both you and she can legitimately believe completely different things. You can legitimately believe you're being generous, and your spouse can legitimately believe you're being a piker. Being able to see the living-standard facts of different settlement arrangements may quickly resolve many disputes. Stated differently, why should couples spend, in some cases, years arguing over who is getting mistreated, when one can determine precisely and objectively how each party is being treated in terms of the bottom line: future living standards.

PART 4

Pricing Your Passions

We've already suggested how economics can calculate your living standard under different circumstances, thus helping you price and make lifestyle decisions. This part of the book considers six such decisions in some detail. They are whether to get married, whether to get divorced, when to retire, whether to have children, whether to make financial contributions to children, and what it really costs to make charitable contributions.

To be clear, none of these decisions is solely financial, but each is largely financial. If money weren't a factor, the divorce rate would surely be much higher than 50 percent, and most workers would likely retire before they started their first job. Values, passions, love, and friendship all enter into lifestyle decisions, but these decisions invariably come at a financial price—a price that now can be calculated before making the decision.

25. Ciao, Baby

EVER HEAR THE old saw (no doubt coined by a jilted sociologist) "Economists know the price of everything and the value of nothing"?

Well, it's half true. Economists don't know the price of everything. But with some effort, they can find out. As we've been arguing, they can even determine the price of love.

Here's a Starbucks example: You love your grande cinnamon dolce espresso frappuccino latte. But do you know the price of this love? Do you know how much your daily $3.79 Starbucks fix is costing you per week, per month, per year, per lifetime? Do you know how much of your lifetime living standard you are sacrificing to spend a quarter hour each day pretending to speak a Romance language?

A lifetime Starbucks addiction isn't cheap. It costs the same as a 3 Series BMW, which won't keep you up at night.

Pricing your Starbucks love is easy compared with pricing your other passions. Take your passion for your red-hot Italian lover, Stallissimo. Suppose your Wonder Bread husband just discovered your dalliance and has threatened you with divorce unless you break it off. What to do? For all the emotional turmoil this no doubt entails, you also face an economic choice and have to start thinking like an economist. What will happen to your living standard if you ditch Wonder Bread and continue seeing Stallissimo? If Wonder Bread is making a lot more money than you and if Stallissimo is unemployed, a divorce will certainly mean a drop in your living standard.

Suppose it's a 10 percent drop? That's not so much. Maybe you're willing to sacrifice this much of your living standard for Stallissimo. But what if you're facing a 50 percent drop? At this price, your passion for grande cinnamon dolce espresso frappuccino lattes, which you will no longer be able to afford, may outweigh your darker desires.

Let's assume that's the case. Then there's some loss in your living standard—say 26.37 percent—at which you're just indifferent between (a) staying married and kissing Stallissimo good-bye and (b) getting divorced and kissing Wonder Bread off.

So your passion for Stallissimo is worth exactly 26.37 percent of your living standard. Who said you can't put a price on love?

Prices, it's important to realize, don't stand on their own. They are swap rates. They tell you how much of one thing you need to hand over to get something else. It makes no sense to say, "My love for my Aunt Tilly is worth $10,000" or "I have $10,000 of love for my Aunt Tilly."

On the other hand, you can say, "The maximum I'd pay a kidnapper to release my Aunt Tilly is $7,538." In this case, you're talking about a swap of money (which really represents a general claim to goods and services) for your Aunt Tilly.

The prices of things you love don't necessarily have to be positive. If you hate Aunt Tilly, your price for freeing her is negative; that is, you're willing to pay the kidnappers to keep her.

If you think about your myriad lifestyle decisions—how hard to work, where to live, whether to get married, whether to have a child, whether to stay married, when to retire, whether to visit your guru in Nepal, whether to buy a vintage RV trailer (Scott can help you there), whether to buy a Martin guitar (Larry recommends this) . . . these are all affairs of the heart, but they also all involve swaps or trade-offs. In each case they involve swapping (giving up) part of your living standard for something you love.

Take the decision of how hard to work. That means swapping your leisure for your living standard. Or think about getting married. In marrying you are swapping some (all?) of your personal freedom and some (all?) of your sanity to enjoy a higher living standard. Or think about visiting the guru. Going to Nepal will set you back a bundle and require sacrificing a chunk of your remaining lifetime spending power. But you may achieve enlightenment.

Although neither you nor anyone else can place an absolute dollar figure on love, you can certainly put a price tag on love whenever you need to make a decision about something you love. Indeed, it's absolutely imperative that you place a price tag on love if you are going to make financially correct lifestyle decisions.

Suppose, for example, that you underprice the living standard cost of ditching Wonder Bread. Suppose you think your living standard will fall by only 20 percent if you get divorced, but it actually falls by 30 percent. In this case, you screwed up. You made the wrong choice. Better you should have stuck it out with Wonder Bread. Yes, he would have left you wanting in some dimensions, but overall you would have been happier.

26. Shacking Up

*All marriages are happy. It's the living together
afterward that causes all the trouble.*

—RAYMOND HULL

FOR AN ECONOMIST, it's called "economies of shared living." Others would call it a cheap date. Here's how it works when you're in college: she offers to rent the DVD; he brings the pizza. The total cost of the movie and pizza, if each person were having an evening alone, would be $18 each. But the cost per person, shared, is only $9.

The same amazing principle applies on a much larger scale when we say, "Why don't we live together?" or "Will you marry me?" Married or not, once you are living together, you are enjoying the economies of shared living.

Let's see what happens when George meets Lela. George lives in Dallas with what seems like millions of other twenty-somethings who couldn't find a way to stay in Austin after graduating from the University of Texas, or who couldn't wait to leave Lubbock after graduating from Texas Tech University. George is single and earns $35,000 a year at age twenty-one. He rents a pretty marginal apartment for $500 a month, has no debt, has $9,000 in the bank and $30,000 in taxable mutual funds. He has nothing in qualified plans, but he's starting to save 6 percent of his salary, and his employer is putting up a 50 percent match. Sadly, George is not getting raises that do any better than inflation. He doesn't know it yet, but that's the way it will be for the rest of his life.

How much can he spend? What will his lifetime standard of living be? Can he improve it?

The consumption-smoothing answer: after shelter, taxes, and saving, he can consume $23,740 a year. He can do this, in constant purchasing power, every year for the rest of his life, which we assume will end for sure at age one hundred.

Fortunately, George meets Lela. She has the same salary and the same type of job that George has. She also rents a marginal apartment for $500 a month and has the same assets. Perhaps this remarkable similarity causes their instant bond.

"Why don't we live together?" Lela suggests one morning. She doesn't want to move into his apartment; he doesn't want to move into hers. So they pool their rent money and find a better apartment for $1,000 a month. Actually, it gets them a pretty trendy apartment, so we're already seeing a benefit of shared living: the quality of their shelter has improved, although each is spending the same amount as before.

The real improvement, however, comes from sharing living expenses. Consumption smoothing tells us that after shelter, taxes, and saving, they will enjoy an adult standard of living equivalent to $28,227 a year each.* That's an 18.9 percent increase in their standard of living.

Even though their combined savings are $18,000 in the bank, $60,000 in taxable mutual funds, and access to credit equal to $140,000, they are liquidity constrained. They can't fully smooth

---

* Their actual consumption is $45,163, but assuming that two can live for the price of 1.6, the actual dollars are the equivalent of 25 percent more—$56,454, or $28,227 each. Needless to say, this 1.6 figure is not a universal constant; it's up for debate.

their lifetime consumption. When George retires at sixty-seven and Lela retires at sixty-four, they will enjoy a small bonus. Their adult standard of living will rise to $29,943 a person. That's a 6.1 percent increase on top of the 18.9 percent rise.

Can it get better? Will getting married and filing a joint tax return instead of two single returns improve their standard of living still more?

Yes, but not by much. Once they are married, their adult standard of living rises to $28,874 from the $28,227 they enjoyed as live-togethers. That's a 2.3 percent increase. At retirement the marriage benefit rises from $29,943 each to $31,128, an increase of 4 percent. In other words, the so-called marriage tax—the so-called tax disadvantage in being married—is actually a marriage credit.

Would things be different if George and Lela had unequal earning power? Yes. To see how this can matter, suppose that George earns $70,000 a year and Lela stays home and eats bonbons. Also assume that George and Lela's total starting assets and total annual retirement account contributions don't change.

Since Lela earns nothing and, we'll assume, would earn nothing even if George died young, George now has to buy more life insurance (and pay more premiums) to protect her. This reduces the couple's living standard before retirement.

After retirement, however, the couple enjoy a higher living standard compared to the case where both spouses earn the same amount. The reason is Social Security, which provides spousal benefits to Lela for free. Together, George and Lela receive $41,020 in annual Social Security benefits in retirement when only George works. This is $6,584 more than they collect if both work and earn $35K each. Note that in both cases, George and Lela collectively pay exactly the same Social Security payroll taxes.

If this seems unfair, it is. It's all part of the marvelous mess you get when you construct a government pension system with 2,728 (and counting) rules. Because their Social Security benefits are higher when George makes all the money, and because these benefits are subject to federal income taxation, George and Lela end up paying higher income taxes in retirement. But on balance the couple are better off in retirement.

The bottom line is that when George is the sole breadwinner, the couple have a 2.1 percent lower living standard before retirement and a 10.7 percent higher living standard after retirement.

Buying a Boy Toy

Betty is twenty-seven years old. She lives in Dallas, has a graduate degree, works hard, works out, and pulls down $70,000 a year. She's got $18,000 in her checking account and $60,000 in taxable mutual funds. (Just like her neighbors George and Lela.) She rents a nice one-bedroom apartment for $1,000 a month in the trendy West Village area. What she hasn't got is a boyfriend.

"What I need," she says to herself, "is a boy toy."

That's when she meets Barry, working on his second margarita at the corner Chipotle, where he has had dinner, sans margaritas, for $7.95. The margaritas, like the beers, are $3 each. Barry is three years younger, attractive, and funny. Think a young Jeff Bridges with a Texas accent. A young Big Lebowski. He can fix her car. He can fix her computer. He can make her laugh.

Barry is unemployed and has virtually no money. For the last week, he has been sleeping in the back of his aging Ford Expedition. It may be a gas-guzzler, but he is increasingly grateful that it's not an econo-box because, well, he can sleep stretched out. This is fine in spring, when Dallas temperatures are reasonable, but sleeping in his car won't be an option come July.

Is this a match made in heaven, or what?

Betty takes Barry home. In the morning, she realizes that he is not a prince, but she is more grateful that he hasn't turned into a frog. He can be fixed and made better. He has a lot of potential. She suggests he can move in while he gets his act together.

No one has to think very long about how moving in with Betty improves Barry's prospects. If the relationship works and they share their lives together, it's all upside for him. Her apartment, for instance, has indoor plumbing. He's going from being homeless to living in a $1,000-a-month apartment.

But it gets better. Barry's adult standard of consumption is going to soar from iffy to about $25,045 a year as he and Betty share her wages. What's not to like?

Betty, on the other hand, faces a significant drop in living standard. Her shelter will remain the same, so there is no change there—in fact, some might argue that she has lost something with Barry living there. Others could argue that she has gained something because her apartment feels better with Barry in it.

But the big change is in her adult consumption level. Her living standard falls from $40,472 to $25,045, a decline of $15,427. That's a big drop. It could, however, be considered the price of companionship. Is Barry worth it? We're tempted to leave that decision up to Betty, but we can't help tinkering. Betty can reduce the cost of companionship by marrying Barry. Even though this Lebowski lookalike may never do a lick of work in his life, marrying him will lower Betty's tax payments (she'll file as married) and increase both her and Barry's standard of living to $28,260 each year before Betty retires.

That means Betty's cost of taking in Barry drops to $12,212 a year.

And that isn't the end of it. By marrying Barry, Betty is endowing him with spousal Social Security retirement benefits. Just as Lela gets a freebie spousal benefit if George is the sole earner, so does Barry. Indeed, once they retire, Barry's companionship will be costing Betty only $5,994 a year.

Whether Betty or George is the single earner in a marriage, measuring the dollar price of companionship raises another question: Is it possible for a spouse who produces no cash income to earn his or her keep by doing things like shopping and making repairs that are valuable, but not income producing? The answer is obvious: even without Barry's working, the cost of his companionship is so low that it's easy to see the economic utility of having a nonworking spouse.

Barry, after all, costs only $6.11 an hour—roughly today's minimum wage. And he'll cost less than $3 an hour when they have both retired. Even sweeter, while Barry costs Betty $6.11 to $3 an hour throughout his lifetime, Barry feels as if he's being paid far, far more because his living standard is so much higher.

That's the economics of it. Put the tiniest value on the joys of companionship, and it's clear that marriage is a great institution, which is why so many people try so hard to make it work.

27. Take the Leisure and Run

TIME IS MONEY. The more time you spend not working, the more it costs you. But money is also time. The more time you spend making money, the less time you have to enjoy life.

What would it really cost you in terms of your ongoing living standard to work forty hours a week rather than forty-five, to take three weeks of vacation rather than two, or to retire at age sixty rather than at age sixty-two?

If you don't know, you may be working too much or too little.

Knowing is very tough. Take retiring early. You need to translate the income loss into an ongoing spending loss. In this regard, as we have said before, you'll need to think about your own maximum life span and that of your spouse/partner. Because you could make it that far.

Next you need to think about taxes. Retiring early means paying less in taxes after you stop working but more in taxes before. Suppose you're now forty-five. Retiring early—say, at age sixty rather than sixty-two—will necessitate saving more. Let's say you do this by increasing your regular assets. Then you're going to have more taxable regular-asset income and pay more taxes until you retire. At that point, you'll start to eat up some of the assets to help cover the two extra years of retirement. At ages sixty-one and sixty-two, you'll pay less in taxes on balance because you'll have no labor income in those years. After age sixty-two you'll have fewer regular assets (remember, you're now targeting a lower living standard and need fewer assets to support that reduced living standard) and thus will pay less in taxes for the rest of your life.

Third, you need to check whether retiring early will reduce your Social Security benefits.

Most of us don't fire our jobs at thirty-five or forty. That's when we're trying our hardest to make more money just to keep up with the cost of raising the kids. But if we're lucky enough to have a choice—as opposed to being shown the door in a downsizing—most of us start thinking about firing our job when we turn sixty-two. That's when we're first eligible for Social Security retirement benefits. From that point on, we're constantly trying to figure which is worth more: money or leisure.

And guess what? Most people choose leisure. Even as the financial services industry puts out warning after warning telling us that we're all going to be eating cat food unless we save and invest more money while working more years, any examination of the choices people age fifty-five and over make leads to only one conclusion: we like leisure more than we like money.

For some, this is a no-brainer. Others are slower. Scott, for instance, has retired and collects a corporate pension. He and his wife own their Santa Fe, New Mexico, house free and clear. Ditto their Prius, Suburban, Airstream trailer, and shared ownership of a sailboat in Maine. Expenses that the pension doesn't pay can be covered by Social Security and/or investment income.

Yet Scott still writes his syndicated column and works on other projects, such as this book. Now sixty-seven, he is beginning to question his sanity, knowing that working longer won't do that much for his standard of living and each additional week of work could be spent doing something else.

Yet Scott isn't alone. He has been meaning to call Humberto

Cruz, another syndicated columnist. Famous for his advocacy of frugal living, Humberto announced quite a few years ago that he had a million dollars (a sum most journalists can only dream about) and was going to retire from his newspaper job.

He did.

But he continues to write a syndicated column on personal finance, just as he did before—advocating frugality and telling his readers about all the lousy deals available from the financial services industry.

Let's consider someone who is not a journalist—someone who is closer to normal. Take John and Jane Noworlater. They live in California, are fifty and forty-eight, respectively, and have raised their children. Both work and both earn pretty good money: $60,000 a year each. Both get inflation increases but nothing more. Their savings are modest, about $120,000, and they contribute only $3,000 each to their company 401(k) plan. The plan is typical and has a 50 percent employer match. Finally, the house they bought for $250,000 is now worth $500,000, and they expect the mortgage to be paid off by the time John turns sixty-two.

Should they retire at sixty-two? Or should they work until full retirement age, sixty-seven?

The consumption-smoothing approach tells them they can retire at sixty-two with $51,200 in annual discretionary spending money after paying all taxes and covering all their shelter expenses.

If they work another five years, something strange happens. Unless they can borrow a great deal of money, they are liquidity constrained. As a result, their consumption will start at $58,679. Then it will rise as they age, providing them with $69,238 a year through their retirement years.

If you focus on the dollars, working longer seems like a pretty good trade-off. If they work another five years, their living standard in retirement will increase by $18,038, or 35 percent. Some couples would look at this increase and call it salvation. Without that increase, their future would be hopeless. And if you read the personal finance press—magazines like *Money*, *SmartMoney*, and *Kiplinger's*—one of the most common recommendations financial

planners make for "money makeovers" is that people short on savings should consider working longer.

Real people, however, take the leisure and run.

The Noworlaters apply a different analysis. "Jane," says John,
"do you realize that we gain only $3,607 a year of lifetime spending
for each additional year of work?"

"How do you figure that?"

"I divided the $18,038 gain by 5, the number of extra years we're
going to work."

"And?"

"Well, think about it. Which would you rather have, $3,607
more to spend each year for life, or forty-eight more weeks of vacation *this year*?

"Are you telling me that we're working forty-eight weeks this
year so we can increase our lifetime consumption by a measly $3,607
a year? Are you telling me that all we'll gain from the next year of
work is $3,607 for life?"

"It looks that way."

"That means we're really working for $75 a week, kind of. Both
of us," Jane opines.

"Doesn't look too good on an hourly basis, does it? I mean, if I'm
putting in forty hours, and you're putting in forty hours, we're working eighty hours a week to gain $75 a week for life. *That's only 94
cents an hour for our time!*"

"Well, it is for life. But you know, I think I can put my time to
better use than that," Jane says.

"How?" John asks.

"Well, it's not exactly a big hurdle. We can eliminate the cost of
going to work. We can take care of more things on our own. We can
be more careful about how we spend money. I think there is a lot we
can do with our leisure time that will be worth a lot more than the
dollars we'll gain by working."

For all the anxiety about having enough money in retirement,
most people retire early. Are we supposed to believe they are all
crazy? We don't think so. They simply choose leisure over money.

And interestingly enough, the 2007 Retirement Confidence Survey done by the Employee Benefit Research Institute found that most retirees were able to spend either the same amount of money or more in retirement.

TABLE 4. POST-RETIREMENT VERSUS PRERETIREMENT SPENDING

Post-Retirement vs. Preretirement Spending

Spending Level	Workers (Expected)	Retirees (Actual)
Much lower than before you retired	20%	20%
A little lower	34%	24%
About the same	34%	42%
A little higher	8%	7%
Much higher than before you retired	2%	6%

Source: Employee Benefit Research Institute.

Needless to say, many people will continue to work because they simply have to. Having mismanaged their finances, they still have mortgages, car loans, and credit card debt. And they have little or no savings.

Many more—the majority, which excludes Scott and Humberto—will make a tough examination of the stress of work versus the pleasure of leisure. And they will choose leisure.

Takeaways

- Don't work yourself to death.
- Price your retirement in terms of your living standard.
- Retiring early may be cheaper in terms of your living-standard reduction than you think.

28. Pricing Procreation

Love is not the dying moan of a distant violin.
It's the triumphant twang of a bedspring.

—S. J. PERLMAN

IN MUCH OF the developed world, the sizzle of sex has replaced its steak. There are fewer and fewer children. The zero population growth fertility rate—the average number of children each woman needs to bear, absent immigration, to maintain a stable population—remains at 2.1 children per woman. American women are hitting this target right on the nose. But in Europe it's another story altogether. The birth rate for the European Union is only 1.5 children per woman. In Germany the rate is 1.4 children per woman. A stunning 30 percent of young German women will never have children. In Spain the figure is 1.3 children per woman. In Italy it's 1.2. Today most European children are only children. Tomorrow the definition of *aunt* and *uncle* will have to be carefully explained.

The decline has been blamed on television, among other things, but others think it's a matter of economics. So does Philip Longman, for the most part. In *The Empty Cradle,* one of many books written about the consequences of changing birth habits, Longman points out that modern urban couples are presented with a tough choice. They can have a shot at the sophisticated, mobile, affluent life they see on television and in magazines—the world of Starbucks, casual dinners out, a spare SUV topped with kayaks and filled with cases of wine one day, brand-new rock climbing gear another. Or they can have a life of profound struggle as both work full-time to "have it all"—material success and children—while suffering from time poverty.

In *The Two-Income Trap: Why Middle-Class Mothers and Fathers Are Going Broke,* Harvard Law School bankruptcy expert Elizabeth Warren and her daughter Amelia Warren Tyagi argue that modern families are in financial peril because it now takes two earners to buy a house in an area with good schools that will, in turn, help their kids get into good but frightfully expensive schools of higher education. And long before you start to deal with the expensive preschool, the luxurious primary school, the pricey prep school, and the gilded college or university, the U.S. Department of Agriculture informs us that raising an old-fashioned simple child, sans tuitions, now costs a small fortune. An update of its figures puts the cost at $124,800 for a family with income of $39,100 in 2001 and up to $249,180 for a family with an income over $65,800.

Add some of the pricey goodies—like the BMW for kids at the Hockaday School, Phillips Exeter Academy, St. Mark's School of Texas, or their equivalents elsewhere; the family Christmas trips to the Caribbean; not to mention pedestrian needs like orthodonture—and having a child can appear to be a terrifying financial commitment.

Or not. Consumption smoothing tells us a very different story about the cost of kids, at least if you're willing to utilize public goods and state universities and let them take the bus. Indeed, if your income is low enough, making babies can be profitable as well as entertaining.

Skeptics should consider Lou and Lucy Low Income. They barely make ends meet, each earning only $10,000 a year. The thirty-five-year old couple live in New Bedford, Massachusetts, a poor maritime city and former home of Lizzie Borden, the famous parental ax murderess, immortalized by this tender poem:

Lizzie Borden took an axe
And gave her mother forty whacks.
And when she saw what she had done,
She gave her father forty-one.

For their part, Lou and Lucy Low Income count themselves lucky—lucky to be alive, given where they are living, and lucky to be earning a combined $20,000, which, compared to the incomes of their neighbors, puts them high on a very skinny hog.

If Rent-A-Center were to repossess the wide-screen television set they bought on a payment plan with an effective interest rate that would make a Mafia juicer envious, or if the local tire rental shop repos their treads, Lou and Lucy might rediscover more traditional entertainment and have a child. The birth of a child, notwithstanding having an extra mouth to feed, would actually raise their individual living standard from $6,571 to $8,264 each. That's a 26 percent increase!

What makes the difference? Once little Lucky shows up, Lou and Lucy become eligible for the IRS's child tax credit and refundable earned-income tax credit, as well as food stamps. In Lucky's first year of life, Lou and Lucy get a $3,416 federal income tax refund and pay only $21 in Massachusetts state income taxes rather than the $360 in federal income taxes and $283 in Massachusetts state income taxes that they had been paying. In addition, they receive food stamps worth $4,400.

Alas, having more kids beyond Lucky is a money loser. The advent of Lucky's sibling, Loser, lowers Lou and Lucy's living standard to $7,692 each. And were Liability to pop out as well, Lou and Lucy would see their own living standards drop to $7,218. Note, however, that they are still 10 percent better off with three children than with none.

For Mike and Mary, a middle-income couple earning $50,000 a year, having children doesn't solve any financial problems but doesn't create huge ones either, thanks, again, to federal tax breaks for kids. Their living standard does decline from $12,514 to $11,155 with the birth of Here's-Looking-at-You-Kid, but this is a drop of only 10 percent.

The second child, Come-to-Us-Baby, is free. Their lifetime living standard rises slightly to $11,174 with her birth. But their living standard takes another hit when Go-Back-Where-You-Came-From shows up—it declines to $10,603. These figures assume that each child costs 70 percent of what an adult costs. Other assumptions about the relative costs of children, as well as the degree of economies of scale in shared living, would produce different results. What is clear, however, is that the cash cost of rearing a child is often offset by reduced need for retirement saving, because adult consumption is lowered throughout life and taxes are lower.

Even Harry and Hallie, a high-income couple earning $200,000 a year, wouldn't be too greatly discouraged from having one child in the consumption-smoothing analysis. As a childless couple, their lifetime adult consumption is $28,291 each. It falls 8 percent to $26,101 with the birth of their first child, Thank-the-Lord, and then falls to $24,282 with Break-the-Bank and to $22,779 with Not-You-Too.

Note that our high-income couple experience a 19 percent cut in living standard in going from zero to three children, while our low-income couple experience a 10 percent gain. Could this help explain the much higher fertility rate of the poor?

In any case, if you are trying to figure out what to do tonight, consider the following table before taking the plunge:

TABLE 5. THE VALUE (OR COST) OF PROCREATION

(Living Standard Per Person)

Combined Annual Earnings	No Children	One Child	Two Children	Three Children
Lou and Lucy $20,000	$6,571	$8,264	$7,692	$7,218
Mike and Mary $50,000	$12,514	$11,155	$11,174	$10,665
Harry and Hallie $200,000	$28,291	$26,101	$24,282	$22,779

Takeaways

- Procreating can pay.
- Even when kids come at the cost of your living standard, that cost can be surprisingly low.
- You might want to think through the living-standard cost of kids before having them.

29. Can We Help the Kids?

WHEN IT COMES to our kids, we're remarkably similar. Whatever our hopes for their work lives, we want them to be happy. We don't want anything to stand between them and a good life, material and otherwise. We don't want them to suffer or want. So we make great sacrifices while they are kids.

Studies have shown, however, that we do much less when they are older. Although many parents could easily provide financial help to struggling adult children, it seldom happens. We don't think this is selfishness. We've talked with too many older people to take those "I'm Spending My Kids' Inheritance" bumper stickers seriously.

What we see is an uncomfortable standoff. We see older people not spending because they want the kids to inherit more, but not giving today because they are anxious about the stock market, medical expenses, inflation, and all the other realities of daily life. The result is both parents and kids living a lesser life today because of fears about tomorrow.

The consumption-smoothing approach can break this paralysis. It can help determine the costs and benefits of our giving decisions by showing how much gifting lowers our own living standard and raises that of our kids. You can see this in the extreme if you measure the potential impact of being a generous grandparent to lovely little Darling, whom you are going to help by giving a low-cost tax-deferred annuity. Vanguard's variable annuity, for instance, combines its low-cost funds with a very low insurance charge for a total expense of about 50 basis points (or half of 1 percent). That's a fraction of the typical cost in the industry. It allows a gift to accumulate tax deferred for years, but it puts a penalty on withdrawals before age fifty-nine and a half—exactly how you'd like it.

Combine Darling's life span and your gift, and you can estimate the future value of the gift by counting doubling periods. If the money grows at a real rate of 7 percent (the long-term geometric average real return on large cap stock), it will double every ten years. Thus, a gift of $10,000 today to a ten-year-old is likely to become about $320,000 valued in today's dollars by the time Darling is sixty.* That's what happens when you double $10,000 five times.

To accumulate the same purchasing power, Darling would need to put about $40,000 into an unmatched 401(k) plan by the time she was thirty or make really hefty contributions over the next thirty years. We're doing a lot of casual assuming here, but the basic reality is that giving generously to a young grandchild will carry the kid through many years of uncertainty in her future.

A somewhat larger gift to a young married child—about $40,000 at age thirty—would grow to $320,000 in real purchasing power by age sixty. A gift like that can do double duty. By reducing the need to save for retirement, it can make it easier for your children to pay for the education of your grandchildren—even as it makes it easier for your children to retire.

These are not enormous gifts. As of 2007 you can give $12,000 without any impact on your lifetime gift-tax exemption. Make it a joint gift with your spouse, and you can give $24,000. And you can do that for *each* child and grandchild. At worst, a generous grand-

---

* You can play with the real and nominal value of being a generous grandparent on Scott's Web site at www.assetbuilder.com.

parent might have to make gifts over two years to make a big contribution to the retirement of a child or grandchild.

But how much would it cost you?

Let's price it for George and Georgina Generous, a recently retired Texas couple. He's sixty-six; she's sixty-four. They own a $300,000 house free and clear, have $100,000 in regular assets and $800,000 in retirement accounts. They hope to earn a nominal 8 percent return (5 percent real) on their financial assets. George collects $1,950 in monthly Social Security benefits; Georgina collects $1,200.

If they give no gifts, the (not so) Generouses will enjoy $66,193 of annual consumption for the remainder of their lives after taxes, Medicare premiums, and shelter spending. That makes them better off than most Americans without even considering that they no longer have to work. If they make an $8,000 gift to a grandchild, their annual consumption will fall by $355 to $65,838.

That's not exactly a big hit, about 0.54 percent. Even if George and Georgina make the gift to four grandchildren at age seven, it will ding their standard of living by only about 2 percent a year. They could gain some wiggle room simply by being generous at birth rather than at age seven.

The same principle works for other gifts. The most common gift between generations—other than education—is money for the down payment on a house. It's the equivalent of a table stake for entry into the American middle class. Here again, the benefits to children relative to the cost to their parents are enormous.

If George and Georgina, for instance, give $24,000 to Darling and her new husband as part (or all) of the down payment on a house or condo, that gift will cut their consumption to $65,128 a year—a decline of $1,065 a year, or 1.6 percent, which is not much at all. Moreover, there's a good chance that Darling loves her parents as much as they love her. In this case, the money George and Georgina give to Darling may come back their way with more than standard interest if George and Georgina end up in financial need. "One hand washes the other," as the saying goes. By helping those in need, including members of our own families, we create mutual assistance insurance societies that we can likely draw on for support at a later date. Indeed, we might think of our kids as part bank, part insurance company and our contributions to them as part deposits, part premium payments.

Trust plays a big role here, but if we fully trust our kids, we can make beautiful financial music together. One example is parking our taxable assets with children who are in lower tax brackets. Suppose you are in the top federal tax bracket, where the marginal tax rate is 35 percent, and your kids are in the bottom bracket, where the rate is 10 percent. There's a big difference with respect to after-tax return that can, if need be, be split between you and your kids—at Uncle Sam's expense, of course.

A second example is dealing with the possibility of going onto Medicaid to cover nursing home costs. Medicaid covers close to half of all such costs and does so by hitting up its nursing home beneficiaries with essentially 100 percent income and asset taxes. If you like your kids more than you like Uncle Sam or the corporations running the majority of the nation's nursing homes, it makes sense to transfer most of your assets to your kids well in advance of your moving into a nursing home. (You'll do this to avoid being disqualified because of recent asset transfers.) This way you can go onto Medicaid, the government pays for your nursing home stay, and your kids spend your money. That spending could well be on you. For example, your kids may decide to use the money to pay for private aides to assist you in the nursing home.

Takeaways

- Thanks to the miracle of compound interest, small gifts to children and grandchildren can make a huge difference to their retirement assets if made early.
- The cost to your own living standard of helping your kids may be less than you think.
- Don't forget, there's a good chance that your kids will pick your nursing home.

30. Charity Stays at Home

WHEN SCOTT RETIRED from the *Dallas Morning News,* he did something that shocked his wife. He started a Charitable Gift Fund.* "I just didn't think we had that kind of money," his wife said.

"We don't if you're thinking family foundations, Bill Gates, and Warren Buffett," he told her. "But we can end the uncertainty of our regular giving—and give more—if we do this *because* we don't have that kind of money."

The secret here is simple: Social Security benefits and our tax system work together in pernicious ways for retirees. Creating a charitable gift fund turns out to be a good way for a retired couple

---

* Fidelity Investments started the first Charitable Gift Fund in 1991, allowing donors to give cash or securities, get an immediate tax deduction for the value of their donation, and have the money managed by Fidelity. Fidelity charges a fee for operating the fund, as well as fees for managing the actual assets, but donors are saved the cost of establishing a personal foundation. The Fidelity CGF now boasts over $3.5 billion in assets contributed by 39,000 donors. Many financial services companies have established their own charitable gift funds, with Vanguard and Charles Schwab being the next largest at $1.25 billion and $1.06 billion, respectively. Once a donor account is established, donors can instruct the fund to issue checks to any qualified charitable organization. The minimum initial donations for the Fidelity, Vanguard, and Schwab gift funds are $5,000, $25,000, and $10,000, respectively. You can learn more at www.charitablegift.org (Fidelity Gift Fund), www.vanguardcharitable.org, and www.schwabcharitable.org.

to increase their giving and increase the amount they spend on themselves. Here's an example.

Jack and Jill Giver live in Nashville and are about to retire. Like many couples, they have been diligent savers in qualified plans, but their other savings are limited. They've got $1.5 million squirreled away in the company 401(k) plan and an IRA. They also can look forward to healthy Social Security checks.

Jack has been a good earner; Jill has been a homemaker. The kids are off the payroll. The couple own their house mortgage free. When Jack checks the impact of giving $10,000 a year to charity for the next twenty-five years, he learns that after paying taxes and Medicare premiums, he and Jill can jointly spend $63,447 on consumption, which will deliver a living standard per adult of $39,654.

An alternative strategy is for Jack and Jill to make a onetime gift. Given how he's investing his money, Jack figures that the present-value equivalent of contributing $10K a year is $107,000. Running this option through ESPlanner shows the couple's living standard rising to $40,754 per adult. Thus a big gift today will let Jack and Jill fulfill their charitable giving hopes. But it will also increase their lifetime living standard per adult by $1,100, or 2.8 percent!

Sound penny ante? It isn't. Remember, this is a *lifetime* increase, a constant purchasing-power benefit they will enjoy as long as they live. The immediate increase in their household's total consumption expenditure is $1,760, to $65,207. (To purchase a lifetime inflation-adjusted income benefit of this size would cost about $29,659, based on a single life quote for a sixty-five-year-old male from the Vanguard inflation-adjusted life annuity program.)

The economic magic here comes from tax savings. You can see how this happens—and see a more dramatic result—if you examine it in the more conventional framework of year-to-year taxes.

Suppose you are retired and drawing Social Security benefits. You cover additional expenses by making withdrawals from your IRA rollover account. At year's end you withdraw $1,000 for a charitable donation.

What happens?

The American Lung Association, the Salvation Army, the Nature Conservancy—your chosen charity—gets your check for $1,000. The world improves a little bit.

Your taxable income, however, just rose by $1,000. Unless other deductions from your taxes total at least $10,700, that $1,000 won't provide any tax benefit. Many middle-income retiree households don't have enough deductions to itemize. This is particularly true for those who live in states with no income tax, those who rent, and those who have no home mortgage.

Result: if you don't itemize deductions, your tax bill increases by your marginal tax rate. For most retirees that would be 15 percent. So it costs you an additional $150 in taxes to give away $1,000.

Worse, the same $1,000 gift also caused some of your Social Security benefits to be taxed. A couple with $36,000 in Social Security benefits, for example, can have only $14,000 of other income without paying taxes on their Social Security benefits. Every dollar of income over that triggers benefit taxation. The next $1,000 of income will cause $500 of benefits to be added to taxable income. This will increase the couple's income tax bill by another $75. So it really costs them $225 in taxes to give away $1,000.

And that's getting off easy.

If this couple withdraw more than $26,000 from their IRA, an additional $1,000 withdrawal to make a donation will trigger taxation of $850 in Social Security benefits. They will have to pay $150 on the additional $1,000 and another $127.50 on the $850 in Social Security benefits—a total of $277.50. Republican or Democrat, we think you'll agree that's not fair. But that's the way it is. It gets worse every year because Social Security benefits are inflation-indexed, but the thresholds beyond which Social Security benefits are taxable are not. This policy dates to 1983, the last major "reform" of Social Security.

In taking out $107,000 of their retirement account money this year and giving it away to charity, Jack and Jill can't avoid paying taxes on the $107K withdrawal. But they can save taxes in two ways. First, by clumping together their donations in one year, they can push themselves far above the threshold for the standard deduction;

in other words, they can ensure that their every dollar of their $107K contribution will be deductible. In addition, the clumping limits their Social Security benefit taxation in two ways. First, they'll be withdrawing less from their retirement accounts in each future year and thereby triggering less taxation of Social Security benefits in those years. Second, in the current year they'll end up maxing out with respect to taxation of their Social Security benefits, so that much of that $107K won't trigger additional Social Security benefit taxation. Why? Because the taxation of benefits is limited to 85 percent. In this case, that's $30,600. Jack and Jill will hit that level when their income from other sources is about $58,000.

Using a Charitable Gift Fund to Clump Deductions and Spread Giving

If Jack and Jill don't want to make all their charitable contributions in a given year, they can still clump their retirement account withdrawals and their charitable deductions by withdrawing the $107K and contributing it to a charitable gift fund. Over time, they can direct the contributions from the fund to the charity of their choice.

Millions of retirees who are making annual charitable contributions may be in Jack and Jill's position—able to help themselves in addition to helping their favorite charities by either making a one-time large contribution to the charities they'd otherwise contribute smaller amounts to through time by putting it in a charitable gift fund.

You're probably one of those millions if you say yes to these five questions:

1. Are you retired?
2. Are you collecting Social Security benefits?
3. Do you regularly give to charity?
4. Are your deductions too small to permit itemization?
5. Do you have enough income from IRA accounts and other sources that part of your Social Security benefits is taxed?

Answer yes, and you're in the Social Security gauntlet, the corridor of middle-class retiree income that generates taxes on Social Security retirement benefits. Have enough additional income, and you'll exit the gauntlet and be back to normal income taxes. You're also likely to have enough itemized deductions that your charitable giving will be tax deductible.

Takeaways

- Charity can stay, in part, at home if you're careful about taxes.
- Withdrawing retirement account assets annually to make charitable contributions may increase taxation of your Social Security benefits relative to clumping these withdrawals in a single year.
- Making annual charitable contributions may limit their deductibility relative to clumping the contributions.
- Setting up a charitable gift fund permits you to clump in one year your potentially nonitemizable future contributions but still make annual contributions from the fund.

PART 5

Preserving Your Living Standard

We've spent a fair amount of time telling you how to raise your living standard. Now we want to make sure you preserve it. Unfortunately, life is very uncertain, so we can recommend ways only to limit the uncertainty you face, not eliminate it. We'd also be doing you a disservice were we to scare you to death and suggest that you never take any risk, no matter how high the payoff. Consumption smoothing is a balancing act. It's about balancing future and current spending, but it's also about balancing safety with opportunity.

There are lots of outstanding risks well worth taking, just as there are lots of awful risks well worth avoiding. Investing in a low-cost, fully diversified stock market index fund is a terrific risk to take, but only up to a limit. Knowing that limit and how it changes as you age are two of the issues we raise in this section.

Portfolio risk is one of the more controllable risks we face. So are longevity and mortality risk. Annuity insurance is a marvelous hedge against living too long. And life insurance is a very loving exit strategy. We've discussed annuity and life insurance earlier, so we won't belabor those self-protection plans here.

The other major risks of economic life are inflation uncertainty, health expenditure uncertainty, public policy risk, and earnings uncertainty. The first two of these—inflation risk and health expenditure—are controllable, but at a price that may be more than you are willing to pay. Deciding not to buy insurance may make you feel queasy, but think of it from the perspective of having bought it. Once you own an expensive policy, you have the option of canceling it. Doing so brings you a stream of income (your premium savings) plus the potential for a big future loss. This is like buying a stock that pays a high dividend but whose price can fall through the floor. If the dividend is high enough and the current price of the stock low enough, buying that stock and taking the gamble of experiencing an even lower price in the future may be the smart move. So too might be canceling a long-term care policy you own, which would be equivalent to not buying it in the first place.

Unfortunately, our book is too short to catalog all aspects of the principal economic risks we face or all ways to avoid or mitigate them. Our goal in this part is much narrower: namely, to consider some issues of personal financial risk management that may come as a surprise.

Our first topic is managing your money, specifically when to hold stocks, how much to hold, and how these decisions should affect your spending behavior. Next we'll consider public policy risk, followed by earnings uncertainty, health expenditure uncertainty, and inflation uncertainty.

31. Are Stocks Safer Than Bonds in the Long Run?

A LOT OF people, even some economists, have come to the conclusion that stocks are safer than bonds in the long run and that there is relatively little risk in holding stocks, provided that you hold them long enough. Their reasoning goes like this: stocks have a higher average real return than bonds, so if you start with equal amounts of stocks and bonds and reinvest all investment proceeds, the longer your holding period, the bigger the gap between the expected or average return on your stocks and the return on your bonds.

This reasoning is correct as far as it goes. Suppose, for example, you start with $100,000 invested in thirty-year TIPs (the only really safe bonds on the market) and $100,000 invested in an S&P 500 equity index fund. Let's assume that the TIPs you buy yield 2 percent per year after inflation and that you can reinvest the interest over time at the same rate. Given our assumptions, your TIPs investment has a smooth ride, growing at 2 percent per year. After one year, you'll have $102,000. After ten years, $121,899. After twenty years, $148,595. And after thirty years, $181,136.

How about your equity index fund? Historically, the S&P 500 has yielded 9.1 percent per year, on average, after inflation.* This is miles above 2 percent. Given the statistical properties of the stock return (actually, the logarithm of the stock return), you can expect your stocks to be worth $109,172 after one year. After ten years, you can expect them to be worth $240,515. After twenty years, they should be worth $578,477. And after thirty years, you can expect $1,391,326.

From this perspective, stocks seem to be a much better bet than bonds the longer you invest. After all, the ratio of the money you can expect from stocks to that you can expect from bonds is 1.07 after one year, 1.97 after ten years, 3.89 after twenty years, and 7.68 after thirty years.

While it's true that the mean of where you end up with your stocks increases with your holding period, so does the variability (the variance) of your stocks' final value. This increasing spread of where you will land makes it more likely that your stocks will end up below unpleasant values. Indeed, as you increase your holding period, it's always possible to find worse and worse outcomes that have higher chances of occurring.

To see what's going on here, imagine playing the following game with us. We give you $100 and ask you if you'd like to play our flipping game up to ten times, with the option of stopping at any time. The game works like this: You flip a quarter. If it lands heads, you get $20. If it lands tails, you lose $10. On average you make $5 per flip.

If you flip ten times, you can expect to make $50. But the longer you flip, the bigger the downside. The most you can lose after one flip is $10. After two flips, it's $20. After ten flips, you can lose your entire $100. So this long-term investing (flipping ten times) entails a

---

* This is an arithmetic average, not a geometric average. The geometric average, which reflects the compound annual growth rate, is 7.2 percent.

small but positive risk of your coming up with ten tails and being entirely wiped out, something the short-term investing (flipping one time, for example) does not.

If you are highly risk averse, you'll take the $100 and say ciao, baby. If you're not super risk averse, you'll probably flip all ten times, since each flip has a high expected payoff. But there's nothing wrong or cowardly about taking your money and walking away, particularly once you understand the downside risk, including the possibility of losing everything. Lots of gamblers effectively limit their flips by going to the casino with a fixed amount of money in their pockets.

To summarize, a longer holding period makes stocks look safer than bonds in some ways. In other ways, the relative risk of stocks doesn't change. And in yet other ways, stocks look riskier the longer you hold them.

What should one make of this?

Nobel Laureates Weigh In

In 1969 two economic Nobel laureates, Paul Samuelson and Robert Merton, independently showed that stocks do not, on balance, offer a better risk-return deal the longer you hold them. Nor do they offer a worse deal. From an economics perspective, the risk-return deal looks the same whether you invest for twenty minutes or twenty years. Consequently, economics prescribes the same stock-bond split for long-term as well as short-term investors.*

So whether you intend to hold your money for one year and then spend it all at once or hold your money for thirty years and then party big-time, Samuelson and Merton are saying, Hold your money the same way. If you hold a third in stocks and two-thirds in bonds when investing for one year, do the same when investing for thirty

---

* Samuelson's and Merton's analyses go beyond simply considering the statistical properties of the returns on stocks and bonds. They also consider how investors evaluate risk—their risk aversion. For an outstanding analysis of the risk of equity investment, see Zvi Bodie's *Worry-free Investing*.

years. And choose the fraction in stock based on your degree of risk aversion—your concern about risk. If you are very risk averse, don't hold stock.

Of course, we don't manage our money in order to spend it all in a single year. In light of this, Samuelson and Merton also considered portfolio choices for typical investors who spend money each and every year. The two economists arrived at the same conclusion: we should maintain the same portfolio year in and year out, both before and after retirement.

Life-Cycle Funds

How does the Samuelson-Merton prescription square with the current investment rage, known as life-cycle funds, which start young households with a very high share of equities and automatically reduce their equity share over time? The life-cycle funds amount to a replay of one of the oldest known rules of thumb for investing: that your equity share should be equal to the number 100 minus your age. By that rule, a twenty-five-year-old would be 75 percent in equities while a sixty-five-year-old would be 35 percent in equities.

Are Samuelson and Merton wrong in arguing that your portfolio should stay fixed as you age? And are the purveyors of life-cycle funds right in claiming that your portfolio should be invested in safer assets as you age?

Actually, neither is right. Samuelson's and Merton's work is impeccable, but it's predicated on a mathematically convenient assumption that happens to be irrelevant for the vast majority of households. The assumption is that all of our economic resources are in the form of financial assets, which we are free to invest in whatever financial securities we'd like. In fact, for most young folks, the majority of economic resources is represented by future labor earnings. For most old folks, the majority of economic resources is represented by claims to future Social Security, Medicare, and, if needed, Medicaid benefits.

So most of our economic resources are in forms that we can neither sell nor invest (a good thing for the spendthrifts among us). We can't, for example, sell our claims to future Social Security or private pension benefits and invest the proceeds in derivatives. This fact has important implications for how we allocate the resources that we can invest—namely, our liquid financial assets.

The most important implication is this: as we age, we should change how we invest our financial assets (the resources we can invest) in light of the resources we can't invest (our current and future labor income, pension income, and government benefits net of taxes).

This means that our financial portfolios should change over time—but not in the way the financial industry, which is selling us life-cycle funds, suggests. The funds on the market neither change appropriately with age nor utilize the right bonds to reduce risk. What they do offer is oversimplicity, which makes for easy marketing. The unfortunate disadvantage of investing based on life resources is that it is complicated. And messy. And it's truly meaningful only if it can be hand tailored.

The fundamental mistakes of the life-cycle funds do not, however, preclude the industry from selling them at handsome expense ratios. While federal employees can invest in life-cycle funds at an annual cost of 3 basis points (.03 percent) of assets, the best deals available to most 401(k) participants come from Fidelity, T. Rowe Price, and Vanguard. They charge as much as twenty-five times more. Other fund companies charge still more.

Takeaways

- Nobel laureates Paul Samuelson and Robert Merton independently developed the basic economic model of portfolio choice.
- The basic economic model assumes that all economic resources are marketable or tradeable.
- The basic economic model recommends diversification, with the share of risky assets depending on your concern about risk.

- The basic economic model recommends no change in one's portfolio with age.
- But the basic model's assumption that all resources are marketable doesn't hold.
- Consequently, as we age, we need to diversify the resources we *can* diversify, based, in part, on the resources we *can't* diversify.

32. Diversify Your Resources, Not Your Portfolio

WHAT HAPPENS TO our *total* economic resources, not just our financial assets, determines the average level and variability of our living standard over time. By "economic resources," we're referring to your current and future income from working, your current and future employer-provided pension benefits, your portfolios of regular and retirement account assets, the equity in your homes and real estate holdings, and your current and future government benefits net of current and future taxes. Indeed, *diversify your total resources, not your portfolio, stupid* is the common thread of much current research in finance that previously seemed to have missed Samuelson's and Merton's broader point.

Their broader point is that the allocation of one's *total* resources between safe and risky assets should be independent of one's age.

Understanding that you are investing your overall resources, not just your portfolio, can dramatically change the way you think about asset allocation. Let us help you down this path by transposing you into someone else—namely, Justin, a thirty-year-old ne'er-do-well.

You/Justin have a $1 million inheritance you can invest as you please and a $1 million trust fund that pays you two things: $20,000 a year after inflation and $1 million you'll receive in thirty years, also adjusted for inflation. You like to roll the dice, but having been burned many times in the past, you've decided that the best investment strategy entails a 50-50 split between stocks and bonds, specifically long-term TIPs. Given this, how should you invest your portfolio—the $1 million inheritance over which you have discretion?

Your first instinct is to invest half of it in TIPs and half in stock. But then you realize that your trust fund is no different from an investment in TIPs. Indeed, after calling the trustee, you discover that the $1 million fund is, in fact, invested exclusively in thirty-year TIPs yielding 2 percent real. You're not surprised. It was left to you by your dear Aunt Flora, who was fairly cautious.

If you follow your first instinct and invest half your $1 million portfolio in stock and half in TIPs, your portfolio will be invested 50-50, but your $2 million in *total economic resources,* which includes the trust fund, will be invested 25-75. You'll have $500K in stock in your portfolio and $1.5 million in bonds, with $500K of these bonds being held in your portfolio and $1 million of these bonds effectively being held in your trust fund. So your portfolio will be "properly" diversified, but your resources will not. Scott regularly gets reader e-mail asking whether to count pensions and Social Security as financial assets, an indication that lots of people think planning is about resources, not just financial assets.

Now, suppose you invest 100 percent of your portfolio in stock. In this case, your portfolio will be completely undiversified, but your total resources—the inheritance plus the trust fund—will be diversified in the 50-50 proportion you favor. In this case, diversifying your resources requires *un*diversifying your portfolio.

Next suppose that Aunt Flora instructed your trust's trustee, Uncle Bernie, differently. Suppose she told Bernie to invest the trust 30 percent in stocks and 70 percent in TIPs, but then to reduce the share invested in stocks by 1 percentage point each year for the next thirty years so that by the end of the thirty years, the trust would be invested fully in TIPs. In this case, to achieve the desired constant 50-50 stocks-TIPs allocation of your total resources, you'll need to initially allocate your portfolio 70-30 stocks-TIPs and increase the share invested in stock each year for the next thirty by 1 percentage point. Doing this violates the Samuelson-Merton prescription regarding holding your portfolio allocation constant as you age, but it fully accords with their prescription *if you simply apply it to your total resources*.

Labor Earnings and Government Benefits

If you think about it, your earnings capacity and claims to government benefits, be they Social Security, welfare, or medical benefits, are quite similar in many respects to Justin's trust fund. They are nonmarketable assets that provide a return in the form of income (albeit, in some cases, in-kind income) that ranges from being very safe to highly uncertain but either way is not very well correlated with the return on stock. From that perspective, these nonmarketable assets are similar to TIPs in their return properties. And our financial mantra—*diversify your resources, not your portfolio*—applies to resources defined to include *all* nonmarketable and marketable sources of spending power.

For illustrative purposes, assume that you're middle-aged and that your resources consist of some financial assets plus your current and future labor income and old-age government benefits. Further assume that these nonfinancial resources are perfectly safe. In this case, you'll want to hold much and, depending on your aversion to risk, potentially all of your financial assets in stock because you have so much of your other resources tied up in what are for all intent and purposes TIPs.

Of course, you don't have access today to all your future nonfinancial income flows. When you are young, your labor earnings grow, if you're like most workers, and peak around age forty-eight. After that they decline through retirement. Once you retire, Social Security and Medicare kick in. So if you think of these nonmarketable resources (labor income, Social Security) as implicit holdings of TIPs, the amounts of these implicit holdings of TIPs rise through middle age, then fall as you approach retirement, and then rise again in retirement.

The right way to measure these remaining future holdings at any point in your lifetime is in terms of their present discounted value. Consider, for example, the present value of your labor earnings. When you're, say, twenty-eight, the present value of your labor earnings is less than when you're, say, thirty-eight, when you're closer in time to your peak earning years. At fifty-eight the present value of your earnings is less than at thirty-eight because your earnings are below their peak and won't continue for much longer.

The other key factor that determines the relative size of your financial assets (your marketable/investable resources) and your nonmarketable TIPs-like resources is simply how much of the former you accumulate and expend over time. As you approach retirement, you naturally build up financial assets to help pay for your old age. As you proceed through retirement, you naturally spend down these assets. During the preretirement saving phase, you are raising the ratio of financial assets to nonmarketable assets. During the postretirement spending phase, you are lowering this ratio.

Consequently, sticking to the Samuelson-Merton rule of maintaining through time fixed shares of your total resources in stocks and bonds (either explicit or implicit) requires increasing through middle age the share of your financial assets invested in stock, then reducing the share leading up to retirement, and then increasing the share once you're retired—with the actual share, again, depending on your degree of risk aversion.

Thus, the economic prescription for your life-cycle pattern of stock holding by age is at odds with that generated by standard life-cycle funds. In such funds, the equity share of assets starts high and declines smoothly over time. It doesn't rise, fall, and then rise again, as Samuelson and Merton tell us it should.

Of course, what major financial institution would dare tell the elderly that they should increase their equity position as they age?

This runs completely counter to traditional financial advice. But, as we've seen, traditional financial advice runs completely counter to *proper* economic advice.

Parenthetically, you should be aware that the typical life-cycle fund, in addition to providing the wrong pattern of equity shares with age, uses nominal bonds (standard bonds, the coupon payment of which is not indexed for inflation), as opposed to TIPs, to reduce risk. But nominal bonds, particularly long-term nominal bonds, are highly risky because of the potential for high future inflation. This potential is really a presumption, given the prospect of the U.S. government's dealing with its impending fiscal/financial insolvency by printing money and thereby running a very high inflation that would dramatically water down the payoff to long-term nominal (conventional) bonds.

Uncertain Labor Earnings and Government Benefits

So far we've claimed that Samuelson and Merton were right, then wrong, then right. They were right in arguing that our stock-bond mix shouldn't vary with age; wrong in assuming that our portfolios of marketable financial assets constituted all our economic resources; and right if we extend their analysis to all our economic resources. Doing so tells us to diversify our resources, not our portfolios.

Now we're going to assert that Samuelson's and Merton's advice that the stock-bond mix of our total resources remain perfectly fixed as we age is no longer correct if you take into account two factors: (1) the uncertainty of our future labor earnings, government benefits, and health expenditures; and (2) the prevalence of liquidity constraints.

These factors make a real dent in the Samuelson-Merton analysis. When we include them, economics no longer recommends a fixed asset allocation by age of your overall remaining economic resources, let alone a fixed allocation of your financial assets through time. The first economists to point this out were—get this—Samuelson and Merton together with Zvi Bodie. However, the Samuelson isn't Paul Samuelson, but Bill Samuelson, one of Paul's sons. Both he and Zvi are finance professors at Boston University's School of Management.

The general message of this more recent research is to reduce the share of your total resources held in stock when you face more uncertainty and when you are liquidity constrained. Our earnings are most uncertain when we are young. We're also most likely to be liquidity constrained when young. Both points suggest an even lower share of stock in our financial portfolios (our marketable resources) when we're young.

Uncertainty about benefits is greatest in our late forties and fifties, when the benefits are close enough to smell and big enough to matter, but not yet available to touch. Once we hit our golden years and start collecting these benefits, it's not likely that the government will snatch them away. This pattern of benefit uncertainty with age suggests reducing your stock holdings as you approach retirement but increasing them thereafter.*

Health expenditure uncertainty is greatest when we reach older old age, roughly age eighty. This uncertainty suggests a smaller allocation to stocks in our advanced years.

Where do these new considerations—uncertainty in earnings, benefits, and health expenditures, as well as liquidity constraints—leave us?

They leave us with the following roller-coaster portfolio prescription for asset allocation with age: When young, invest a small to moderate share of your financial assets in stock. Increase this share dramatically in middle age. Reduce this share as you approach re-

---

* One indication that this idea is moving from deepest academia toward practice is a recent study done for the Research Foundation of the CFA Institute. Written by Roger G. Ibbotson, Moshe A. Milevsky, Peng Chen, and Kevin X. Zhu, *Lifetime Financial Advice: Human Capital, Asset Allocation, and Insurance* may be the first book to try to integrate the idea of human capital into our use of financial assets over our lifetime. It's a long way from being conventional wisdom, but it's likely to be seen as the first attempt to put long-accepted theory into practice. Please note: No need to buy it. *Lifetime Financial Advice: Human Capital, Asset Allocation, and Insurance* is available as a free download on the CFA Institute's Web site at www.cfapubs.org/toc/rf/2007/2007/1.

tirement. Increase the share modestly in early retirement, and reduce this share dramatically in late retirement.

Also, at any age, set the stock share based on your risk aversion. If your risk aversion is high, make your roller coaster very flat, meaning that you should hold TIPs exclusively or almost exclusively.

Figure 2. The Roller-coaster Portfolio Prescription

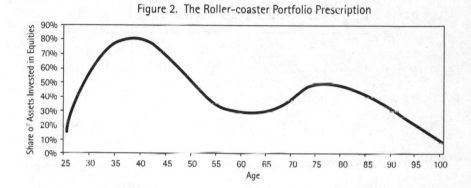

33. Spending Down

MANAGING YOUR MONEY in line with consumption smoothing has three aspects: determining your portfolio allocation, determining how it should change through time, and determining how much to spend each year. Bungling these decisions when you're young is less problematic than doing so when you're old. There's always the option of working harder and longer to make up for mistakes when you're young. And when you are young, you have only modest amounts of savings at risk.

When you're old, things get a lot trickier. Riding the stock market can, as we've seen, continue to make sense, especially for lower-income households with more downside protection from Uncle Sam. But don't take our word for it. If you are retired and reading this, make sure you think through the deepest living-standard downside of investing in anything risky.

By "downside" we refer, of course, to a major decline in your *living standard*. This can happen to the nicest retirees even if they invest solely in TIPs and never experience any uninsured medical or nursing home bills. All they need do is spend too much or too little.

Spend too much you understand. But spend too little? How can that be risky for a retiree? Well, bear in mind that retirees had a life before they retired, and if they needlessly underspend in retirement, they will be the instruments of their own pre- to post-retirement living-standard decline. Yes, there is a risk of running out of money and suffering a decline in your living standard. There's also a risk of never spending your money and dying rich. Think of Scrooge McDuck having a heart attack while swimming in his pool of cash.

The 4 Percent Rule of Dumb

The investment/planning nexus will tell you that the smart asset-spending rate—the ratio of fixed annual real retirement spending to the value of your assets *as of the date of retirement*—is 4 percent no matter how long you might live, the nature of your investments, the size of your Social Security benefits, whether you have a pension, whether the kids are still in college, the age of your spouse, the mix of your assets between taxable and nontaxable, your off-the-top housing expenses, your taxes, and so on. (While this is the broad rule-of thumb rate, it should be noted that financial planners such as William Bengen have devised simple rules that allow significantly higher, "safe" withdrawal rates. The real problem with any of these rules, however, is that they treat the portfolio in a vacuum and ignore all other life resources.)

Remarkably, this strategy of spending 4 percent of your *initial* retirement assets each year come hell or high water makes no sense even for a single person with no Social Security, no housing expenses, no Medicare premiums to pay, no tax obligations, no kids, no nothing except for a cool $1 million that she can invest with no risk whatsoever at 3 percent real from her current age of sixty-five right through age one hundred—her maximum age of life.

The 4 percent spending rule for this person—let's call her Sally— implies annual consumption of $40,000 though age one hundred. The appropriate consumption-smoothing spending level, in contrast, is $46,565. If Sally follows the 4 percent rule, spends only $40,000 each year, and makes it to one hundred, she'll enjoy a living standard that's 14 percent lower than it need be for thirty-five years, and she'll leave close to $330,248 in unspent assets (measured in today's dollars) when she dies.

Now, who does this benefit? Maybe the company or person managing those assets?

What if Sally has Social Security benefits ($15K per year) and housing expenses ($5,500 per year) and pays taxes (including Alabama state income taxes) and Medicare Part B premiums? In this case, her annual spending on consumption plus housing is not $46,565, but $49,871. But that good ol' spend-down rule doesn't change a bit. It still says to spend $40,000. Were Sally to follow it, she'd experience a 22.2 percent lower living standard every year of her life and leave over $450,000 (in today's dollars) unspent at age one hundred.

And what should we make of *initial* retirement assets? If Sally retires on January 1 and her assets are $1 million, but the market crashes the next day, leaving her assets at $800,000 (because she was just about to switch to TIPs), is the rule telling her to spend 4 percent of $1 million ($40K) in each of next thirty-five years, or is it telling her to spend 4 percent of $800,000 ($32K) for the next thirty-five years?

There's a big—20 percent—difference between the two spending recommendations. If the market doesn't recover or Sally switches to TIPs on January 2 but sticks to the "spend $40K a year" rule, she'll come up broke well before reaching one hundred.

Would the rule work better if it were "spend 4 percent of your *remaining* assets each year" instead of "spend 4 percent of your *initial* assets"? Many people, hearing the rule but missing the emphasis on *initial* assets, are likely to get the latter version into their brains rather than the former.

"Spend 4 percent of your remaining assets" at least tells you to adjust your spending up and down as market forces move their value. But this alternative rule raises its own problems. If you think about it, consumption smoothing implies a constant level of spending by Sally over time as well as a declining amount of assets over time. So consumption smoothing says that Sally's spending rate—the ratio of her constant spending to her declining assets—should rise over time, not remain permanently at 4 percent. Indeed, in the no-nothing case, the ratio starts at 4.6 when Sally is age sixty-five, reaches 5.7 when she's seventy-five, hits 8.3 when she's eighty-five, equals 21.8 when she's ninety-five, and culminates at 100.0 at one hundred—Sally's terminal year.

Were Sally to follow the modified "spend 4 percent of your remaining assets" each year, she'd clearly violate consumption smoothing. Her living standard would start at $40,000 at age sixty-five and decline each year, reaching $32,000 at age eighty-five and ending up just above $27,000 at age one hundred. Thanks to her ever-greater underspending, Sally would end up at age one hundred with over $680,000 in unspent assets.

Consumption-Smoothing Spending Rates

As we've just indicated, consumption smoothing in retirement doesn't entail spending each year 4 percent of your initial retirement assets. Nor does it entail spending each year 4 percent of your current financial assets. Consumption smoothing synthesizes all of your life resources and calculates a time path of withdrawals from financial resources that will sustain a smooth living standard. So if Sally also has a $50,000-per-year non-taxable inflation-indexed pension, her annual sustainable consumption rises from the $46,565 sustainable amount from her investments to $96,565.

As another example, suppose that Sally has no pension but invests all of her assets in stocks rather than in TIPs (which we assumed were yielding 3 percent). Does consumption smoothing still say to spend $46,565 at age sixty-five, which was based on the TIPs return? Or does it say to spend more because Sally can expect to earn more than the TIPs rate? Or does it say to spend less because the return on stocks is uncertain?

The answer is certainly not to spend the same amount when holding stocks as when holding TIPs. But whether to spend more or less depends on Sally's degree of risk aversion—her concern about the downside.* But even moderate concern for the downside will lead Sally to be *really* cautious about how much she spends.

What constitutes "really cautious"? Try this: Plugging such a degree of risk aversion into the appropriate Samuelson-Merton-type formula, we find that Sally's spending rate at age sixty-five should be 3.2 percent rather than 4.6 percent if she holds large-cap stocks. So instead of being able to spend more because she is targeting a higher return, she actually has to spend less—if she wants to be sure to avoid a very painful downside. The good news is that this stock-holding spending rate will also rise with age and is extremely sensitive to what else is going on in Sally's economic life. For example, if Sally were to have a $50K inflation-indexed pension, her proper spending rate at age sixty-five for an all-large-cap stock portfolio would be dramatically higher than 3.2 percent.

Although there are no simple rules of thumb to use in setting your spending rate, setting it right can make an absolutely huge difference in your future living standard. As we'll next discuss, this is particularly the case if you invest in risky securities. But before pushing on, let us summarize.

Takeaways

- "Spend annually in retirement 4 percent of your initial assets" is a really dumb rule of dumb.

---

* Economists assume that people get utility (pleasure) out of their living standard, but because of diminishing returns (recall the six-year-old becoming sated on cupcakes) the loss in utility from suffering a given reduction in consumption exceeds the gain in utility from an equal-size increase in consumption. This heightened concern about downside risk is called *risk aversion*.

- "Spend annually in retirement 4 percent of your current assets" is an equally dumb rule of dumb.
- Consumption smoothing implies a rising ratio of spending to current assets in retirement.
- Spending rates consistent with consumption smoothing depend on a plethora of factors. In particular, your proper spending rate depends critically on what assets you hold and the riskiness of your nonfinancial resources.

34. Beware of Averages

WE HOPE THAT most retirees have the good sense to ignore the strict 4 percent drawdown rule. Sadly, those who do ignore it run the risk of selecting an even more dangerous spend-down strategy. Take Sally's twin sister, Ruth, who invested all her money in the stock market when young and was lucky enough to end up at sixty-five with $2 million in assets—twice Sally's stash. Ruth is a student of the stock market and knows that since 1926, large caps have returned 9.1 percent per year on average after inflation. During her own years of investing, the S&P averaged an even higher return, so Ruth is confident that the true average lies above 9.1 percent. In any case, she thinks it's prudent to assume she'll earn at least a 9.1 percent real return, on average, throughout her retirement.

Ruth has a degree in accounting and is mighty quick with a hand calculator. For simplicity, let's assume that she lives in the nothing-but-assets world mentioned in the last chapter. After some tinkering on her calculator, Ruth figures out that if she's able to earn 9.1 percent real each year, she can spend $195,359 each year. (Remember, she's going to be spending some of her principal each year.) Mind you, this spending level is over twice the $93,130 she can actually spend *for sure* each year were she to invest in TIPs yielding, we'll assume, a certain 3 percent after inflation.

The problem with Ruth's thinking and spending plan is that she's forgetting that the return on large-cap stocks is both irregular and highly skewed, meaning that there is a higher probability of receiving returns below 9.1 percent than there is of receiving returns above 9.1 percent. Moreover, the probability of getting very low returns is much higher than that of getting very high returns. Consequently, if Ruth pursues this spending strategy over time—always spending out of her remaining assets based on the 9.1 percent average—the chances get larger and larger that her living standard will get smaller and smaller.

Figure 3 below shows what awaits Ruth as she follows her spend-down strategy. The vertical axis shows Ruth's living standard (expressed in thousands of dollars), and the horizontal axis shows the remaining years of her life. The flat horizontal line in the middle—the projected trajectory—shows the $195,359 that Ruth, as of age sixty-five, thinks she'll be able to spend each year.

The top curve shows the potential upside. It shows, for any given year, that Ruth has a 5 percent chance of having a higher living standard than the living standard level demarcated by the height of the curve for that year.

Now look at the lowest square-dotted curve. It shows the downside of Ruth's spending strategy. If you start at a given year, go up to this curve and mark off its height, you'll learn that in that year Ruth's living standard has a 5 percent chance of being below that height. The other curves have the same interpretation if you substitute 25 percent, 50 percent, and 75 percent, respectively, for 5 percent.

Here's the problem: four of the five percentile curves head down-

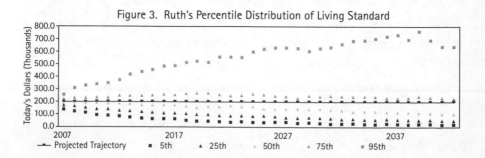

Figure 3. Ruth's Percentile Distribution of Living Standard

hill. So with each passing year, Ruth's chances of having a low living standard increase. For example, at age seventy-five Ruth's living standard will be below $56,452 (the height of the bottom square curve in that year) 5 percent of the time. At age eighty-five her living standard will be below $32,757 5 percent of the time. Both the $56,452 and the $32,757 (let alone values below them) are far below the $195,359 Ruth expected to be able to spend each year. More important, they are also well below the $93,130 Ruth could spend for sure were she to invest solely in TIPs.

What could lead to such bad times for Ruth? Answer: a run of below-average rates of return on her stocks combined with her far too aggressive spend-down behavior. Each year under this scenario, Ruth eats up too much of her remaining assets and discovers that the market has failed her yet again. She is repeatedly forced to drop her living standard because when she goes to spend a big chunk of her remaining wealth, she'll find there isn't much there.

The 5th percentile outcomes occur, of course, only 5 percent of the time. So let's consider the 25th and 50th percentile outcomes for Ruth at age seventy-five. According to the chart, 25 percent of the time Ruth's living standard at age seventy-five will be below $104,661, and 50 percent of the time it will be south of $168,433. At age eighty-five these 25th and 50th percentile values are $75,793 and $138,031.

All this means that Ruth has a very good chance of experiencing major consumption disruption—a giant drop in living standard—if she sticks blindly to her trust in averages and ignores the substantial variability and skew of stock returns.

This was, we should tell you, foreordained. Ruth, you see, decided in college that statistics was too boring a subject with which to bother. She took history of the opera instead.

A Parallel Universe

From what we gather, there are serious physicists who believe strongly in the likelihood of a near infinity of parallel universes, some of which differ from our own only in minor details. So let's consider the particular parallel universe in which Ruth took statistics instead of the history of the opera. This led Ruth to courses in economics and an eventual PhD in the subject. With this PhD, Dr. Ruth was able to absorb Samuelson's and Merton's work and quickly realize that her old-age living-standard risk depended both on what assets she held in retirement and how aggressively she spent down (and, thus, withdrew) those assets.

In this alternative universe, Dr. Ruth, at age sixty-five, chooses (in the nothing-but-assets setting) to spend not $195,359 but only $64,090—the amount suggested by Samuelson's and Merton's work. As table 6 shows, Dr. Ruth maintains much more conservative spending rates (spending as a share of wealth) than Ruth right through age one hundred.

TABLE 6. COMPARING DR. RUTH'S AND RUTH'S SPENDING RATES

Age	Dr. Ruth's Spending Rate	Ruth's Spending Rate
65	3.2%	9.5%
75	4.3%	10.2%
85	6.6%	12.4%
95	17.0%	25.7%

Figure 4 is the counterpart to figure 3 but based on Dr. Ruth's spending behavior. Dr. Ruth's initial spending of $64,090 starts at a dra-

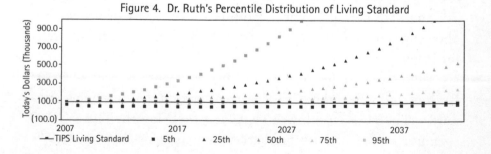

Figure 4. Dr. Ruth's Percentile Distribution of Living Standard

matically lower level than Ruth's $195,359 amount. Indeed, the $64,090 is almost one-third below the TIPs $93,103 spending level denoted by figure 4's solid black line. This completely changes the nature of Dr. Ruth's living-standard risk. Now all five percentile curves head uphill rather than four or five heading downhill.

Dr. Ruth is making her stock investment work for her by spending prudently. She realizes that investing in stocks is very risky. In light of this risk, she intentionally cuts her initial spending to limit her future downside. But the reason she invests in stocks in the first place is for the upside, and figure 4 shows that the upside of such prudent spending can be very large indeed. Recall that spending at any age equals Dr. Ruth's quite low spending rate multiplied by her wealth at that age. But if she ends up, at a given age, with a huge amount of wealth due to high past returns and spending forbearance, she'll get to consume a great deal because she'll be multiplying a low spending rate by a very big value of wealth.

Consider the 75th percentile value at age eighty. It's $263,740, meaning that a quarter of the time, Dr. Ruth's living standard will be above $263,740, which is almost three times the TIPs living standard. The 95th percentile shows that 5 percent of the time, Dr. Ruth's age eighty living standard will be north of $550,256.

No question, Dr. Ruth's upside looks great, given this spending behavior. But does this strategy of holding stock, but spending cautiously, clearly dominate the option of holding TIPs and not having to worry about what one spends each period?

The answer is no. TIPs are certainly not dominated. First of all, if she goes with stocks, Dr. Ruth consumes almost one-third less in the very short term than she does if she goes with TIPs. Secondly, the 5th and 25th percentile curves both lie either below or just slightly above the TIPs line and, in the case of the 5th percentile curve, pretty far below.

Although the scale of the chart makes it hard to see, when Dr. Ruth is eighty-five, there is a 5 percent chance that her living standard will be $45,476 or lower. That's very far below the TIPs $93,103 spending level. The 25th percentile value at age eighty is $94,879.

This means that one-quarter of the time, Dr. Ruth will be, roughly speaking, living at roughly the same or a lower level than she would have enjoyed by investing in TIPs! Of course, three-quarters of the time she'll be doing better, and that may—repeat, may—be worth the gamble. There's an important message here: stocks can be pretty damn risky even if you spend very prudently while holding them.

Telepathy

If parallel universes exist, maybe Dr. Ruth could communicate with Ruth in ways that might appear to both as telepathy. If so, Dr. Ruth would surely tell Ruth that she's completely nuts investing just in stocks and spending at the rate she's spending. Ruth would respond, of course, that averages occur on average, and they will for her as well. Like most people, Ruth doesn't feel comfortable thinking about her life as a big probability table. She'd rather focus on the average and hope for the best. But Dr. Ruth would reply that Ruth should put at least half her money in TIPs and base her spending on the average of the stock and TIP return if she's so stuck on averages.

Maybe this did happen, because Ruth woke up one morning and sold half of her stock and bought TIPs with the proceeds. As a result, her living-standard level/variability diagram now looks like the figure below:

Figure 5 looks a lot like figure 4, but the scales have changed. Careful examination shows that figure 5 entails much less upside as

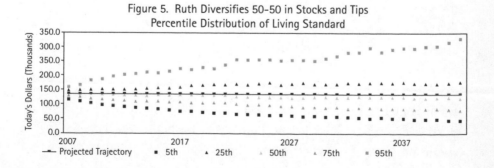

Figure 5. Ruth Diversifies 50-50 in Stocks and Tips
Percentile Distribution of Living Standard

well as downside risk. For example, if Ruth invests solely in stocks, she can expect, at age seventy-five, to spend $56,452 or less 5 percent of the time. But if she diversifies, the downside is reduced, and the worst 5 percent of outcomes, as of age seventy-five, start higher—at $74,272. The upside is also moderated. In figure 3, the top 5th percentile value at age seventy-five is $488,276. It's only $233,722 in figure 5.

True, Ruth now starts out spending $135,614, not $195,359. But she's drinking less and saving money on the Valium co-pays.

Takeaways

- Your living-standard risk depends on the riskiness of your resources and your spending rate.
- Economics says spend defensively if you invest aggressively.
- Don't consider only average returns in setting your spending rate. Worry about the downside, too.
- Failure to spend cautiously can make stocks extremely risky in the long run.
- Holding stocks can be highly risky in the long run even with very cautious spending.

35. Portfolio Choice

FIGURES 3, 4, AND 5 in the preceding chapter may not look like much, but diagrams like this represent a true revolution in portfolio analysis. They provide us with the means to make spending decisions and portfolio choices based on what really counts—not the statistical properties of our portfolio returns per se, but the level and variability of our actual living standards in the future.

We mention the statistical properties of portfolio returns, specifically the mean (average) portfolio return and its variance (variability), for a reason. These two variables alone have formed the basis of portfolio analysis by the financial planning and investment industry for decades. If financial planners learn anything about portfolio choice in their certification programs, it's based on the *mean-variance frontier* (also called the *risk-return frontier*)—a diagram showing the highest portfolio return that you can expect on average to receive over a period of time if you're willing to live with a given amount of risk.

Each point on the frontier corresponds to a different portfolio—a different combination of stocks and bonds. For example, combining stocks with bonds in a 60-40 split is one portfolio and is associated with one point on the frontier. A 55–45 split is another portfolio and is associated with another point. If *all* your resources are financial, the mean-variance frontier is really a mean-variance frontier for the total resources you'll end up with after a year. And since total resources determine how much you get to spend, the mean-variance return frontier also constitutes a mean-variance living-standard frontier.

Moreover, in the simple Samuelson-Merton "all resources are financial assets" world, each year looks like the next, so the same mean-variance frontier can be consulted whether you're age thirty-seven or age eighty-two. In this framework, portfolio choice comes down to choosing a point (the same point each year) on this frontier and then finding the particular portfolio associated with that point.

That's the simple world that Samuelson, Merton, and other economists assumed in the 1950s, 1960s, and 1970s in order to develop some basic financial theory. *But it's not the world we live in.* As we discussed earlier, most of our resources aren't financial assets, so they can't be diversified. They can't be sold in exchange for (swapped for) other assets with different risk-return properties. And because we have lots of nonmarketable assets whose sizes and composition change over time, one year is not like every other year. When we're age thirty, we have earnings but no Social Security. When we're eighty, it's the reverse. Consequently, the conventional risk-return frontier graph doesn't show us our risk-return living-standard frontier. It is a small part of a much larger picture.

In contrast to the standard mean-variance frontier, the new *living-standard risk diagram* provides a dynamic picture of what can happen to our bottom line—our living standard. This is very important. The idea (and implementation) of living-standard risk amounts to what radio personality Paul Harvey calls "the rest of the story." It also tells us that the proper place for the traditional mean-variance frontier diagram isn't in personal financial planning. It is more appropriate for strictly financial entities such as pension funds and endowments.

Consider Dr. Ruth. By checking figure 4 she can determine whether the highly likely long-run gain from investing in stocks coupled with spending prudence is worth the downside risk when compared to

(1) simply investing in TIPs, (2) not having to take a short-run living-standard cut, and (3) not having to worry about losing her blouse in the market.

Economics analysis alone can't tell Dr. Ruth if the sure-thing TIPs line in figure 4 beats the initially low but sharply upward-tilted percentile living-standard curves. Nor can it tell her whether she should hold stocks and TIPs in a 50-50 or some other diversified ratio. She must apply her own feelings, preferences, tolerance for risk, impatience, and other factors. But for the first time, she can actually see in a simple diagram what's involved in her choice—the average level and variability of her living standard.

Moreover, by comparing figures 3 and 4, Dr. Ruth sees that stocks can be extremely risky in the long run if one doesn't spend cautiously. She also sees that successful risky investing mandates conservative spending. She has to make a short-run sacrifice to help raise her chances of living like a queen down the road.

The Best of Times and the Worst of Times

Dr. Ruth also realizes that even if she does really well, on average, in the stock market, she's not going to do well every year. That's hoping for too much. There will be some years with really poor returns and some years with fantastic returns. In years when returns are really poor, she'll have to cut back her spending, and in years when they are really good, she'll be able to raise her spending. Hence, by investing in stock, Dr. Ruth knows she's going to experience a pretty bumpy living standard even if things work out as hoped.*

The Curse of Dimensionality

As more and better consumption-smoothing tools are developed for commercial use, you will be better able to judge explicit portfolio recommendations. Such tools are already in full use by economic

---

* ESPlanner's Monte Carlo trajectory reports show these living standard bumps.

researchers. The new tools will show you the living-standard risks arising from the combination of uncertain earnings, life span, investment returns, health expenditures, and even government policy. They'll also figure out your best risk-mitigating and risk-taking moves, given these types of uncertainties and your tolerance for risk.

The new tools will go a long way in helping you manage risk, including providing portfolio advice with respect to holding stocks, bonds, real estate, foreign equities, and other broad classes of risky assets.* But economics will never be able to deal fully with all the risks you face or help you pick individual stocks or mutual funds. There is too much uncertainty. And there are too many individual assets to consider.

Economists call this computation problem *the curse of dimensionality*. It sets real limits to the questions that economists or anyone else (particularly your stockbroker) can answer.

Takeaways

- The average level and variability of your living standard are key to assessing risky investing.
- Economic software can now generate dynamic mean-variability living-standard diagrams.
- Traditional portfolio analysis has been based on the static risk-return financial assets frontier.
- The traditional risk-return financial assets frontier assumes a world that doesn't exist—one in which all our resources are marketable.
- Investing in risky assets entails a bumpy living-standard ride even when one's assets generally perform well over time.

---

* ESPlanner is being modified to incorporate the aforementioned uncertainties as well as to provide general portfolio guidance.

36. Public Policy Risk

ONCE YOU EXPAND your view from portfolio risk to living-standard risk, you open the door to considering the impact of changes in public policy that can have a major effect on your living standard. Remember, you have to have accumulated substantial wealth in financial assets before programs like Social Security and Medicare are reduced to a small portion of your overall standard of living. For most people—at least 90 percent of all households—changes in Medicare benefits or in the formula for Social Security benefits are likely to have a bigger impact on their smooth-consumption path than changes in interest rates, the price-to-earnings multiple of common stocks, or other financial changes.

That's why the greatest vulnerability of most Americans isn't to gyrations in the stock market or even to declines in the housing market, but to public policy. Our government has promised far more in benefits than it will ever receive in taxes. At some point, this must change. The more we rely on government benefits, the more we imperil our futures.

The fiscal gap—the difference between the government's projected future spending and taxes, measured in present value—exceeds $70 trillion. That is far greater than the net worth of all

Americans put together.* The problem can be traced to two events. First, 77 million baby boomers will retire over the next twenty-five years. Our elderly population will more than double. Second, we'll be spending more money on each elderly person. By 2030 the government expects to pay, on average, at least $50,000 (measured in today's dollars) to each surviving boomer in Medicare, Medicaid, and Social Security (MMS) benefits annually. The change will more than double the percentage of gross domestic product (GDP) spent on the elderly.

How big is $70 trillion, really? Well, consider the immediate and permanent tax hikes or spending cuts needed to eliminate it. The options include an 80 percent increase in personal and corporate income taxes, a 120 percent hike in payroll taxes, the complete elimination of federal discretionary spending, and a 50 percent cut in Social Security and Medicare benefits. Adopting any one of these policies or any combination of them would be incredibly painful.

What about economic growth? Can the United States outgrow its obligations? Theoretically, yes; practically, no. The postwar norm is for oldsters' benefits to grow roughly twice as fast as the economy. There are, of course, radical ways to restructure U.S. entitlements to limit benefit growth and save the day. But so far neither the voting public nor the folks we elect have shown any interest in change.

---

* This $70 trillion estimate of Uncle Sam's fiscal gap comes by way of a highly reliable source: the U.S. Treasury Department. Former Federal Reserve and Treasury economists Jagadeesh Gokhale and Kent Smetters initially measured the U.S. fiscal gap in a highly detailed 2002 U.S. Treasury study, "Fiscal and Generational Imbalances," commissioned by then Treasury Secretary Paul O'Neill and then Federal Reserve Chairman Alan Greenspan. Their study, which showed a $45 trillion gap, was censored the day O'Neill was fired by the White House. To their eternal credit, Gokhale and Smetters quit the government and published their study (see www.aei.org/books/bookID.426.filter.allbook detail. asp). Today, after more tax cuts, huge military and other discretionary spending hikes, the dramatic expansion of Medicare to cover prescription drugs, and the accrual of interest, the fiscal gap appears to lie above $70 trillion. This massive figure is, if anything, an underestimate, since it relies on highly optimistic longevity and health-care spending assumptions. Gokhale and Smetters's most recent fiscal gap study is posted on the National Bureau of Economic Research Web site at www.nber.org/papers/w11060. It reports a $63 trillion fiscal gap for 2005.

Japan, Italy, Germany, the U.K., and France all face far worse demographics than the U.S. But each country has enacted major pension reforms, and each has much better control of its health-care expenditures. In contrast, the U.S. has made no serious changes to Social Security since 1983, has a unique fee-for-service system in which most government health-care spending is on autopilot, and has recently taken steps to dramatically and permanently expand its health-care spending. Add it all up, and the U.S. may be in worse fiscal shape than countries like Turkey, Mexico, Brazil, Russia, and Argentina, which have reputations as fiscal miscreants.

Public policy risk also means financial market risk. We believe the future holds more inflation and higher taxes, with the attendant effect on financial assets. Others believe the issues can be handled, though we think they are relying on the tooth fairy. Either way, consumption-smoothing software allows us to test the impact of possible policy changes on our long-term living standard.

Hedging Policy Risk

Public policy risk is something over which we seem to have the least control. You can't buy insurance against tax hikes, Social Security benefit cuts, or Medicare premium increases. On the other hand, you can modify your saving in light of their eventuality. Deciding to commit more of your saving to a Roth IRA, as discussed in chapters 15 and 16, is one possible option. Deciding to hold a long-term mortgage rather than paying it down is another. If inflation takes off, it will reduce the real value of your mortgage payments.

Some readers, more convinced of public policy risks, may want to be more aggressive about hedging that risk by investing in assets that will appreciate as a result of government fiscal woes. An example of such defensive investing is buying a financial security with a value that rises when interest rates rise. Larry bought such an asset several years back. He still holds it today. It's a mutual fund, called the Rydex Juno Fund, that invests in put options on long-term U.S.

Treasury bonds.* The fund does well when interest rates rise and long-term Treasurys do poorly.

Larry figured that Uncle Sam will have to print money to meet all the benefit promises he's made and that this will lead to higher interest rates, a lower value for bonds, and a higher value of the Rydex Juno Fund. So far, Larry has lost money year after year. Inflation has remained very low, and long-term interest rates have climbed only modestly.

We're not recommending that you adopt Larry's strategy. Scott didn't. He'd rather diversify than make a negative bet. What we are recommending is that you consider steps to limit the risks you face from unpleasant future policy changes.

For example, if you think that taxes are going to rise, particularly at the top end, consider:

- working more now, when the tax rates are relatively low
- contributing to a Roth rather than a regular retirement account
- converting your regular retirement accounts to a Roth
- withdrawing your regular retirement account assets before your Roth assets
- giving money to your kids if they are young now and will remain in a lower tax bracket
- buying a bigger home or putting on an addition (remember, the implicit rental income on owned homes isn't taxed)
- realizing the capital gains on your investment portfolio and real estate holdings
- withdrawing all of your regular retirement account assets before tax rates are raised

---

* A put option written on a stock or bond provides the owner of the option with the right to sell it at a prespecified price. For example, you might own a put on ABC Corp. that allows you to sell ten shares of ABC Corp. at $100 per share. If the price of ABC Corp. shares falls to $70, you can buy ten shares for $700 on the market and then exercise your option and sell them for $1,000, pocketing $300 on the transaction.

If you think that inflation will take off in the United States, consider investing more of your assets in:

- U.S. inflation-indexed bonds (TIPs)
- foreign equity index funds
- foreign inflation-indexed bonds
- commodities, minerals, natural resources, and other assets likely to be inflation proof
- real estate, including your own home

If you think Social Security and Medicare benefits will someday be cut or Medicare premiums will rise, consider:

- buying more inflation-indexed annuities
- buying long-term care insurance
- taking Social Security somewhat earlier
- buying stock in HMOs, nursing homes, drug companies, and other assets that do well when health-care costs rise

Takeaways

Preserving your living standard can be as important as earning it. Indeed, as you enter retirement, it becomes ever more important to anticipate the various downsides you may experience and attempt to insulate yourself from each. In particular, think about policy risk and how to avoid it. Specifically:

- Invest in assets that do well when Uncle Sam does poorly.
- Pay your taxes before Uncle Sam raises them.
- Lock in your benefits before Uncle Sam cuts them.
- Work with other family members to minimize the family's collective taxes.

37. Sell Your Boss Short (or Long)

OUR EMPLOYER-BASED SAVING system is melting down. Everywhere you look, you see a mess. Collectively, private-sector pension funds are underwater to the tune of $450 billion. State and local pension funds are short some $800 billion. That's $1.25 trillion in total! This situation didn't happen by accident. The federal government, with its own $11 trillion unfunded Social Security liability, has condoned the underfunding of private pensions for decades. It's also encouraged pension funds to invest in risky assets to cover their funding shortfalls. Those gambles generally haven't paid off. And it has sat silent as state and local governments turned pension underfunding into an art form.

Who's going to take the hit?

Not rich stockholders. They know how to protect their interests. No, it's America's workers and retirees. Over one million private pension participants have already watched their pension funds go belly-up. True, their pension benefits are "guaranteed" by the Pension Benefit Guaranty Corporation (PBGC), a government-established insurance company. But since the PBGC limits the amount of benefits it insures, most of these participants have seen or will see tremendous benefit cuts. And there's no guarantee of the PBGC's guarantee. The corporation is short $23 billion and needs another $150 billion to deal with pending defaults.

To be sure, most companies with pension plans are solvent and have enough assets to pay the benefits they legally owe. But these legal obligations, technically called accrued liabilities, are much smaller than what they have promised their workers.

What corporate America has promised their workers until now is this: "We're not paying you what you're producing now. But stick with us, and we'll pay you a lot more than you produce as you approach retirement. We'll do this through our pension benefit formula, which makes your pension accruals rise dramatically with your seniority." Economists refer to such informal promises as implicit long-term labor contracts. To improve retention and enhance work incentives, workers are underpaid when young and overpaid when old.

About 44 million American workers now participate in employer-provided pension plans. But these implicit contracts are now being ripped up left and right by the biggest, most profitable companies in the country. Verizon, Hewlett-Packard, Motorola, IBM, Sprint, Alcoa, Sears, Roebuck and Co., and DuPont are among the growing number of Fortune 500 companies that have frozen their pension plans, thereby denying their workers the ability to accrue additional pension benefits. In the opinion of many, they have swindled their workers.

Yes, many of these companies have increased their contributions to their workers' 401(k) plans. But their higher contributions are far less than the roughly 10 to 15 percent of pay needed to make their workers whole. The companies engaging in this great pension swindle claim they need to remain competitive. But the future accruals they are cutting represent payment for past work, not current or future work. The cuts are nothing less than legal theft, because the implicit contract was never written down in black and white and signed.

Virtually every company with a pension plan is now considering a freeze. The Pension Protection Act of 2006 will likely accelerate the trend. It requires companies with well-funded pensions to pay higher premiums to the PBGC to cover the losses of poorly funded ones. State and local governments are now copying this "best business practice." As we write, six states have already frozen their pension plans for new employees.

The demise of employer-provided pensions doesn't just mean worse work and retention incentives. It also puts millions of future retirees at much greater risk of outliving their money. Retiree and survivor pensions are, after all, generally paid as annuities—securities that keep paying until the recipient dies.

What about 401(k)s, IRAs, and other defined-contribution plans? Can't these accounts be converted into annuities at retirement and substituted for traditional pensions? Not quite. Many private-sector workers are either not covered by such plans, don't participate if they are covered, don't contribute much if they do participate (even accounting for employer contributions), don't invest sensibly, or won't use their assets to buy annuities when they hit retirement.

Here's the bottom line: Don't count on employer-provided pensions. Count even less on your employer-provided health insurance. There is nothing preventing employers from suddenly dropping this coverage, not only for their current workers but also for their retirees.

Healthy Balance Sheets or Healthy Workers?

Rising health-care costs are quite literally driving American companies broke. The average premium costs to employers of insuring the health expenses of their employees and their families is now over $12,000 per worker for large firms with large numbers of employers.

Collectively, American companies are now paying close to $500 billion each year in employee and retiree health insurance premiums and health expenditure claims (if the companies self-insure). It's no coincidence that Ford Motor Company is spending over $3 billion per year for health care for its retirees and current workers, that these costs are rising annually, in real terms, at roughly 6 percent, and that Ford is laying off 40 percent of its workforce.

Nor is it a coincidence that employers are starting to eliminate health insurance coverage for their workers. In 2000, 66 percent of nonelderly Americans were covered by employer-based health insurance. Today's figure is 59 percent. Employers that continue to offer their employees health insurance are asking them to pay for ever-larger shares of the premiums. As a consequence, millions of U.S. workers are declining coverage in their employer's plan, thereby swelling the ranks of the uninsured (currently 47 million). Employers are also cutting back on health insurance for retirees. Only 13 percent now offer such coverage. A decade ago the figure was 20 percent.

Hedging Your Employment Bet

Like public policy uncertainty, earnings uncertainty seems like another tough thing to hedge. Many, if not most of us, get fired, laid off, phased out, closed down, canned, pink-slipped, riffed, shown the door, given the boot, or declared redundant at some point in our careers. Even tenured professors can see their real earnings slip if their salaries aren't adjusted for inflation. The good news is that for all the millions of workers losing their jobs each year, there are other millions finding new ones. But finding a new job, particularly late in life, doesn't guarantee you'll get paid the same.

In recent years Scott has witnessed hundreds of journalist colleagues around the country handed corporate buyouts as newspapers lost advertising to the Internet. Scott thought himself lucky in wanting to retire just as the *Dallas Morning News,* owned by the Belo Corporation, was urging one-fifth of its employees to depart.

Now he wonders if he and his fellow employees would have had an offsetting defense had they taken a speculative gamble and bought Belo stock at the time of its restructuring. In keeping with the idea presented in this book—that our total resources are much broader than our financial assets—he wonders if it is too extreme to think

SPEND 'TIL THE END

about being short your employer's shares while being employed and buying them while leaving.

That's a bold step that we think few people would take. Scott, for example, sold his Belo shares years earlier, when he turned sixty. He did not do this out of prescience; he did it as a prudent move to minimize the risk exposure of his total resources (job and financial assets). He sold his company's stock in order to better diversify his overall resource position.

Remember, the worst of all worlds is to lose your job and see your assets sink at the same time. Another way to limit earnings risk is to spend your free time learning skills in areas completely different from your current area of work, which may come in handy if your own skills lose their value. It's worth noting, in this regard, that the U.S. Department of Labor, which keeps a close eye on career and job changes, counsels young workers to anticipate three to five major career changes during their work spans.

Takeaways

- Don't go down with the boss's ship.
- Diversify your earning capacity.

38. The Troll Under the Bridge

DRIVE SOUTH FROM Yuma, Arizona, and you're on a straight shot to El Golfo, an RV resort at the north end of the Sea of Cortez in Mexico. Just west of Yuma, a string of billboards advertises inexpensive dental work, cut-rate pharmaceuticals, and low-cost eyeglasses. The billboards lead to an isolated border crossing that takes you into Los Algodones, a tiny Mexican town devoted to serving the medical and margarita needs of older Americans.

Thousands of retirees regularly cross the border seeking inexpensive health-related treatments. They go from San Diego to Tijuana, from El Paso to Juárez, and from Brownsville to Matamoros. While those visits are usually short, there are also large enclaves of American expats living full-time all over Mexico and Central America. When Scott writes about retiring in Mexico, describing San Miguel de Allende, Lake Chapala, and other colonies, readers on the verge of retirement send in questions for months.

The primary question is always the same: Yes, yes, yes—but what about Medicare? How will I get my treasured Medicare benefits if I'm living in Mexico? Or Belize? Or Costa Rica? Or Panama?

The answer: you won't. If you want U.S. government–supported health-care benefits, you'll need to get your health-care services in the United States. Many of the expats organize their lives around regular medical trips back to the States, making the rounds of their various specialists, getting prescriptions renewed if necessary, and then heading back to Oaxaca, the suburbs of Puerto Vallarta and La Paz, and dozens of other communities where life is relatively inexpensive and simple.

The day is coming, however, when some, perhaps many, older Americans will slip across the border having never registered for Medicare. When the time is right, they'll sign up for Social Security retirement benefits, but whatever the exhortations of the Social Security agent, they'll say "Thanks, but no thanks" to Medicare.

The Big Gray Wave—the biggest demographic shift in human history—will cause this to happen. Successive cohorts of retiring Americans will discover that the American health-care system has become the equivalent of a Soviet-era department store. Everything is offered, but nothing is available. Retirees will discover that they have been invited to play a giant game of medical musical chairs. While the music plays, an increasing number of retirees circle a diminishing number of medical chairs as the ratio of retirees to doctors rises and, in the case of frontline doctors, like general practitioners and internists, the absolute number of doctors declines.

As access diminishes, the main price of admission—the Medicare Part B premium you pay—will continue rising. More important, it will rise faster than inflation, so it will rise faster than Social Security benefits, the primary income source of most retirees. Skeptics can see the future by visiting Scott's Web site at www.assetbuilder.com and running the Social Security benefits versus Medicare calculator. It's called this because Uncle Sam simply subtracts your Medicare premiums from your Social Security benefit check.

Enter your current Medicare premium, your Social Security benefit, an assumed inflation rate, and a rate of increase for the Medicare premium, and the calculator will show you how the rise of the Medicare premium will slowly reduce the real value of your Social Security benefit check after the premiums have been deducted.

For 2008, the basic Medicare Part B premium is $96.40 a month, and the average Social Security retirement benefit is $1,078.50 a month. So a typical retiree pays nearly 9 percent of benefits in Medicare premiums and has a net income of $952 a month after Medicare.

But if the Medicare premium rises at its historical rate—4.6 percent over the rate of inflation—the premium will be 11 percent of benefits in five years, 14 percent in ten years, 17 percent in fifteen years, and 21 percent in twenty years. Those with higher retirement incomes from other sources will be hit harder because the feds are now basing your Medicare premium increase on the level of your taxable income.

Take our friends the Earners, the young couple we met in chapter 20. While the Medicare Part B premium is $1,157 a year today, it will be $10,830 a year (in today's dollars) by the time they start taking Medicare thirty-five years from now if the historical rate of increase continues. The premium will be larger than the $9,163 they'll pay that year in federal and state income taxes, assuming no changes in tax laws, and it will absorb 19 percent of the Earners' combined $57,600 Social Security benefit—double the current take. Viewed another way, the insurance premium will absorb a full third of the $32,924 they receive in asset income from their life savings.

Remember, this doesn't include the premiums for Medigap insurance, currently running somewhat higher than the Medicare Part B premium,* or the new Medicare Part D premiums,† currently about a quarter of the Medicare Part B premium. Add the deductible, copays, and exclusions for eye care, dentistry, and hearing aids, and millions of retirees will be looking for an alternative—like turning on, tuning in, and dropping out to Mexico.

Far-fetched? We don't think so. American medicine is good, but not that good. For all our sophistication, technology, and spending, the United States ranks forty-fifth among nations in overall life ex-

---

* Currently $117 a month for Medigap "F" from AARP/UnitedHealthcare.
† Currently $26 a month for Medicare Part D from AARP/UnitedHealthcare.

pectancy. That puts us just behind places like Jordan (fortieth) and Bosnia/Herzegovina (forty-second) and modestly ahead of Albania (fiftieth) and Costa Rica (fifty-fifth). So who knows? Maybe we can do just as well health-wise in Panama.

For those who can't speak Spanish or are too light-skinned for the tropics, sticking it out in America requires saving to deal with Uncle Sam's problems. A happier, but improbable, alternative would be if health-care costs rose no faster than inflation. Were that miracle to occur, the Earners would face Medicare Part B premiums of $2,244 a year, a stunning $8,586 less at age sixty-five than they will pay if the historical growth rate continues. This and subsequent savings on Part B premium payments translates into a 1 percent *lifetime* living-standard gain for the Earners starting at their current age, thirty.

Saving Doesn't End at Retirement

Between 2004 and 2007, the real Part B premium increased by a whopping 50 percent! Medicare trustees predict additional "significant increases" in coming years. How should the Earners react to the prospect of higher Medicare benefit growth in the future than the 4.6 percent annual growth rate they're now assuming?

The answer is that they need to save a lot more, but not for a while. Remember, right now they are age thirty. They have two small mouths to feed, a mortgage to pay off, and significant 401(k) contributions to make. Moreover, their earnings are rising by 1 percent a year after inflation. They are, in short, borrowing constrained.

Their consumption-smoothing plan, based on an assumed 4.6 percent real growth rate of the Medicare Part B premium, entails no regular saving until age forty-five, at which point they start saving in earnest. By the time they reach retirement, they'll accumulate over a half million dollars (measured in today's dollars). The annual saving needed to build up this stock of assets is impressive. At age sixty, for example, the Earners must save $43,484.

Now suppose that Medicare Part B premiums grow at 6 percent real, rather than the historic 4.6 percent real, into the future. This is a pretty modest fillip in assumptions, given what's happened in recent years to these premiums. Yet required saving shoots up substantially. The Earners' saving at age sixty must now be $48,984—almost 13 percent higher than in the base case. And the couple's assets at age sixty-five rise by almost $80,000.

The additional saving to deal with the higher Medicare premium doesn't end at retirement, however. Since the Earners are smoothing their living standard over *all* their postliquidity-constrained years, they have to cut back on consumption in middle age, old age, and old-old age to pay for the higher premiums. This means spending less in early retirement. The flip side of spending less is, of course, saving more. At age sixty-five Ernest and Eleanor save $1,958 more because they know that Medicare premiums will be a lot higher when they reach old-old age than they are now. (More precisely, Ernest and Eleanor run down their assets by $1,958 less at age sixty-five than they'd do otherwise.)

Thus far we've had the Earners collect Social Security starting at age sixty-five. But if they wait until age seventy to collect, they'll raise their living standard in retirement by 4.5 percent. Doing so will dramatically change their postretirement saving behavior. Now they'll dissave (use savings for current expenses) substantially before age seventy, but once they reach seventy and Social Security kicks in, they'll start to do positive saving in anticipation of ever-higher Medicare Part B premiums. This positive saving will continue through age seventy-six.

Saving in retirement and consuming less may seem strange, but that's what future retirees will have to do if government health-care spending is not controlled.

Takeaways

- Medicare premiums have been growing like crazy.
- Medicare premiums are likely to continue to grow like crazy.
- Medicare premiums are now assessed on a progressive basis.
- When you can, raise your saving dramatically in light of Medicare premium hikes. Or plan to move to Mexico.

39. Should I Care About Long-Term Care?

RECENTLY A FORTY-YEAR-OLD colleague named David contacted Larry to ask how much he and his wife should save for retirement, given that they had very few assets apart from $600,000 in retirement accounts. The couple have two kids in elementary school, plans to finance four years of college at $40,000 per year, and a moderately expensive home.

Larry did a quick run and told Dave to save $2,169. He also pointed out that they were borrowing constrained and would end up with a higher living standard in retirement, but nothing too dramatically different. The colleague looked crestfallen and asked if there was anything they could do.

"Sure," Larry said. He then showed how taking Social Security at age seventy and buying an inflation-indexed annuity at sixty-five could generate an 11 percent higher living standard once they hit age seventy. Dave brightened up a bit. But on the way out the door, he raised the question of long-term care. Specifically, "Should I care about long-term care? Can't I simply self-insure?" Larry said, "Don't leave. Let's check this out."

"Given the way nursing home costs are rising," said David, "I think I should plan to spend $150K in today's dollars for five years starting at age eighty. Can you stick that into the program?"

"No problem," said Larry. "Here's what you're looking at. You need to save close to $11K this year and reduce your current living standard by almost 10 percent if you want to self-insure."

"That's a big hit," said Dave.

"Sure is," said Larry.

"I guess most people are ignoring this problem. No one's saving this much money for nursing home care," said Dave.

"You're right," replied Larry. "Most people appear to be relying on Medicaid. Problem with Medicaid is that they grab all your assets to help them pay the bills. Your wife can stay in the house, but if you get sick, you'll both go down the financial tube together. They even go after the equity in your house once your wife moves out or dies. To avoid this vicious asset test, you can give your assets to your kids or divorce your wife and give her all the assets, but you have to do this at least five years before going onto Medicaid."

"Sounds grim. What about buying a long-term care policy?" asked Dave.

"Glad you asked," said Larry. "I had my research assistant check into the cost of these policies recently. They are actually relatively cheap if you buy them at a young age. Of course, you're forty, and you may spend forty years paying premiums before you collect. Or, if you're lucky, you'll never collect. From what I gather, you could buy a policy for about $1,500 a year that would give you about $150K a year in coverage for up to five years, with the $150K rising by 5 percent annual to account, albeit imperfectly, for rising nursing home costs. The $1,500 annual premium would likely rise at least with inflation. Understanding the fine print of these policies isn't easy. Anyway, paying $3K a year for policies for you and your wife beats having to save an extra $7K each year."

"Right. But if we self-insure and never have to spend the extra savings on a nursing home, we can leave it to the kids," said Dave.

"Yes, but the better move," said Larry, "is to buy the policy and just give the kids a couple thousand a year. This way you give them money for sure, deal with your nursing home concerns, and have a couple thousand left over to spend on yourself."

"Makes sense," said Dave.

Don't Take Our Word for It

Dave's case is instructive. It suggests that we should all check out the costs of buying long-term care very carefully. But in so doing, you need to ask a lot of questions and try to get the answers in writing. Here are a few:

- What will the policy cost me in today's dollars now and down the pike?
- What happens if the insurance company goes belly-up? Who pays my claim?
- Is the benefit fully adjusted for inflation? If not, is the nominal benefit graded so it at least rises in nominal terms each year?
- What if I need home health care, not nursing home care? Can I get coverage for both?
- Will the premium depend on my preexisting medical condition?
- How long will coverage last?
- Is there a maximum daily benefit?
- If I have a short stay in a nursing home followed, a year or so later, by a longer stay, will my policy stay in force?

Worry About the Insurer and Get Competitive Quotes

There has been a lot in the news lately about home health care and nursing home insurers not processing claims, denying claims, and jacking up premiums on the elderly. It seems like you need insurance against your insurance company. But no such insurance exists. Our advice is to be very cautious about whom you deal with. Look at their track record and ask lots of questions. Most important, keep them honest by getting competitive quotes and having them explain why their policy beats the competition. This may reveal some dirty little secrets about the policies you're considering that you'd otherwise not discover until it was too late.

Most important, make sure you understand by how much premiums could rise. It's one thing paying $1,500 a year in today's dollars when you're seventy-five for a "renewable" policy that you purchased at age forty. It's another thing to pay $10,500 in today's dollars at age seventy-five for the same policy. We mention these numbers because that 7-to-1 ratio ($10,500 divided by $1,500) is the ratio of current premium prices for new policies now being issued to healthy seventy-year-olds and forty-year-olds. The current premium being charged eighty-five-year-olds for the same coverage is $21,750.

These quotes, by the way, are high because we are thinking about 50 percent higher nursing home costs by the time Dave is likely to need nursing home care. Currently, a policy paying $300 a day would provide excellent nursing home cost coverage. The premiums being charged right now for such a policy, with the same five-year coverage and 5 percent grading as referenced above, range from $1,000 for a forty-year-old, $2,700 for a sixty-five-year old, $6,700 for a seventy-five-year-old, and $14,000 for an eighty-year-old. Not cheap by any means, but these policies may still be well worth buying.

Takeaways

- Except for the super-rich, saving against a future nursing home stay is a Herculean task.
- Almost all middle- and low-income households rely on Medicaid for nursing home care.
- Medicaid will wipe you and your spouse out financially.
- Do care about long-term care. Yes, the policies cost a fortune. But buying one may be the best of a set of bad options.
- If you do buy a long-term care policy, check it out very carefully in advance.

40. A Safety-First Strategy

LIFE IS SIMPLE at the extremes. If you are destitute and destined to remain so, there are few financial decisions because, well, you don't have much in the way of finances to make decisions about. You have government promises of income benefits, in-kind benefits (food stamps, subsidized housing), and health-care benefits. These benefits won't impress The Donald or Paris Hilton. Nor will they put your lifestyle on the pages of the *Robb Report* or *ForbesLife*. But they will keep body and soul together. The benefits will be more than adequate, for instance, to live a life of contemplation and beauty at any number of spiritual centers around the country. And not a bad idea, at that. In our observation, spiritual organizations occupy some of the most beautiful locations in the country, such as the Green Gulch Zen Center in Marin County, California, or the Upaya Zen Center in Santa Fe.

Being super-rich also makes your life simple. You need never worry about job loss or tear your hair out commuting. Your financial life is about treasuring your stocks and bonds, your real estate, your art collection, and your antique cars. It's about trust funds and estate planning, not about retirement decisions, Social Security benefits, Medicare premiums, or even spending money.

But that's life for the desperately poor and the filthy rich. What about the rest of us, the vast majority who wonder how much we can earn, how long we can work, and whether the government will judge us rich when it starts cutting back on its promises? Sadly, the consumption-smoothing problem we face is vastly more complicated. It's also psychologically very difficult.

We can follow the artificially precise prescriptions of the financial services industry and experience very bad results that are very good for them. Or we can follow the guidelines of economics, respond to circumstances with flexibility, and get much closer to a smooth lifetime living standard. We call the risk-reducing guidelines of consumption smoothing our safety-first strategy. Here are the broad strokes:

Secure your housing. Housing is the major albatross (off-the-top expenditure) limiting our ability to spend our resources on other goods and services. For most of us it's also a source of tremendous pleasure. The hard part is paying for it, which can be risky business. Buying rather than renting can mitigate this risk. If we buy, we have protection against rising housing costs. Yes, property taxes and homeowners insurance will go up. Yes, the house may develop termites or flood on occasion. But if rents go up, homeowners won't have to pay more for the housing services they receive from living in their own homes. So buy your home rather than rent it, unless the cost of buying is far higher than the cost of renting—measured, of course, in terms of your living standard.

Secure your mortgage. Interest rates can rise dramatically over a relatively short period of time. Between 1977 and 1982, short-term rates rose from 5 percent to 14 percent. That was no time to be holding a variable-rate mortgage. Today is no time to do so either. If you have one, refinance immediately at a fixed rate. Then sit back and pray that inflation will erode your real repayment costs. But unless you are pretty sure inflation is about to take off, the best mortgage is no mortgage, and paying off your mortgage is the highest-yielding safe return you can earn in the market. So if you find you have extra money to invest, use it to pay down your mortgage.

Secure your longevity. Now that inflation-indexed annuities are readily available, consider purchasing them to insure against excess longevity. Of course, shop around for the best deal, and make sure that any annuity you buy is fully protected against inflation. If you can find multiple vendors selling them at comparable rates, buy some from each. This will help protect you against insurance company default.

Get married and have kids. Remember the bumper sticker "Be nice to your kids. They will choose your nursing home." Even better, they may take you in and keep you out of a nursing home. Getting married and having kids lets you establish an implicit family insurance market—a mutual assistance society/arrangement—that may be vital in insuring you against unemployment, earnings loss, health expenses, and so forth. Most developing countries have no formal insurance markets or very poorly developed ones. What they do have is a highly sophisticated system of extended family support that substitutes remarkably well for regular insurance markets.

Be flexible. Most of us think binary. We want a yes-or-no, all-or-nothing answer. We don't want to hear "on the one hand and on the other." We don't like ambiguity or uncertainty. But the best we can do is mitigate the odds in life. We can do this on several levels. The primary level is something every person on the planet can achieve without any knowledge of investments. We can work hard to be flexible, multitalented human beings. This means being prepared to do more than one kind of work, being willing to ponder changes in how and where we live, and avoiding fixed ideas of what our lives should be like.

Consider investing just in TIPs. TIPs are yielding 2.4 percent after inflation as we write. This is a very respectable rate of return with essentially no downside short of the federal government publicly defaulting on its official debt. Before you invest in anything else, read Boston University Professor Zvi Bodie's *Worry-Free Investing* and consider holding simply TIPs. There is nothing wrong in playing it safe. On the contrary, that's a major part of the consumption-smoothing goal: a smooth but *very* safe living standard.

Diversify your resources. Starting from a position of holding just TIPs in your financial portfolio, consider the riskiness of your overall resources. Even though your financial assets are fully secure, your overall resources may be anything but. You may, for example, work for an embattled company like GM, which could fold in coming years. If it does, this will wipe out in one fell swoop your earnings, your current health insurance coverage, your employer 401(k) match, and, depending on what happens to the UAW, your retiree health insurance coverage.

While there are financial ways (put options and so on) to hedge this risk, few people are likely to use them. The best protection is to remain marketable and difficult to replace, yet few workers make much effort to broaden their skills. We believe that constant skill building is a life necessity.

Beyond loss of our jobs, the second major resource risk we face is that our taxes will rise or our government benefits will be cut. These fiscal changes will likely occur when the United States is perceived to be in fiscal trouble and the dollar is falling. So if you have purchased inflation-adjusted bonds, foreign bonds, foreign stocks, or domestic stocks with significant foreign earnings, you will have some protection.

For all the discussion of international markets, for all the attention to obscure exchanges, for all the billions of dollars that have flowed to mutual funds and exchange-traded funds that invest in foreign equities, most Americans still have the majority of their equity investment dollars tied up in domestic equities. According to the Hewitt Associates 401(k) Index, which tracks asset allocation in a large number of major plans, international equities account for only 8.8 percent of portfolios and emerging markets for only 1 percent.*

---

* Readers can follow this regular report at www.hewittassociates.com/Intl/NA/en-US/OurServices/IndexObservationList.aspx.

There are other asset classes to consider as well if you want to go beyond TIPs and raise the expected level of your future living standard at the price of higher future living-standard variability. These include REITs (real estate investment trusts); natural resources, including oil and timber; and commodities, including gold.

It isn't difficult to diversify. One of us (Scott) has been writing about couch potato investing for nearly two decades. His approach is based on the single idea that simple and cheap are better than complicated and expensive. In its most simple form, this means that you invest equal amounts in a *very-low-cost* domestic equity index fund and a TIPs index fund.

Over the years, Scott has added asset classes and built portfolios with more moving parts. He calls his three-part portfolio "the margarita portfolio" because, like a margarita, it is three equal parts—in this case, a TIPs index, a domestic equity index, and an international equity index. Still very simple, and if you need to practice dealing with parts, you can always do it with lime juice, triple sec, and tequila. Today the "building block" portfolios have up to ten parts, so you can be as diversified as you choose.* But always keep in mind that diversifying your portfolio is not the same as diversifying your resources—and that diversifying your resources may preclude diversifying your portfolio (see chapter 32).

Risky investing requires defensive spending. As we've seen, consumption smoothing requires that you gear your spending to your overall resource risk. If you are investing in risky assets in order to reduce your overall resource risk and you succeed in that objective, then you can be secure in spending at a higher rate. But if your financial investment strategy is intended to increase your resource *and* living-standard risk in order to raise the average level of your living standard, you need to cut back your current spending *a lot!*

---

* For more information about costs, trailing returns, and platforms for putting the portfolios together, check Scott's Web site for regular reports, www.assetbuilder.com.

Worry about inflation. Since 1926 inflation has run at an average 3 percent annual rate. Since 1950 it has run at a nearly 4 percent annual rate. With $70 trillion in unfunded spending commitments, it is reasonable to believe that our government will soon start printing more money and that future inflation will be greater, not smaller. That means we should plan and invest accordingly. We think there is plenty to worry about, and we laid it all out, with portfolio recommendations, in our book *The Coming Generational Storm.* Our approach to financial planning and consumption smoothing in this book allows you to test the impact of different events on your long-term standard of living so that you can come to your own conclusions and plan accordingly. We ask that you remember that a 3 percent inflation rate will cut the purchasing power of dollars in half every twenty-four years. At 15 percent it's five years. That's why we recommend TIPs. They'll pay off in real terms each and every year precisely what's promised. Yes, their market value fluctuates, just like other bonds', on a continual basis. But if you hold these bonds to maturity, the annual real payments are guaranteed.

Second, consider what other nominal income streams you have, such as a fixed pension. Then consider buying foreign stocks, gold, REITs, or energy stocks that may rise to offset your purchasing power losses. Third, make sure you don't buy any nominal bonds, nominal annuities or make any long-term loans that pay back in nominal (in other words, not inflation-adjusted) dollars.

Avoid complicated insurance products. One way the insurance industry collects gigantic fees is by creating complicated products and making big claims for them—offering higher than average returns at lower than average risk. These claims are invariably baseless, and the products invariably incorporate very high but hard-to-understand fees as well as highly adverse redemption conditions.

That's why we recommend avoiding cash-value life insurance, conventional variable annuities, variable annuities with "living benefits," and most equity index annuities. Instead, buy renewable term life insurance with the length of time for renewing tied to the period your earnings need to be replaced by insurance. By buying renewable term, you in effect buy insurance against life insurance premiums rising over time, perhaps because you contract a disease that makes you look highly risky to life insurers.

Consider buying long-term care insurance. Nursing home costs are, quite frankly, the biggest risk most of us face in retirement. If you can afford it, buy long-term care insurance. If you do buy it, buy it at an early age and with as much inflation protection as you can get. Make sure you buy it from a company in sound financial shape and fully understand how much your premium can be raised through time.

Now you have it, our safety-first strategy, summarized as follows:
- Secure your housing.
- Secure your mortgage.
- Be flexible in your employment options.
- Consider investing just in TIPs.
- Diversify your resources.
- Spend defensively if you invest aggressively.
- Worry about inflation.
- Avoid complicated insurance products.
- Consider buying long-term care insurance.

Epilogue:

Is There an Economist in the House?

ECONOMICS IS A social science, but economists are much more interested in the science than the social. They are fascinated by the search for optimal solutions to ever-more-intricate economic problems regardless of the fact that no real economic actors are remotely capable of computing these optimums or behaving according to the dictates of their formulas. The idea of climbing down from their ivory towers and actually treating the financially sick has been intellectually unappealing. Until recently, it has also been technically infeasible.

Ministering to the public on financial matters has been left to investment and insurance companies, who hawk their expensive elixirs on their Web sites and through armies of brokers, dealers, and financial planners with fancy initials that include CFP, CFA, CFC, and so on.

Although most financial professionals are well meaning and seek to do the best by their clients, they make their money the old-fashioned way: by selling you more financial products than you need and charging you a tremendous price to mismanage your money. They are itinerant medicine men selling cures. The quicker they make a diagnosis, the quicker they make a sale. This impetus to provide quick/easy/simple/fast plans has culminated in a conventional wisdom that is at complete odds with consumption smoothing—economic science's prescription for financial health.

Is All Conventional Financial Advice Wrong?

Here's the short answer:

Yes.

Here's the long answer:

Yes.

Just contrast the standard financial mantras with economic advice below.

CONVENTIONAL WISDOM	ECONOMIC ADVICE
Put your saving on autopilot.	Smooth your living standard, not your saving.
Set your own retirement spending target.	This is dangerous. Small targeting mistakes lead to huge consumption disruption.
Target to replace 75 percent to 85 percent of preretirement income.	Do this and you'll likely save and insure far too much.
You can never save too much.	Not true. You can squander your youth rather than your money.
You can never have too much life insurance.	Don't overinsure. You can't count on dying young.
Diversify your portfolio.	Diversify your resources and concentrate your portfolio as required.
Hold stocks when young and bonds when old.	Put your portfolio on a roller coaster. Hold mostly TIPs (Treasury inflation-protected securities) when young, more stock when middle age, less stock when approaching retirement, more stock in early retirement, and little or no stock in late retirement. And hold very little to zero stock at any age if you are very risk averse.

CONVENTIONAL WISDOM	ECONOMIC ADVICE
Bonds are safer than stocks.	Nominal bonds, particularly long-term nominal bonds, are highly risky when, as now, inflation can shoot up at any time. TIPs are the only safe asset.
The longer the holding period, the better stocks will do compared to bonds.	The probability of stocks beating bonds rises with time. So does the probability of your stocks losing all their value.
Stocks are safer the longer you hold them.	"Safe" references your living standard, not your portfolio return. Your living standard risk from holding stock depends on both the extent of your stock holdings and your spending behavior. If your spend-down rate is too high, stocks will be riskier the longer you hold them.
Ordinary people should hold bonds, and the rich should hold stock.	Ordinary people should hold stock, and the rich should hold TIPs. The poor have much better downside protection—that is to say, their total resources are better diversified.
Life-cycle funds are a safe bet for young savers.	Hardly. Life-cycle funds start out highly concentrated in stock and hold very risky nominal bonds.
Spend 4 percent of initial retirement assets each year in retirement.	This is a prescription for running out of money, particularly if you invest in stock. You can't set your retirement spending on autopilot when you invest in risky assets or experience unexpected expenses or other economic shocks.
Your asset spend-down rate should stay fixed in retirement.	Your spend-down rate should start low and rise with age. It should be much lower at any age if you are investing in risky assets and have significant resource risk.
Take Social Security as early as possible.	Take Social Security as late as possible unless you fear benefit cuts or can double dip.

CONVENTIONAL WISDOM	ECONOMIC ADVICE
Withdraw your 401(k) as late as possible.	Withdraw your 401(k) early to permit taking Social Security late and avoid higher future tax rates.
Defer your taxes as long as possible; withdraw from your Roth before your 401(k).	Not if you think tax rates will be increased or if you are in the top AMT bracket now but may be in a higher regular income tax bracket later.
Higher education pays.	Higher education costs—a lot. Plumbing may offer a higher lifetime living standard than some well-paid professions after all educational and professional costs are considered.
Mortgage deductions make home ownership cheap.	Mortgages offer no fundamental tax breaks. Pay yours off ASAP unless you see high inflation coming.
Contributing to retirement accounts is a slam dunk.	Most workers are borrowing constrained and must trade off short-run living standard cuts against long-run living standard gains in deciding whether to contribute. But do what it takes to get your employer match.
Any financial planning is better than no financial planning.	Don't count on it.

A Revolution in Financial Planning

The status quo is a rest stop for the mind. It's certain, it's expected, it's understood, and it can't get worse. Beyond the status quo, anything can happen, including things that are unpleasant to contemplate, let alone experience. So thinking outside the box comes at a psychic cost.

This may be why revolutions—political, technological, or commercial—are hard to spot. Seeing them is uncomfortable. Recall Western Union's disdain for the telephone, Decca Records' disregard for the Beatles, and Irving Fisher's trust in the stock market—all soothing, wishful, biased thoughts.

But things do change, think it or not. And things are changing big-time when it comes to financial planning.

Thanks to breakthroughs in dynamic programming, computer processing, and desktop computation, each of us, by ourselves, in our own homes, without breaking a sweat or using any math, can now make extraordinarily complex financial and personal decisions that are consistent with the prescriptions of economic science.

These decisions include what education to acquire, which career to pursue, which job to take, where to live, whom to marry, whether to procreate, how much to spend, how much to save, where to save, how much to insure, how to invest, where to invest, whether to buy a house, when to move, where to move, whether to divorce, when to retire, when to take the 401(k), how to order Roth versus non-Roth withdrawals, whether to annuitize, when to take Social Security, whether to take a reverse mortgage, how much to donate, how much to help the kids, how much to bequeath, and what size funeral to schedule.

Each of these decisions requires knowing how it affects our living standard, now and in the future. This includes decisions of the heart, which invariably come with a living-standard price.

ESPlanner is the first publicly available living-standard machine. It handles the above decisions and more. Over time, expect even more powerful living-standard machines to measure, raise, and preserve your living standard. Know that you can "follow your bliss," but you can also assess the living-standard costs of doing so. (You may be surprised to discover that it costs less than the passion killers say it costs.)

You Can't Know if You Don't Ask

ESPlanner makes its living-standard calculations in less than five seconds, but it requires an initial time investment of a half hour to answer straightforward questions, such as "What's your monthly mortgage payment?" A half hour is less time than it takes for a physical exam in your doctor's office and far less than you'll wait in the nearest emergency room, and you'll invest that time far more usefully than the half minute or so you'll spend on questions posed by thousands of calculators based on simple programs and conventional wisdom.

In reality, most of the planning tools used by the financial services industry are sales tools. They were designed, whether by laziness or intent, to have you save and insure far beyond your means and then, by necessity, invest in stocks to beat the odds. Indeed, the industry's quick saving and insurance solutions and promotion of risk constitute nothing less than financial malpractice. These are strong words, but they are fully justified given the massive economic harm being perpetrated by the industry's so-called solutions.

From Describing to Prescribing

We included the word *revolutionary* in the subtitle of our book for three reasons. First, we wanted to reference the introduction to financial planning of radically new technology that can diagnose and help cure financial illness. Second, we wanted to convey a truly crazy notion: namely, that financial planning can be liberating and fun. In fact, when done right, it offers a free path to a higher living standard, both now and in the future, and the opportunity to pursue our passions without going broke in the process.

The third and most significant motivation was to signal that economists are finally moving from *describing* personal financial problems to *prescribing* solutions. These problems are simply too important and too complex to leave to the self-interested guesswork of a financial services industry whose primary goal is to make money rather than provide appropriate financial advice. Economists have spent the better part of a century cataloging financial disease, understanding its causes, and identifying its cure. In recent decades they've assembled a big black bag full of financial medicine based on thousands, if not tens of thousands, of highly sophisticated dynamic programs and Monte Carlo simulation models. Economists are now starting to open that bag. They may at last become financial MDs, and, in the process, revolutionize the standard of care in financial planning. Our lives will be better for it.

Index

age
  and expected age of death, 167
  and maximum age of life, 167
  and retirement account
    contributions, 144–52, 154
  See also retirement; Social
    Security: when to take
alimony, 199–201
Allianz Life Insurance Company of
  North America, 29
Alternative Minimum Tax (AMT),
  50–51, 138, 157, 158
American Economic Association,
  62
American Lung Association,
  230
Andrew and Jessica (example),
  128–32
annuity/annuities
  and charity, 229
  and employer pension funds,
    274
  equity index, 103
  failure to have, 175–79

and fees, 102
and helping children, 225
income from, 176
and inflation, 177, 182
and inheritances, 175–76, 178,
  180–82
and long-term care insurance,
  283
and maximizing your living
  standard, 25, 26
and nursing home costs, 176
and preserving your living
  standard, 234, 271, 274, 283,
  289, 292
and pricing your passions, 225,
  229
and public policy, 271
and raising your living standard,
  10
and revolution in financial
  planning, 299
risk of, 176–77, 181
and safety-first strategy, 289,
  292

annuity/annuities (*cont.*)
  Social Security as, 172–73, 177,
    178
  and solvency of insurance
    companies, 176–77
Aon Corporation, 37, 95, 97, 98,
  100
Armand and Alice (example),
  134–35, 136–37
assets
  allocation of, 237–42, 243–49,
    250
  importance of using, 99
  and replacement rates, 99, 104
  spending of, 99, 104
  See also type of asset
Aunt Judy (example), 49
Austin, Texas, homes in, 135–36
averaging, 256–62, 266

Bank of America, 36
Barber, Brad, 83–84
Barry (example), 211–13
Bart and Beverly (example),
  135–38
Becker, Gary, 89
behavioral finance, 9, 88–91
Belo Corporation, 275–76
Bengen, William, 251
Bernheim, Douglas, 12, 67, 79, 89
Betty (example), 211–13
bidding wars, 61
Bill (example), 40–41
Bill and Hillary (example), 169–70
Blow, Joe and Sally (example),
  32–34, 35, 36
Bob (example), 89
Bodie, Zvi, 42, 247–48, 289
bonds
  and asset allocation, 247–48
  and conventional wisdom versus
    economic advice, 296, 297
  and life-cycle funds, 240–41
  municipal, 190
  and portfolio choice, 263–66

and preserving your living
    standard, 237–42, 247–48,
    263–66, 271, 292
  and public policy, 271
  and raising living standard, 10
  and safety-first strategy, 292
  and taxes, 186–90
  See also TIPs
borrowing
  and choosing careers, 109, 110,
    112, 114
  and college, 116, 117
  constraints on, 143, 144, 149,
    150, 161, 165, 283
  expansion of, 58–60
  and financial pathology, 57,
    58–62, 75
  and keeping up with the Joneses,
    60–61
  and lending practices, 59
  and mind-benders, 48–49
  and raising your living standard,
    116, 117
  and retirement account
    contributions, 48–49, 143,
    144, 149, 150
  and Social Security, 161, 165
Boston College, Center for
  Retirement Research at, 56
Boston University, saving
  experiment at, 81
boy toys, 211–13
brain-imaging studies, 89–90
bubbles, 70, 84
Buffett, Warren, 228

Camerer, Colin, 90
capital gains, 187, 270
careers
  changing, 276
  choosing, 109–14
  and choosing not to work, 114,
    118–21, 162
  and preserving your living
    standard, 276

and raising your living standard, 10, 107, 109–14, 118–21
and revolution in financial planning, 299
See also work
Carman, Katherine, 67
Carnegie, Andrew, 29
cars, 58, 59, 60
cash, 42, 48–49, 58
catch-up provisions, 56, 72
Cedar Rapids, Iowa, 122–26, 133
Center for Retirement Research (Boston College), 56
Center for Retirement Research (Vanguard), 56, 72
Center for Risk Management and Insurance Research (Georgia State University), 95–96
Center for the Study of Brain, Mind, and Behavior (Princeton University), 90
charitable gift fund, 228–29, 231–32
charity, 10, 203, 228–32, 299
children
    and consumption smoothing, 220, 224–25
    financial contributions to, 203
    and financial pathology, 97
    gifts to, 284–85
    helping, 224–27, 270, 299
    and long-term care insurance, 284–85
    and mind-benders, 47
    and preserving your living standard, 269–70, 284–85, 289
    and pricing your passions, 10, 203, 219–23, 224–27
    and replacement rate, 98, 104
    and revolution in financial planning, 299

and safety-first strategy, 289
and taxes, 221
See also inheritances; life insurance
Choi, James J., 71
Chuck and Corinna-Corinna (example), 136–39
Cohen, Jonathan, 90
collectibles, 70
College Board, 115–16, 117
college. *See* education
common sense, 4
communication, lack of financial, 87
company stock, 57–58, 67–68, 75, 91, 92, 275–76
compound interest, 24, 227
compulsive behavior, 86, 89, 93
computational limitations, 92–93
Congress, U.S., 136, 158
Congressional Budget Office, U.S., 57, 75
Consumer Expenditure Survey, 95
consumer sovereignty, 77
consumption
    and choosing careers, 112–14
    competitive, 61–62
    definition of, 33
    disruptions in conventional, 27–38, 44, 87, 258
    maximizing lifetime, 131
    See also consumption smoothing
consumption smoothing
    as balancing act, 233
    characteristics of, 18–19, 23, 26, 42
    and consumption disruptions, 38
    drug dealer example of, 21–25
    and ESPlanner, 13
    and financial sickness, 18–19
    Fisher as father of, 85
    and gambling, 62
    and lack of financial communication, 87
    and living life to the longest, 22

consumption smoothing (*cont.*)
  as mantra, 104
  and maximizing your living
    standard, 25
  overview about, 21–26
  and preserving your living
    standard, 10–11, 265–66
  and pricing your passions,
    224–25
  as target, 30–31, 38
  and three commandments of
    economics, 2–3
  See also smoothing your living
    standard; *specific topic*
Corzine, Jon, 39
credit cards, 58, 75
Cruz, Humberto, 215–16, 218
curse of dimensionality, 265–66

Dallas Morning News, 13, 228,
  275, 278
David (example), 283–84
day-trading, 58, 69–70
death
  expected age of, 167
  as factor determining financial
    future, 8–9
debt
  distribution of national, 60–61
  hatred of, 60
  U.S. consumer, 58, 59
  See also borrowing
derivatives, 197, 241
designed neglect, 81–83, 93
dimensionality, curse of, 265–66
disruptions, consumption, 27–38,
  44, 87, 258
diversification
  and basic economic model of
    portfolio choice, 239–40,
    241–42
  and company stock, 276
  and conventional wisdom versus
    economic advice, 296
  of funds, 66

  of portfolios, 5, 45–46, 92,
    243–49, 264, 290–91, 296
  and preserving your living
    standard, 239–40, 241–42,
    243–49, 264, 270, 276,
    290–91, 293
  and public policy, 270
  of resources, 243–49
  and risk, 243
  and safety-first strategy, 290–91,
    293
dividends, 187, 234
divorce, 10, 199–201, 203, 205–7,
  299
doctors
  economists as, 78, 300
  plumbers compared with,
    109–14
Dow Jones Industrial Average,
  79
downsizing, 196–98
drug dealer (example), 6, 21–26

early retirement, 10, 56–57, 203,
  214–18
earned income, spending of, 99
Earner, Ernest and Eleanor
  (example), 191–95, 279–81
earnings
  and asset allocation, 247–48
  median college graduate,
    116–17
  and preserving your living
    standard, 234, 245–49, 275,
    276
  and retirement account
    contributions, 144–52
Econometric Society, 84
economic efficiency, 77
economic schizophrenia, 88–91,
  93
Economic Security Planning, Inc.,
  12
economic theory, 6
economists, 19–20, 78, 295–300

education
  and choosing careers, 109–10,
    114
  and consumption disruptions, 27
  and conventional wisdom versus
    economic advice, 298
  and helping children, 225, 226
  and pricing your passions, 220,
    225, 226
  questions about, 3
  and raising your living standard,
    10, 115–17
  and replacement rate, 97, 104
  and revolution in financial
    planning, 299
  self-, 79
Eisenberg, Lee, 95
emergencies, 167, 176
emotions, 5–6, 9, 84–85
Employee Benefit Research
  Institute, 56, 218
employee stock ownership plans
  (ESOPs), 92
employers
  matching funds from, 57, 65,
    70–72, 75, 142, 143, 144–48,
    153, 154, 216, 272, 273
  and preserving your living
    standard, 272–76
  reliance on, 91
  See also company stock
Enron Corporation, 68, 91, 197
equities, 101, 186–90, 290–91. See
  also stocks
equity index annuity, 103
ESPlanner, 9, 12–14, 114, 156–57,
  163, 173, 197, 229, 299
Excel program, 12
Executive Life, 176

fears
  grab bag of, 55–57
  and pricing your passions, 224
  See also specific fear
Federal Reserve Board, 59, 60

fees, 102, 191–95
Fehr, Ernst, 90
Fidelity, 7, 8, 28–29, 36, 56, 98,
  176, 241
financial disease, understanding,
  76–93
Financial Engines (Vanguard), 36
financial illiteracy, 57, 78–80, 93
financial pathology
  causes of, 76–93
  overview of, 9, 53, 55–75
  and replacement rate, 94–101,
    104–5
  scope and depth of, 75
financial planning/planners
  and asset allocation, 247
  benefits of, 26
  choices offered by, 104
  and consumption disruptions,
    28–38
  conventional, 4, 6, 7–8, 51,
    296–98
  and conventional wisdom versus
    economic advice, 298
  and designed neglect, 83
  failure of, 6
  fees of, 101–3, 295–96
  functions of, 26, 295
  influences on, 81
  lack of, 56, 75
  and life-cycle funds, 241
  as marketing tool, 30, 295–96
  revolution in, 298–99, 300
  and risk, 7, 39–40
  and three commandments of
    economics, 4
  types of, 7
  See also targets
financial sickness, 8, 17–20, 295
financial tools, 31–32, 36, 92–93,
  265–66, 269, 299–300. See
  also specific tool
First Capital, 176
Fisher, Irving, 84–85, 298
529 college accounts, 88

Forbes, 13, 21
Forbes' Retirement Guide, 172
Ford Motor Company, 274–75
foreign countries, retirement living
    in, 277–78
Foreman, George, 15–16
Fortune 500, 273
Fortune, 13, 21
4 percent spend-down rule, 11,
    251–53, 254–55, 256, 297
401(k) plans
    average return from, 192
    and charity, 229
    and company stock, 67–68, 91,
        92
    contributions to, 48–49, 64,
        70–72, 142–55
    and conventional wisdom versus
        economic advice, 298
    and conversion of retirement
        accounts, 158
    and early retirement, 216
    and economic schizophrenia, 88
    enrollment in, 91
    fees for, 102, 192–95
    and financial pathology, 64, 65,
        67–68, 70–72, 75
    and framing, 65
    and indifference to money, 70–72
    and life-cycle funds, 241
    and preserving your living
        standard, 241, 272, 273, 290
    and pricing your passions, 216,
        229
    questions about, 3
    and reliance on others, 91
    and revolution in financial
        planning, 299
    and safety-first strategy, 290
    and taxes, 103, 141–55, 187
    when to take withdrawals from,
        162–63, 164, 165–68, 298,
        299
    See also matching funds,
        employer

403(b) accounts, 64, 92, 102, 156,
    187
framing, 65–66, 75
Frank, Robert, 62
Frazier, Joe, 15

Gallo wine, 89
gambling, 11, 57, 62–65, 75, 86,
    88, 239
gender, and stock trading, 83–84
General Electric, 82
Generous, George and Georgina
    (example), 226
George and Lela (example),
    208–11
Georgia State University (GSU)
    Center for Risk Management
    and Insurance Research at,
    95–96
    replacement rate study by, 37,
        100
Gokhale, Jagadeesh, 12, 67, 119
gold, 68, 69, 291, 292
Goldman Sachs, 39
government
    benefit programs of, 118–20,
        125–26, 160–68, 243, 245–49,
        267–71, 287, 290
    and choosing not to work,
        118–21
    and defaults on student loans,
        117
    fiscal gap of, 267–68
    laissez-faire, 77
    reliance on, 91, 92
    See also Medicaid; Medicare;
        Social Security; taxes
government workers, 56–57, 102,
    193, 241
Grand, Guy (fictional character),
    70
gratification, instant and deferred,
    18
Great Depression, 85
greater fool theory, 70

Green, Hetty, 16
Greenspan, Alan, 59
Gruenberg, Dan, 187–88, 189, 190

Harrah's, gambling survey by, 64
Harry and Hallie (example), 222, 223
Harvey, Paul, 264
health care
  and asset allocation, 247, 248
  employer-based, 274–75
  and homes as security blanket, 125
  and inflation, 193, 280, 284, 285
  and preserving your living standard, 234, 247, 248, 269, 271, 274–75, 277–82, 290
  and public policy, 269, 271
  and replacement rate, 98
  and safety-first strategy, 290
  uninsured, 275
  See also Medicaid; Medicare
hedge funds, 69–70
Hewitt Associates, 67, 71, 290
home equity line of credit, 59–60, 134
home health care, 285
homes
  and consumption disruptions, 27
  depreciation of, 60, 132
  downsizing of, 196
  equity in, 126, 131, 132, 243
  and helping children, 226
  and implicit rent, 139
  insurance for, 131, 132, 180, 288
  location of, 122–26, 127–32, 299
  and preserving your living standard, 269–70, 271, 293
  prices of, 127–32, 135
  and pricing your passions, 208, 209, 211–12, 220, 226
  and public policy, 270, 271
  and raising your living standard, 122–26

refinancing of, 60
renting versus buying, 128, 129, 132, 220, 288
and revolution in financial planning, 299
and safety-first strategy, 288, 293
as security blanket, 125
and taxes, 124, 129–30, 131, 132, 133–40, 196, 288
as type of economic resource, 243
See also home equity credit line; mortgages
hospital rounds (example), 53
house poor, 196, 197
household demographics, 98–99, 104
Huffman, Charles, 72–73
Hull, Raymond, 208

implicit rent, 139, 270
index funds, 40, 43, 82, 83, 102, 194, 195, 233–34, 237–38, 271, 291
indifference to money, 70–72
inflation
  and annuities, 177, 182
  and asset allocation, 247
  and careers, 111
  and conversion of retirement accounts, 157
  and health care, 193, 280, 284, 285
  and home-buying, 130–31, 132
  and long-term care insurance, 284, 285
  luxury, 61–62
  and Medicare, 193
  and mortgage interest, 135
  and pimping risk, 42
  and preserving your living standard, 234, 247, 269, 271, 280, 284, 285, 288, 292, 293
  and public policy, 269, 271

inflation (*cont.*)
  and retirement account
    contributions, 144
  and reverse mortgages, 179
  and safety-first strategy, 288,
    292, 293
  and Social Security, 149, 160,
    173
  and stockbroker fees, 193–94
  and taxes, 111
information technology
  and borrowing, 59
  See also financial tools
inheritances
  and annuities, 175–76, 178,
    180–82
  and consumption disruptions,
    27–28
  and helping children, 224–27
  life insurance as, 168
  and maximizing retirement
    account contributions,
    48–49
  and mind-benders, 48–49
  and pricing your passions,
    224–27
  and revolution in financial
    planning, 299
insurance
  avoiding complicated, 292–93
  and choosing careers, 109, 110
  and consumption disruptions,
    30, 37
  family support as, 289
  and financial pathology, 67, 75
  for homes, 131, 132, 180, 288
  Medigap, 279
  and mind-benders, 44, 47–48, 50
  and preserving your living
    standard, 234, 289, 292–93
  and revolution in financial
    planning, 299, 300
  and risk, 50
  and safety-first strategy, 288,
    289, 292–93
  and socioeconomic status,
    47–48
  and targets, 30
  and three commandments of
    economics, 5
  too little, 67, 75
  too much, 5, 37, 50, 67
  and two-income households, 67
  See also insurance companies;
    type of insurance
insurance companies
  and annuities, 176–77, 178
  responsibilities of, 295
  as salesmen, 295–96
  solvency of, 176–77, 285, 289
  target advice from, 7
  worry about, 285–86
interest, 24, 58, 110, 124, 133–39,
    187, 227, 269–70
Internal Revenue Service (IRS),
    139, 141, 189, 221, 229
Investment Company Institute, 64
IRA accounts
  annuitizing, 25, 26
  and charity, 229, 230, 231
  and consumption disruptions,
    27
  and consumption smoothing, 25,
    26
  contributions to, 64, 65
  and employer pension funds,
    274
  and financial pathology, 64, 65
  and preserving your living
    standard, 274
  and pricing your passions, 229,
    230, 231
  questions about, 3
  and raising living standard, 10
  and taxes, 103, 141–55, 187
  withdrawals from, 168, 229
IRS. *See* Internal Revenue Service

J. D. Power and Associates, 59
Jack (example), 76–77

Jack and Jill (example), 229–31
Jansen, Michael and Carolyn
  (example), 196–97
journalists, financial, and gambling,
  63–64
Justin (example), 243–44

Kahneman, Daniel, 88
Kamenetz, Anya, 60
Kasparov, Garry, 8
keeping up with the Joneses,
  60–61
Keogh accounts, 158, 168, 188,
  189
Kiplinger's Personal Finance, 13,
  18, 216
Kotlikoff-Gokhale study, 120–21

La Dolce Vita index, 61–62
Laibson, David, 71, 82, 83, 89,
  90
Las Vegas, Nevada
  economists' meeting in, 62
  journalists' meeting in, 64
law of diminishing returns, 2,
  10–11
leisure, and pricing your passions,
  214–18
lending practices, 59
life insurance
  and consumption disruptions,
    35, 37
  and conventional wisdom versus
    economic advice, 296
  and ESPlanner, 13, 14
  and financial pathology, 57,
    66–67, 97
  goal of, 47
  hawking, 37
  as inheritance, 168
  and mind-benders, 47
  and preserving your living
    standard, 234, 292–93
  and replacement rate, 97
  and safety-first strategy, 292–93

and three commandments of
  economics, 5
  too much, 296
life-cycle funds, 240–41, 246, 247,
  297
Lindal, Bertha and Steven,
  162–68
liquidity constraints, 143, 150,
  209, 247, 248
living standard
  early sacrifices on, 112–13
  as economic's bottom line, 4
  and ESPlanner, 13
  and financial sickness, 18, 19
  and homes, 122–26
  maximizing your, 25
  overview of, 107
  preservation of, 10–12, 233–93
  protection of, 3, 13
  questions about, 3, 4
  raising your, 107–201
  stable, 19
  and three commandments of
    economics, 1, 2–3, 5, 10–12
  See also consumption smoothing;
    smoothing your living
    standard; *specific topic*
living-standard risk diagram,
  264
long-term care insurance, 126,
  176, 234, 271, 283–86,
  293
Longman, Philip, 219–20
Lotus 1-2-3 program, 12
love, and pricing your passions,
  205–7
Loveless, Frank and Stacy
  (example), 199–200
Low Income Home Energy
  Assistance, 119, 162
Low Income Housing Assistance,
  162
Low Income, Lou and Lucy
  (example), 220–22, 223
Lusardi, Annamaria, 56

Luxury Index, Moet and Chandon, 61–62
luxury inflation, 61–62
Lynch, Peter, 8

Madrian, Brigitte, 71
"margarita portfolio," 291
market cap, 41
marriage/marital status
    and preserving your living standard, 289
    and pricing your passions, 203, 207, 208–13
    and retirement account contributions, 144–52
    and revolution in financial planning, 299
    and safety-first strategy, 289
    and Social Security benefits, 167
    and taxes, 210
    See also shared living; two-income households
matching funds, employer, 57, 65, 70–72, 75, 142, 143, 144–48, 153, 154, 216, 272, 273
Maxwell, Robert, 16
mean-variance frontier, 263–66
Medicaid
    and choosing not to work, 119
    as government benefit program, 162
    and long-term care insurance, 284, 286
    and nursing home costs, 125–26, 167, 176, 227, 286
    and preserving your living standard, 240, 268, 284, 286
    and public policy risk, 268
    qualification for, 126
medical savings accounts, 88
Medicare
    and asset allocation, 244
    and expenditure risks, 125
    as factor determining financial future, 8
    as government benefit program, 245
    and helping children, 226
    and inflation, 193
    and living in foreign countries, 277
    Part A of, 184
    Part B of, 162, 177, 183–85, 193, 252, 278, 279, 280–81
    Part D of, 162, 183–85, 279
    and preserving your living standard, 240, 244, 251, 252, 267, 268, 269, 271, 278–79, 280–81, 282, 287
    and pricing your passions, 226
    progressive nature of, 115
    and public policy, 267, 268, 269, 271
    and raising your living standard, 115
    and replacement rate, 98
    and retirement account contributions, 144
    and safety-first strategy, 287
    Social Security benefits versus, 278–79
    and spending down, 251, 252
    when to take, 162, 164
Medigap insurance, 279
"menu effect," 65–66
Merrill Lynch, 29, 79–80, 81, 83
Merton, Robert, 239–40, 241, 243, 246, 247–48, 259, 264
Mexico
    and health care, 269, 277
    and preserving your living standard, 277, 279, 282
Mezrich, Ben, 64
Mike and Mary (example), 222, 223
mind-benders, financial, 4–5, 44–51
misers, 16, 17, 35, 72–74
Mitchell, Olivia, 56
Modigliani, Franco, 13

Moët & Chandon, 61–62
Money magazine, 13, 18, 216
money management
  and asset allocation, 237–42
  and averaging, 256–62
  and diversification, 243–49
  and portfolio choice, 263–66
  and preserving your living
    standard, 237–42, 243–49,
    250–55
  and spending down, 250–55
money market funds, 42, 68–69
Monte Carlo analysis (simulation),
  7, 40, 41, 300
Morgan Stanley Dean Witter, 29
mortgages
  and borrowing, 58
  and consumption disruptions, 27
  and conventional wisdom versus
    economic advice, 298
  and debt haters, 60
  and early retirement, 216
  and financial pathology, 58, 60
  fixed versus variable-rate, 288
  and home location, 124
  interest on, 124, 129, 133–39
  and mind-benders, 50–51
  paying down, 10, 133–39, 140,
    269, 288
  and preserving your living
    standard, 269, 288, 293
  and pricing your passions, 216
  and public policy, 269
  questions about, 3
  and raising your living standard,
    10
  and replacement rate, 97, 98,
    104
  and safety-first strategy, 288, 293
  and socioeconomic status, 50–51
  and taxes, 50–51, 298
  and three commandments of
    economics, 5
  See also reverse mortgages
municipal bonds, 190

Munroe, Dick and Jennifer
  (example), 171–74
Mutual Benefit, 176
mutual funds, 101–2, 103, 269–70
myPlan Snapshot (Fidelity), 28–29,
  98

Nasdaq index, 84
National Association of Realtors,
  133
National Bureau of Economic
  Research, 71
Nature Conservancy, 230
neuroeconomics, 6, 89
nonfinancial resources, and mind-
  benders, 45
Novak, Janet, 172
Noworlater, John and Jane
  (example), 216–17
nursing homes
  and annuities, 176, 177
  costs of, 125–26, 167, 176, 177,
    227, 283–84, 286, 293
  and long-term care insurance,
    283–84, 286, 293
  and Medicaid, 125–26, 167,
    176, 227, 286
  and preserving your living
    standard, 283–84, 286, 293
  and safety-first strategy, 293
  stock in, 271

Odean, Terrance, 69, 83–84
operating in the dark, 87, 93
Ormond, Suze, 8
overconfidence, 83–85, 93

parallel universe, 258–61
parents, as financial role models,
  80–81, 93
Pareto, Vilfredo, 77
payscale.com, 114
Pension Benefit Guaranty
  Corporation (PBGC), 272,
  273, 274

pension funds, employer-based,
    243, 272–76
Pension Protection Act (2006), 65,
    274
Perlman, S. J., 219
plumbers, doctors compared with,
    109–14
portfolios
    and asset allocation, 250
    and basic economic model of
        portfolio choice, 239–40,
        241–42
    "building block," 291
    and conventional wisdom versus
        economic advice, 296
    diversification of, 5, 45–46, 92,
        243–49, 290–91, 296
    and life-cycle funds, 240–41
    "margarita," 291
    and mind-benders, 45–46
    and portfolio choice, 265–66
    and preserving your living
        standard, 234, 239–42, 250,
        263-66, 269–70, 290–91
    and public policy, 270
    returns on, 263–66
    and safety-first strategy,
        290–91
    and socioeconomic status, 45
    and spending decisions,
        263–66
    and three commandments of
        economics, 5
    as type of economic resource,
        243
    Wharton School study about,
        81–83
poverty, 66, 67
present value, 150
pricing your passions
    as commandment of economics,
        1, 3, 7, 8, 10
    overview of, 203–4, 205–7
    questions about, 4
    See also specific passion

Princeton University, 90
Principal Insurance Co., 172, 177,
    178, 180–81
Proctor & Gamble, 92
profit-sharing plans, 92
prospectus, Wharton School study
    using, 82
public policy, 234, 267–71

Quinn, Jane Bryant, 8

Rapson, David, 120
rationality, and three
    commandments of economics,
    9
real estate, 243, 270, 271.
    See also REITs
real return, 42
Rebecca (example), 116–17
REITs, 291, 292
reliance on others, 91–92, 93
rent
    home-buying versus, 128, 129,
        132
    implicit, 39
replacement rate, 36, 37, 38,
    94–101, 104–5
resources
    definition of economic, 243
    diversification of, 243–49
    types of, 243
retirement
    financial illiteracy about, 80
    lack of thinking about, 56, 75
    and revolution in financial
        planning, 299
    when to, 299
    See also early retirement; specific
        topic
retirement accounts
    and charity, 230–31, 232
    and consumption disruptions,
        28–30
    contributions to, 5, 10, 28–30,
        48–49, 141–55

and conventional wisdom versus
   economic advice, 298
conversion of, 156–59, 270
defined-contribution, 64–65
and divorce, 201
and mind-benders, 48–49
and preserving your living
   standard, 269–70
and pricing your passions,
   230–31, 232
and public policy, 270
and raising living standard, 10
and taxes, 48, 141–55, 156–59,
   186–90, 230–31
as type of economic resource,
   243
withdrawals from, 186–90, 270
See also 4 percent spend-down
   rule; matching funds,
   employer; type of account
Retirement Confidence Survey, 218
Retirement Goal Evaluator (TIAA-
   CREF), 29, 36, 37, 98
Retirement Index (Fidelity), 56
Retirement Quick Check calculator
   (Fidelity), 36
Retirement Research Center
   (University of Michigan), 19
revealed preference, 77
reverse mortgages, 10, 125, 126,
   177, 179, 180–82, 197, 299
risk
   and annuities, 176–77, 181
   and asset allocation, 243, 245,
      246, 247, 249
   and averaging, 259, 260, 262
   aversion to, 11
   and basic economic model of
      portfolio choice, 239–40,
      241–42
   and buying homes, 129
   and college, 116, 117
   and company stock, 68
   and consumption disruptions,
      37–38

and conventional wisdom versus
   economic advice, 297
and diversification, 243
and employer pension funds,
   272, 274
and financial industry, 7
and medical/nursing home costs,
   125–26
and mind-benders, 45–46, 50
and overinsuring, 50
and oversaving, 50
overview about, 10–12
and paying off mortgages versus
   investing in stocks, 138
pimping, 38, 39–43
and portfolio choice, 264, 265,
   266
and preserving your living
   standard, 233–35, 237–42,
   243, 245, 246, 247, 249, 251,
   254, 255, 259, 260, 262, 264,
   265, 266, 267–71, 272, 274,
   276, 290, 291
public policy, 267–71
and raising your living standard,
   116, 117
and safety-first strategy, 290, 291
and spending down, 251, 254,
   255
and targets, 40, 41–42, 43
and three commandments of
   economics, 7
for two-income households, 61
risk-return efficiency, 11
Roth 401(k) plans, 142–55, 168
Roth accounts
   and conventional wisdom versus
      economic advice, 298
   and conversion of retirement
      accounts, 156, 158, 270
   and equivalent Roth
      contributions, 148–50
   and preserving your living
      standard, 269–70
   and public policy, 269, 270

Roth accounts (*cont.*)
  and revolution in financial
    planning, 299
  withdrawals from, 298, 299
  See also Roth 401(k) plans
rules of dumb, 28, 30, 38, 251–53,
    254–55
Ruth (example), 256–58, 259–62,
    264–65
Rydex Juno Fund, 269–70

S&P 500. *See* Standard and Poor's
    500 index
SABEW (Society of Business
    Editors and Writers), 63
safety-first strategy, 287–93
Sally (example), 251–54
Salvation Army, 230
Samuelson, Bill, 247–48
Samuelson, Paul, 239–40, 241,
    243, 246, 247–48, 259, 264
Samuelson-Merton prescription
    (analysis), 239–40, 241, 243,
    245, 246, 247–48, 254, 259,
    264
San Antonio, Texas, homes in,
    134–35
San Diego, California, homes in,
    127–32
Sandy (example), 89
Sanguine, Sue (example), 177–82
savers credits, 162
savings
  after retirement, 280–81
  catch-up provisions for, 56, 72
  and charity, 229
  and consumption disruptions,
    27, 28, 30, 32–34, 35, 37
  and conventional wisdom versus
    economic advice, 296
  in defined-contribution plans,
    64–65
  and early retirement, 216
  employer-based, 272–76
  of federal workers, 56–57

financial illiteracy about, 80,
    81
  and financial pathology, 56, 59,
    70–74, 75
  influences on, 81
  lack of, 56
  maximum, 70–72
  and mind-benders, 44, 47–48,
    50
  national rate of, 59
  and preserving your living
    standard, 250, 272–76,
    280–81
  and pricing your passions, 209,
    216, 229
  questions about, 3
  and replacement rate, 96,
    99–101, 105
  and revolution in financial
    planning, 299, 300
  and risk, 50
  and rule of dumb, 28
  and socioeconomic status,
    47–48
  and spending down, 250
  and standard economic theory,
    6
  and targets, 30
  and taxes, 186–90
  and three commandments of
    economics, 5
  too little, 32–34, 35, 100–101
  too much, 5, 35, 37, 50, 72–74,
    75, 86, 100–101, 296
  types of, 186–90
  See also insurance; retirement
    accounts; *specific type of*
    account
Scholastic Aptitude Test (SAT),
    115, 116
Schor, Juliet, 60
Schwartz, Barry, 61
Seattle, Washington, homes in,
    123–26
Sebastian (example), 100

securities
  and consumption disruptions, 38
  and downsizing, 197
  high-return, 40
  See also bonds; stocks
Securities and Exchange
    Commission (SEC), 83
self-control, 88–91
seniors, increase in, and public
    policy risk, 268
SEPs (simplified employee
    pensions), 92, 158
shared living
  and consumption disruptions,
    27, 33
  and consumption smoothing, 25,
    26
  and pricing your passions, 10,
    208–13
  See also two income households
Sharpe, William F., 36
SmartMoney, 18, 216
Smith, Adam, 77
smooth financial paths
  and consumption disruption,
    27–38
  and consumption smoothing,
    21–26
  and financial sickness, 17–20
  and mind benders, 44–51
  overview about, 6–7, 15–16
  and pimping risk, 39–43
smoothing your living standard
  as commandment of economics,
    1, 2–3, 7, 8, 9
  and ESPlanner, 13
  See also consumption smoothing
Social Security
  as annuity, 172–73, 177, 178
  and asset allocation, 245–46
  calculation of benefits from, 13,
    14
  and charity, 228, 229, 230, 231,
    232
  and choosing careers, 111, 114

  and consumption smoothing, 24,
    25, 26
  and continuing to work, 171–73
  and conventional wisdom versus
    economic advice, 297
  and conversion of retirement
    accounts, 157
  cuts in, 46, 55
  and defaults on student loans,
    117
  dependence on, 75
  and divorce, 200
  double dipping on, 169–74
  and downsizing, 196
  and drug dealing example, 7
  and early retirement, 215
  as factor determining financial
    future, 8
  fears about, 55
  and financial sickness, 17, 19, 75
  form 521 applications for, 173,
    174
  and helping children, 226
  and inflation, 149, 160, 173
  and long-term care insurance,
    283
  Medicare benefits versus, 278–79
  and mind-benders, 45, 46,
    47–48, 49–50
  overconfidence about, 83
  and portfolio choice, 264
  and preserving your living
    standard, 240, 241, 245–46,
    251, 252, 264, 267, 268, 269,
    271, 278–79, 281, 283, 287
  and pricing your passions, 210,
    212, 215, 226, 228, 229, 230,
    231, 232
  and public policy risk, 267, 268,
    269, 271
  and raising your living standard,
    10, 115
  reapplying for, 171–73, 174
  and retirement account
    contributions, 144, 149

Social Security (*cont.*)
  and revolution in financial
    planning, 299
  and risk, 11, 45
  and safety-first strategy, 287
  and socioeconomic status, 47–48
  and spending down, 251, 252
  spousal and survivor benefits of,
    47, 167, 169–71, 174, 212
  and taxes, 149, 161, 164–65,
    174, 230, 231, 232
  and three commandments of
    economics, 2, 5
  as underfunded, 272
  when to take, 2, 5, 10, 25, 26,
    49–50, 160–68, 169–74, 180,
    184, 201, 297, 299
The Social Security Handbook,
  170
Society of Business Editors and
  Writers (SABEW), 63
socioeconomic status
  and conventional wisdom versus
    economic advice, 297
  and conversion of retirement
    accounts, 158, 159
  and having children, 219–23
  and mind-benders, 45, 50–51
  and mortgages, 50–51, 133–40
  and pricing your passions,
    219–23
  and three commandments of
    economics, 5
Sophie (example), 86, 87
Southern, Terry, 70
Special Supplemental Nutrition
  Program for Women, Infants,
  and Children, 119
spending
  as commandment of economics,
    1, 2, 7, 8
  and consumption disruptions,
    32–34, 35
  and conventional wisdom versus
    economic advice, 296

definition of, 97
economists' quiz about, 19–20
interrelated factors influencing,
  8–9
maximizing, 1, 2, 7, 8
and preserving your living
  standard, 263–66, 291,
  293
and pricing your love, 3
of principal assets, 99
questions about, 4
rates for, 4, 250–55, 262
and replacement rate, 98, 99
and revolution in financial
  planning, 299
and safety-first strategy, 291,
  293
targets for, 5, 7, 30–31
and three commandments of
  economics, 3, 5
too little, 16, 17, 35, 72–74, 87,
  250–51
too much, 15–16, 17, 32–34, 35,
  87, 250
See also spending down
spending down
  and averaging, 256–62
  and consumption smoothing,
    250–55
  and conventional wisdom versus
    economic advice, 297
  and preservation of living
    standards, 250–55, 256–62
Stallissimo (example), 205–6
Standard and Poor's 500 index
  (S&P 500), 82, 103, 192, 237,
  238, 256
Starbucks, 17, 205, 220
Steve (example), 89
Steven and Bertha (example),
  162–67, 168
stock market
  beating the, 39
  gambling on, 11
  volatility of, 45

stockbrokers
  advice from, 191–95
  fees of, 191–95
  use of, 10
stocks
  and asset allocation, 244–45, 246–49
  and averaging, 256–62
  company, 57–58, 67–68, 75, 91, 92, 275–76
  and conventional wisdom versus economic advice, 296, 297
  and gender, 83–84
  large-cap, 41, 256, 257
  and life-cycle funds, 240–41
  and mind-benders, 45, 46
  overconfidence about, 83–84
  paying off mortgages versus investing in, 138
  and portfolio choice, 263–66
  and preserving your living standard, 233–34, 237–42, 244–45, 246–49, 250, 256–62, 263–66, 275–76, 292
  questions about, 3
  and raising living standard, 10
  and revolution in financial planning, 300
  rise and fall of, 46
  risk in, 42, 46
  and safety-first strategy, 292
  and socioeconomic status, 45
  and spending down, 250
  and three commandments of economics, 5
  trading of, 83–84
stress, 61
Strotz, Robert, 89
"superstar cities," 127
Supplemental Security Income, 119, 162
Survey of Consumer Finances, 59, 67, 2004
swapping, 206–7, 264
Swensen, David, 8

T. Rowe Price, 241
Tampa, Florida, homes in, 123–26
targets
  and consumption disruptions, 30–36, 38
  consumption smoothing as, 30–31, 38
  and conventional wisdom versus economic advice, 296
  current spending as basis of, 30, 32, 35, 36
  and mind-benders, 44
  mistakes in, 32–34, 38, 44
  and pimping risk, 40, 41–42, 43
  probability of meeting, 42
  setting your own, 31–32, 38
  as too high, 32–34, 35, 40
  as too low, 34
tax credits, 221
taxes
  and charity, 228, 230–31, 232
  and children, 221, 222
  and choosing careers, 110, 111, 114
  and choosing not to work, 118–20
  and computational limitations, 93
  and consumption disruptions, 27, 34
  and consumption smoothing, 24, 25, 26
  and conventional wisdom versus economic advice, 298
  and divorce, 200
  and downsizing, 196
  and early retirement, 214–15
  and financial industry fees, 102–3
  future rates for, 152–53, 154–55, 157–58, 159
  gift, 225–26
  and helping children, 225–26, 227

taxes (*cont.*)
  and homes, 124, 129–30, 131,
    132, 133–40, 196, 288
  and marriage, 210
  and mind-benders, 50–51
  and mortgages, 50–51, 133–39,
    298
  and preserving your living
    standard, 252, 269–70, 271,
    290
  and pricing your passions,
    210–11, 212, 214–15, 221,
    222, 225–26, 227, 228,
    230–31, 232
  and public policy, 269, 270,
    271
  and raising your living standard,
    115
  and replacement rate, 96
  and retirement accounts, 48,
    141–55, 156–59, 186–90,
    230–31
  and safety-first strategy, 288,
    290
  and savings, 186–90
  and Social Security, 149,
    161, 164–65, 174, 230, 231,
    232
  and spending down, 252
technology, 4, 300
telepathy, 261–62
three commandments of economics
  overview of, 1–14
  and questions to ask, 3–4
Thrift Savings Plan, federal, 102,
  193
TIAA-CREF, 7, 29, 36, 37, 98
timing, and home-buying,
  131–32
TIPS (Treasury inflation-protected
  bonds)
  and perserving your living
    standard, 260–61
  and pimping risk, 40–41,
    42–43

  and preserving your living
    standard, 237–38, 244–45,
    246, 247, 249, 253, 256, 258,
    265, 271, 289–90, 291, 292,
    293
  and raising your living standard,
    177, 188, 189
  and safety-first strategy, 289–90,
    291, 292, 293
Transitional Aid to Families with
  Dependent Children, 118,
  162
Trumpinski, Donald and Ivana
  (example), 123–25, 126
Tusser, Thomas, 39
Tversky, Amos, 88
two-income households, 61, 67,
  119, 220, 221. *See also* marital
  status; shared living
Tyagi, Amelia Warren, 220
Tyson, Mike, 16

Uncle Rich (example), 48–49
University of Michigan, Retirement
  Research Center conference at,
  19–20
University of Pennsylvania,
  Wharton School study at,
  81–83
U.S. Department of Agriculture,
  220
U.S. Department of Education,
  79
U.S. Department of Labor, 95,
  276

Vanguard, 7, 36, 73, 177, 225,
  229, 241
"vig," 64
VisiCalc program, 12

Wall Street
  jobs on, 39
  and sales pressures of financial
    services industry, 102

Warren, Elizabeth, 60–61, 220
Wharton School, designed neglect study at, 81–83
Wonder Bread husband (example), 205–7
work
  after receiving Social Security, 171–73
  and choosing not to work, 114, 118–21
  and early retirement, 216–17
  and not working, 162
  See also careers

Yahoo-Finance, 13

Zagorsky, Jay, 87